GREEK THEATRE PRODUCTION

Greek Theatre Production

T. B. L. WEBSTER

Professor of Greek, University College, London

METHUEN AND CO. LTD

36 ESSEX STREET · STRAND · LONDON WC2

First published in 1956

TO

J. D. B.

CATALOGUE NO. 5815/U

PRINTED IN GREAT BRITAIN BY NEILL AND CO. LTD.
AND BOUND BY HUNTER AND FOULIS, LTD, EDINBURGH

CONTENTS

v

PLATES

AT END

*References at the ends of captions refer to List of Monuments
on page 173*

1   Stage buildings of the theatre of Dionysos at Athens.
    (From photo: E. W. Handley.)

2 *a.* Satyr riding phallos pole (F 2).
    (From photo: Sopraintendenza Antichita, Florence).

  b. Komast riding phallos pole.
    (From *Rylands Bulletin*, 36 (1954), 584, fig. 2.)

3   Men dressed as women dancing (F 3).
    (From photo: Allard Pierson Stichting, Amsterdam.)

4 *a.* Komasts and nymphs (F 6).
    (From *Rylands Bulletin*, 36 (1954), 585, fig. 3.)

  b. Men dressed as maenads (F 4).
    (From *Rylands Bulletin*, 36 (1954), 585, fig. 4.)

5 *a.* Corinthian padded dancers (F 12).
    (From *Rylands Bulletin*, 36 (1954), 584, fig. 1.)

  b. Boeotian padded dancers (F 20).
    (From photo: Göttingen University.)

6 *a.* Female mask from Sparta (F 21).
    (From photo: British Museum.)

  b. Satyr mask from Samos (F 26).
    (From photo: British Museum.)

7   Iphigeneia in Tauris (A 8).
    (From photo: Sopraintendenza Antichita, Florence.)

8   Actors and chorus of satyr play (A 9).
    (From photo: Alinari.)

9   Actor dressed for female part in tragedy (A 20).
    (From photo: Ny Carlsberg Glyptotek.)

10 Men and women in palace setting (A 35).
    (From photo: Martin von Wagner Museum, Würzburg.)

ACKNOWLEDGMENTS

My thanks are due first to my wife and Professor C. M. Robertson, who read my manuscript and made many valuable suggestions, and to Mr E. W. Handley, who read the proofs; secondly to many people who have given me information and particularly to Mrs D. B. Thompson, Mr R. Higgins, Mr A. Seeberg, and Miss L. Asche; thirdly, to the governors of the John Rylands Library for permission to include in a revised form two articles published in their Bulletin, vols. 32 and 36; to them, to the Council of the Hellenic Society, to the Manchester University Press, and to Messrs Methuen for the loan of blocks for illustrations; fourthly to the following for photographs of objects and permission to reproduce them: Mr E. W. Handley; the Allard Pierson Stichting, Amsterdam; the American School of Classical Studies in Athens; the British Museum; Göttingen University; the Martin von Wagner Museum, Würzburg; the Ny Carlsberg Glyptothek, Copenhagen; the Metropolitan Museum, New York; the Soprintendenza alle Antichita of Bologna and Florence. I have learnt much from a recent visit to Athens and should like particularly to record my gratitude to Professor Homer Thompson and his colleagues in the Agora and to Mrs S. Papaspyridi-Karouzou. Sir John Beazley has read my proofs and has allowed me to dedicate this book to him—in gratitude for all that I owe him over the last thirty years.

T. B. L. WEBSTER

October 1955

INTRODUCTION

My purpose in writing this book is to give a general account of the way in which the ancient Greeks produced their plays at different places and at different times. Greek plays were written to be acted, although the Greek playwright always had a reading public also in view, and classical Athenian tragedy of the fifth century and comedy of the late fourth century were revived again and again. My restricted object is to give a chronological and topographical account of costumes, masks, and scenery from the earliest times down to the late Hellenistic period. I have included the various pre-dramatic performances which were developed into drama and survived alongside drama; I have excluded mimes, which were performed by unmasked performers and therefore had no influence on production; nor have I written of acting or music, which would seem to me to need separate and expert treatment.

The material consists of (*a*) plays and ancient writings on the drama, including literary criticism, commentaries, lexica, (*b*) remains of ancient theatres, (*c*) monuments connected with drama—statues, statuettes, masks, paintings, mosaics, and the like. The first source is the most treacherous. Although Greek plays were written to be acted, the Greek playwright could not be certain of more than a single production, and therefore he always wrote for a reading public as well as his audience. I say that he could be certain of a single production because I assume that in Athens the poet did not complete his play until he had been promised a performance at one of the festivals—the City Dionysia or the Lenaia.[1] After this performance the play might be produced again at one of the Athenian country theatres or abroad and might be revived after the poet's death in

[1] On the details of the festivals see Sir Arthur Pickard-Cambridge, *Dramatic Festivals of Athens.*

Athens or elsewhere; but such further productions were unpredictable, whereas already in the fifth century the tragic poet at any rate could count on a reading public. This means that we have to be extremely careful how we use the plays as a source for scenery and costumes; the poet has to create an imaginary visible world for his readers and this world may not coincide entirely with the seen world of the theatre. It is certain that the frequent tears attributed to tragic heroines could not be seen on their masks, and unlikely that a special set of mythological metopes was provided for the chorus of Euripides' *Ion* to describe. On the other hand a poet so interested in spectacle as Aeschylus clearly exploited all the possibilities of production, and certain scenes, as we shall see, imply certain stage arrangements and equipments. We must therefore use the plays but we must use them with caution.

The same is true of the secondary literary sources. Much in our commentators and lexicographers (including Pollux' great work of the second century A.D.) goes back to Alexandrian scholarship and therefore is evidence for theatrical practice in the Hellenistic age, when, as we shall see, drama became international, and this practice was based on the practice of the earlier Athenian theatre. But sometimes we can show that the ancient scholars were guessing from the surviving plays, and this may happen more often than we can now detect.

The remains of ancient theatres are an important source of information, but the experts have differed greatly in the interpretation and dating of the details. The detail of the Athenian theatre can be found set forth with admirable clarity and sanity by Sir Arthur Pickard-Cambridge in *The Theatre of Dionysus in Athens*, which includes much about the other theatres. Fortunately the main lines of development are fairly clear, and for our purposes we can distinguish the pre-Periclean theatre, the Periclean theatre, the theatre of Lykourgos, the late Hellenistic theatre, and the Roman theatre. In the classical period (fifth and early fourth century) the influence of Athens must have been immensely strong, and in the Hellenistic age the guilds of Artists of Dionysos must have tended to standardise theatre layout. We are comparatively well documented from different parts of the Greek world on the all-important change which took place in the second century: the transference of the action from a low stage connected with the orchestra, where the chorus danced, to a stage twelve or more feet above ground level. I have also discussed in some detail the unique series of records of the rebuilding of the theatre at Delos in the third century.

Much work has been done on the monuments connected with the theatre: besides Sir Arthur Pickard-Cambridge the names of Carl Robert, Margarete Bieber, and Antonia Simon must be mentioned. My treatment is based on a list of some 1500 monuments compiled over the last eight years. This started with the list in Bieber's *Denkmäler*, to which she added many more in her *History of the Greek Theatre*, and includes the immensely useful list of monuments of New Comedy in Antonia Simon's *Comicae Tabellae*. I have added a considerable number beyond these, but the list is still far from complete and will gradually be increased. A copy is deposited in the Classical Institute of London University, and the numbers in brackets added after the numbers in the Select Catalogue of Monuments at the end of the book refer to this list. Apart from work done on these monuments as illustrations of theatre practice, mention must be made of the work done on vases and terra-cottas in recent years, which has made it possible to speak much more accurately about them than before. On Athenian vases the pioneer and definitive work of dating, attribution, and interpretation has been done by Sir John Beazley, work which is beyond praise and to which all scholars will remain indebted. Following him Professor A. D. Trendall has mapped out South Italian vases, and I am grateful for the generosity with which he has acquainted me with his results, particularly for his still unpublished list of phlyax vases. On terra-cottas I have profited much from discussions with Mrs Dorothy Burr Thompson, who has impressed on me the importance of using as far as possible material dated and placed by excavation; her study of the Myrina terra-cottas in Boston is fundamental for dating Hellenistic terra-cottas. In the last year Mr R. Higgins has published the excellent first volume of his catalogue of ancient terra-cottas in the British Museum, which includes the very fine series of fourth-century comic actors.

Much of this monumental material can be accepted at its face value as illustration of actors as they appeared in theatres where the artist had seen them perform; and for these monuments we need to know where they were found, where they were produced, and what is their date. They may tell us about local theatre production, and they may tell us what imported drama interested the local inhabitants. The finds at Pompeii and Herculaneum are a special case. They can be divided into three main classes: paintings derived from earlier originals which can sometimes be dated on internal evidence, terra-cottas which may reflect local theatre practice, and decorative masks in all materials which may derive from earlier originals but, as I shall argue, in a theatre-loving town are unlikely to have been much out of touch with contemporary production. I have therefore used this material in two ways: as evidence for standard Hellenistic practice, where the originals can be dated and parallels can be adduced from other parts of the Greek world, and as evidence for the taste of the owners of certain houses in Pompeii who seem to have had a particular love for the theatre.

One other general point must be made in the introduction. For pre-dramatic performances and for classical drama painted vases are an essential source of information. One must never approach a Greek vase expecting to derive the same sort of information from it as one would derive from a coloured photograph of a first night. The Greek vase-painter is an artist and often a very good artist. A Greek artist in the archaic and classical period always wants to tell more than he sees. Realism in the modern sense, the accurate repre-

sentation of a scene as it appears to the eye, became fashion-
able in the Hellenistic age, and we shall see examples of it in
the best paintings and mosaics from Pompeii and Herculaneum which derive from good Hellenistic originals. The
earlier artist (and probably many later artists too) insists on
telling you more about the play than you can see at any one
moment during the production. Sometimes he draws
particular expressions which could never have appeared on
the mask but may have been implied by the acting or
recorded by the poet. Sometimes he forgets the appearance
of the actor and draws the character as he imagines him, or
produces a figure which is partly character and partly actor.
Sometimes he adds figures which did not appear in a
particular scene, because they make the story clear. He may
paint the situation described in a messenger speech and yet
put it in a stage setting and give the characters actors'
clothing to show that the story was told in drama. These
pictures then are seldom completely accurate realistic
representations of a stage scene, but it would be foolish to
reject them because they are the records of an intelligent
artist rather than of a stupid camera. They must be interpreted, and the rules for interpretation are no different from
those used in understanding the scenes on the many
thousands of other Greek vases that have survived.

Such, briefly, is the material. I have organised it under
regions, because, although I believe that pre-dramatic
performances were very much the same in many Greek
cities, that classical drama was created in Athens and therefore that productions elsewhere were dominated by Athenian
influence, and that Hellenistic drama was international, this
case has to be made, and it can best be made by surveying
the regions separately and noting both cross-connections
and local survivals and variations. Athens must come first. I
have then continued with Sicily and Italy because only the West
has given us good and full evidence for theatre production in
the fourth century as well as for the Hellenistic age. Then
follow Mainland Greece, the Islands, Asia Minor, and Africa.

I. ATHENS

IN the modern theatre we accept certain conventions as normal. We expect to sit in darkness and to see what is happening in somebody else's room. The lighting tells us whether it is morning or evening. Furnishing, decoration, and costumes show to what country and to what period the room belongs; but whether we are overhearing Florentines in the sixteenth century or Californians in the twentieth, there are no gradations between our dark world and their light world, except in amateur performances in small communities where Hamlet or Joxer Daly carry with them some of their everyday associations. Although one of their walls is gone, the inhabitants of the room are not dismayed by this except that their actions and their words are directed towards the wall which is missing. A room with a wall gone so that we can see what happens is the normal convention, but by an easy transference we may be present on a mountain path, on a sea shore, in a forest glen, or on board a ship. Nor does it trouble us that the characters are going to go through the same section of their lives again tomorrow and the next day and perhaps every day except Sundays for the next year or more.

In the Greek theatre the conventions were different. The performance was a unique performance to please the god Dionysos, who saw it in the person of his statue. Thus one spectator at least was not confined by the normal limits of time and space. A play was often revived in subsequent years but runs were unknown. Artificial lighting was impossible and there were no footlights to confine the audience in darkness and illuminate the faces of the characters. Indeed in Athens the theatre of Dionysos was so set that the sun shone into the eyes of the spectators. The normal set (as we shall

see) was a palace front, and so the normal convention was that
the audience were the citizens, sitting round the market-
place to watch the royal family conducting its affairs; Greeks
were an open-air people and so it was not too disturbing that
so much of the royal business was conducted out of doors.
The names of the characters showed that they belonged
to the remote past and very often to some other city than
Athens. In the lifetime of Aeschylus, Sophocles, or Euripides,
actors (as we shall see) wore contemporary costume, but
perhaps an Eastern king might be distinguished by a tiara.
Between the royalties and the audience were the chorus—
councillors, confidantes, or faithful retainers. In several ways
they formed a link between the audience and the characters,
and this is true even when they were given a more exotic role
such as the Furies in Aeschylus' *Eumenides*, satyrs in Satyr
plays, birds or clouds in Aristophanes. They were less active
than the characters and less affected emotionally, but still
by their costume, masks, and role they belonged to the
characters rather than to the audience. But their songs in
classical tragedy consisted to a considerable degree of
reflections on the action as it progressed, the reflections that
an ideal spectator might make. Their songs were also
reminiscent sometimes of songs known to the audience from
contemporary cults and festivals. They themselves were not
professionals like the actors but trained amateurs who would
be known in everyday life.

Thus while we are accustomed to a sharp division between
the dark world of the auditorium and the overbright world
of the characters, the Greeks knew a gradation from audience
through chorus to characters, all united under a dazzling sun.
Whereas our normal convention is to look into a room from
which one wall has been removed, their normal convention
was that they were sitting, as they did in the Assembly,
watching the transaction of affairs of state. Like us however
they could also transfer themselves to the sea shore for
Sophocles' *Philoctetes*, to the mountains for a satyr play, to
a street of private houses, or indeed to Heaven or Hell for

Comedy. But whereas we have all the resources of lighting, realistic scenery, and make-up to create the illusion, the Greek dramatist had to rely far more on his words and less on the limited technical means at his disposal. For us today it is often difficult to say where he was relying on words alone and where his words were reinforced by visual or other aids. When in Sophocles' *Antigone* (526) the chorus describe the tears running down Ismene's face and her cheeks ugly-red with weeping, we know that the mask could not show this. When however in the *Andromeda* Perseus flies 'with winged foot carving a path through the middle heaven' (fr. 124 N), we have every reason to suppose that Euripides had him swung over on the crane. To try to make clear what technical means were at the disposal of the Greek dramatist at different times is the chief object of the present study.

Three obvious limitations to which the ancient producer (by this word I distinguish visual effects from descriptions) had to submit are either unknown or only known in a very minor degree to the modern producer. First, lighting effects were impossible. The Greek producer could not show dawn or sunset, except in so far as the first tragedy on each day of the festival was acted early in the morning and the last comedy late in the evening. He could not distinguish the darkness of Hell from the brightness of Olympus. He could however have a torchlight procession even in daylight and he could show that the palace was on fire by burning something in the background to give off smoke. Secondly, changes of scene were severely limited by time. The calculation quoted by Sir Arthur Pickard-Cambridge [1] that in a twelve hour day not more than two hours at most can have been available for intervals between plays assumes an acting time of ten hours for three tragedies, one satyr play, and one comedy, which does not seem excessive. Two hours then were available for changing the scenery four times. Four changes were often unnecessary. In 438 Euripides' *Cretan Women*, *Alkmaion in Psophis*, *Telephos*, and *Alcestis* could all

[1] *Theatre*, 123.

have been acted before the palace front. We may perhaps say that the satyr play would often need a change of scene and the comedy always needed some change of scene unless mythological comedies, a type increasingly common in the last quarter of the century, were played before the tragic set. On the other hand the scene might have to be changed between each tragedy. In 431 Euripides' *Medea* was played before a palace front. The *Philoktetes*, the next play, was set before Philoktetes' cave on Lemnos. The third play, *Diktys*, had again a palace background. The title of the satyr play, *Theristai*, suggests a country setting. At least the sequence palace/cave/palace for the three tragedies seems certain, and as 'scene-painting' (in a sense to be defined later) is attested, it seems probable that there was some visible change. But the limitation of time was severe, and still more severe for changes of scene within plays.

Thirdly, the size of the Greek theatre introduced a limitation of another kind. If for the moment we accept the Periclean theatre as depicted by Pickard-Cambridge,[1] the area between the projecting wings, the 'stage' proper, was 45 ft. wide, the same as Drury Lane; the width was increased in the fourth century to more than 60 ft. The distance from the front of the 'stage' across the orchestra to the front row of spectators was 60 ft. in the fifth century and over 70 ft. in the fourth century; in Drury Lane it is only 48 ft. from the front of the stage to the centre of the dress circle. The back rows of the theatre of Dionysos were about 300 ft. from the stage. This means that an actor 6 ft. high would look about $3\frac{1}{2}$ in. high to the spectator in front and $\frac{3}{4}$ in. high to spectators at the back. On this scale without footlights facial expression would mean little to the front rows, and the advantage of a mask, necessarily slightly larger than the human face and with the features firmly painted, is obvious.

We may think of the theatre at Athens as an immense roughly semicircular auditorium seating 14,000 people,

[1] *Theatre*, 16 fig. 7.

surrounding rather more than half of the 60 ft. diameter circle of the *orchestra* or dancing floor, which touches on its further side the insides of the projecting wings of the wooden stage building, the back-ground of the action; passages, *parodoi*, between the seats of the auditorium and the wings of the stage-buildings give access to characters when they do not come out of the stage-building but from the town or from abroad. This was the classical theatre, which was copied with modifications in all other theatres. But it is difficult to date the details with any precision. Our requirement is however the modest one of knowing what was the kind of theatre for which Aeschylus, Sophocles, Euripides, and Aristophanes wrote their plays. We are only concerned with the theatre of Dionysos. It is true that we have plays of Aristophanes which were produced at the Lenaia, but nothing in them suggests that external conditions at that festival were any different from those under which his plays were produced at the Greater Dionysia or that his plays for the Lenaia were produced anywhere but in the theatre of Dionysos. Within the theatre of Dionysos we are only concerned with the dancing-floor, the 'stage', and the scenery.

We can assume that the theatre of Dionysos was in use before the earliest productions of which we can say anything. It is possible that the theatre was inaugurated after the collapse of the wooden seats in the agora during a performance of Pratinas. This suggestion comes from a combination of two facts: first, the earth which was used to steepen the slope of the hillside for the auditorium of the theatre contained pottery of the very early fifth century; secondly, Pratinas was dead by 467 when his son produced his posthumous plays. It seems reasonable therefore to assume that the two earliest plays [1] of which we know anything, Phrynichos' *Phoenissae* and Aeschylus' *Persae*, which were produced in 476 and 472 respectively, were

[1] Aeschylus' *Suppliants* can be omitted from the discussion since we now know that it was not produced before 466 at the earliest.

performed in the theatre of Dionysos. Unfortunately nothing remains of this earliest theatre of Dionysos except just enough masonry to show that it had a circular *orchestra*.[1] Later, after the building of the Odeion, which was completed by 443, the auditorium was made steeper and the orchestra was moved northwards. Of this theatre, called the Periclean theatre, although it may not have been completed until after Pericles' death, precious fragments remain. About 10 ft. behind the orchestra (as seen from the auditorium) a rectangular platform, 26 ft. wide by 9 ft. deep, is backed by a wall in the surface of which ten grooves have been cut to support vertical posts.[2] On them a stage building about 105 ft. long could be erected. If the front of this building formed a straight line, the outer ends would extend far beyond the circle of the orchestra and would be invisible from much of the auditorium; it seems likely that they were made into projecting wings framing the 'stage' and its background like the stone stage-building in the later fourth-century theatre: buildings with wings were not uncommon in the last quarter of the fifth century and we shall see later that there is some reason for supposing that the same kind of stage-building was used in Southern Italy by the middle of the fourth century. We have therefore good architectural evidence that at least the last three plays of Sophocles (*Electra*, *Philoctetes*, and *Oedipus Coloneus*), the later plays of Euripides from rather before the *Trojan Women*, and all the plays of Aristophanes after the *Peace* were played before a wooden stage-building with projecting wings and a firm stone foundation for stage-machinery. If other evidence

---

[1] Cf. most recently W. B. Dinsmoor in *Studies presented to D. M. Robinson*, I, 309f.; I. T. Hill, *Ancient City of Athens*, 113 f.

[2] The photograph (by Mr E. W. Handley) used for Pl. 1 is taken from the retaining wall of the auditorium (wA) near the west end of the Hellenistic stage-building, looking along its front with the Roman stage and the orchestra on the left. The rough wall on the right is the Periclean wall and the vertical grooves can be seen in its surface. The rectangular platform runs out from it to the tree which can be seen behind the two marble columns in the foreground.

suggests that such a stage-building already existed in the thirties, there is no reason to reject it.

Except for the masonry which shows that it had a circular orchestra our only evidence for the pre-Periclean theatre is the evidence that can be drawn from the plays which were produced in it. When every allowance is made for the dramatist's skill in substituting verbal description for visual presentation, this evidence establishes (1) that communication between the actors and the chorus was easy, (2) that a practicable door faced the audience, (3) that a high platform existed, (4) that the crane could be used, and (5) that scenery was painted. The first point is clear enough: not only can chorus talk to actors freely from the orchestra, but they can enter or leave the stage-building when necessary: both in the *Choephori* and in the *Eumenides* the chorus enter from the stage-building. A high stage is therefore out of the question. The fifth-century theatre had either no stage or a low stage. We have no contemporary evidence, but a low stage would have the advantage of marking the characters off from the chorus while not hindering communication between them. The only surviving picture (B *1*) [1] of audience and actor in Attic comedy shows a low stage reached by a flight of four steps. It is unlikely that a stage was erected every day when the tragedies were over and before the comedy began. The picture is dated about 420 B.C. and therefore only tells us about the Periclean theatre, but such a stage, while not preventing the intermingling of chorus and orchestra, would increase the effectiveness of, for instance, Agamemnon's entry into his palace over the purple tapestry. Late writers who speak of the 'table' used before the time of Thespis, the 'wagon' of Thespis, and the 'platform' of Aeschylus seem to have preserved some memory that from the earliest times the actor was on a somewhat higher level than the chorus.

[1] References are to the list of dramatic monuments at the end of the book, where references to modern views discussed in the text will also be found. Those numbered in *italics* are also illustrated in the plates.

Phrynichos' *Phoenissae*, produced in 476, opened with a eunuch narrating Xerxes' defeat while he arranged the seats for the councillors. This seems to imply a stage-building. Four years later in Aeschylus' *Persae* (140) the chorus of councillors speak of themselves as 'sitting in an ancient building'; part of this is presumably the tomb of Dareios over which the ghost appears (639). The actor who plays the ghost has previously played the messenger. He must therefore have gone off, changed his costume, and then come on again through the building to a point where he can be seen by the audience; in fact, the *Persae*, like all later plays, demands a stage-building with a practicable door, unless we should think rather of Dareios appearing on the roof of his tomb. In the *Oresteia*, produced in 458, the audience must be able to see at the end of the *Agamemnon* Klytaimnestra standing over the dead bodies of Agamemnon and Kassandra and at the beginning of the *Eumenides* Orestes sitting on the omphalos, Apollo, the ghost of Klytaimnestra, and at least three members of the chorus (the others can come out from the back before they start to dance; Hermes also can come out from the back when he goes off with Orestes—he is not an essential part of the tableau). This requires that the practicable door should be of considerable width to accommodate the tableau, but it must not be so wide that the doors take too long to open or occupy too much space as they open. A twelve-foot opening (half the width of the rectangular platform in the Periclean theatre) would seem to be the minimum desirable.

Two further questions may be raised at this point. Was there any sort of platform on wheels which could be rolled out of the central door to display tableaux of this kind, and were there any other doors in addition to the central door? The question of the platform on wheels (or *ekkyklema*) has been very fully discussed by Sir Arthur Pickard-Cambridge,[1] who argues that we have no evidence for its use before Hellenistic times. In the two passages of Aristophanes

[1] *Theatre*, 100 f.

(*Ach.* 408f.; *Thesm.* 95f.) in which the verb 'to roll out' occurs, the reference may be to a sofa on wheels, since Euripides is too busy and Agathon too effeminate to walk, but it should be noted that both of them have a considerable number of properties. It is therefore possible that when the ancient commentators on plays refer to the *ekkyklema,* they are thinking of Hellenistic and not of classical practice. We must however remember that if a wheeled sofa is possible a wheeled platform is also possible. The limiting factor would seem to be the space required. In the Periclean theatre (we know nothing of these dimensions in the pre-Periclean theatre), if the reconstructions are to be trusted, the total depth of the stage-building is at most 12 ft., and as room must be left for manoeuvring inside the stage-building, the platform could scarcely be more than 6 ft. deep; its width would be determined by the door opening, for which we have assumed 12 ft. We must therefore concede that a wheeled platform 10 ft. wide by 6 ft. deep could have been used in the practicable door. It would not be used for the entry of a single figure or even for the display of a single corpse (like that of Eurydike at the end of the *Antigone*) but for tableaux such as those in the *Agamemnon* and *Eumenides* (described above), Ajax sitting among the dead bodies of the sheep, Herakles with the dead bodies of his wife and children in the *Hercules Furens,* the disciples of Sokrates in the *Clouds.* We must admit this possibility although we have no certain fifth-century evidence for it. The great advantage would be better illumination and acoustics.

If the central opening was 12 ft. or more wide, the doors with their framework and decoration would occupy at least a third of the front wall of the stage-building. If therefore there were side doors as well as a central door, they were narrow. Doors in the projecting wings would not have been visible to much of the audience and would not have given on to the 'stage' but on to the passages leading to the *orchestra.* (In the fourth century an extra 20 ft. of width was added to the stage-building and extra doors would have been more easily accommodated.) It is not however clear that any door except the central door was needed for fifth-century tragedy. The aesthetic factor to be considered here is the Greek love of symmetry; when the action centred on the middle door, it is unlikely that a side door was used occasionally. The instances quoted are not convincing; in the later scenes of the *Choephori* it seems at first that one entrance leads to the men's quarters, where Orestes is lodged and Aigisthos killed, and another to the women's quarters, whence Klytaimnestra is fetched after Aigisthos has been murdered. But this is impossible. The central door must be used for displaying the corpses of Aigisthos and Klytaimnestra, and Orestes must knock at the central door when he first arrives —to be met by Klytaimnestra. Klytaimnestra's quarters are therefore behind the central door and have not a separate entrance. In the *Alcestis* (543 f.) Admetos breaks Herakles's resistance by saying that the guest room is away from the main rooms and can be shut off from them, but this in no way implies that they were not reached through the front door. In the *Hecuba* (1109) Agamemnon arrives because he has heard Polymestor's cries, but this does not mean that he enters through a door on the stage: 'shouting can be heard a long way off', as Odysseus says when he makes a similar entrance in the *Ajax* (1318). In the *Trojan Women* Kassandra and Helen both come out of the central door and no other door is needed. If any of the palace miracle in the *Bacchae* (597) is visible, it must be seen through the central door, and Dionysos must go in and come out through the central door; no other entrance is possible for him at this crisis.[1]

Nowhere in tragedy is the use of a side-door necessary or even desirable. In comedy the question is more difficult to decide. The spectators of Aristophanes were certainly

[1] Pickard-Cambridge, *Theatre*, 52 f. also quotes E. *Hel.* 1180–4 (an abortive cry which leads to no action), *Iphigenia in Aulis* (which plays entirely before Agamemnon's quarters), *Rhesus* (which plays before Hektor's quarters).

expected to use their imagination and 'houses' changed
their owners with lightning rapidity, but in some plays at
least different doors would avoid confusion; and the fragment
of Eupolis' *Autolykos* (42 K) 'they live in three huts, each
with his own dwelling' is best interpreted literally. We may,
I think, reasonably distinguish certain plays in which two
or more doors would be extremely convenient. In the
Acharnians, Euripides is rolled out of the central door and
the wider opening is needed for the various stage properties
which Dikaiopolis collects from him; the side-doors represent when needed the houses of Dikaiopolis and Lamachos.
In the *Clouds* the arrangement must have been asymmetrical
since the middle door was needed for the tableau of Sokrates'
disciples and one of the side-doors for the house of Strepsiades: in the first scene (91) Strepsiades says: 'Look this
way. Do you see this doorway, the little house?', and at the
end (1485) he calls Xanthias out of his own house to burn
down the house of Sokrates: this would be difficult without
two practicable doors. The later scenes of the *Peace* also need
a door for Trygaios' house as well as the central opening
which has become the shrine of Eirene (see below). Finally,
the *Ecclesiazusae* requires two practicable doors for Blepyros
and his neighbour and later for the old woman and the girl.
The other plays would lose nothing by being played with
only the central opening. As the *Acharnians*, produced in
425, requires three doors, this arrangement may have been
made possible by the Periclean rebuilding. We should
have then to conclude that the new stage-building with wide
central door and two narrow side-doors was completed by
425, and we should not have to assume more than a single
practicable opening for the pre-Periclean theatre.

   The plays also show the need of a high platform in the
pre-Periclean theatre, and it may be that the crane was used.
For the high platform the opening lines of the *Agamemnon*
—'lying on my elbows on the roof of the Atreidae'—are
sufficient evidence. It is in fact the roof of the stage-building:
so later in the Periclean theatre, in the *Acharnians* the wife of

Dikaiopolis watches her husband's procession from it, in the *Wasps* Bdelykleon lies on it to prevent his father escaping, in the *Phoenissae* Antigone and the paidagogos climb to it to see the Seven, and in the *Ecclesiazusae*, as Fraenkel [1] has shown, the hag and the girl stand on it to attract their lovers. This high platform may also have been used by the chorus of the *Prometheus Vinctus* during their first scene when they enter in a winged car or cars; this is perhaps the least unsatisfactory of the many interpretations that have been given; the only certainty is that the chorus do not, when they enter, take their normal place in the orchestra; they only appear there after the departure of Okeanos.

In Aeschylus' *Psychostasia* Zeus weighed the souls of Achilles and Memnon with their mothers Thetis and Eos standing beside the scales. The later lexicographer Pollux quotes this as an instance of the use of the *theologeion* high above the stage; this may be the same high platform as is used by the watchman in the *Agamemnon*. Pollux continues: 'the crane is a device which descends from above to remove a body, used by Eos removing the body of Memnon'. This does not necessarily imply that Eos actually removed the body from the stage; she may have appeared in the air carrying it. A late fifth-century South Italian vase (A 26) shows Sleep and Death carrying off Sarpedon, and this has been reasonably used as evidence for the crane in Aeschylus' *Carians or Europa*. We cannot quote any other certain use in Aeschylus or Sophocles unless it was used for the four-legged bird of Okeanos in the *Prometheus Vinctus*. This is possible but not necessary. From the time of the *Medea* the crane was often used and became proverbial. Medea appeared above the palace with her children in her Sun-chariot, Bellerophon flew to heaven on Pegasos and was parodied by Trygaios on his beetle in Aristophanes' *Peace*, Sokrates swung in his basket, Iris flew into Cloudcuckooland, Perseus flew to Andromeda and was parodied in *Thesmophoriazusae*. In several plays a divine figure or figures is seen above the

[1] *Greek Poetry and Life*, 261 f.

palace or temple, usually at the end of the play but once, *Hercules Furens*, in the middle. In most either the high platform or the crane could be used, but the high platform must have been used in the *Hercules* and the crane in the *Orestes*. In the *Hercules* Iris and Lyssa arrive together 'over the house' (817); at the end of the scene (872) Iris goes up to Olympus, Lyssa goes down into the house of Herakles; if, as has been suggested, they came on together in a winged chariot on the crane (of which there is no hint), Iris would have to drop Lyssa on the high platform; if both come on at one end of the high platform, Iris can go off at the same end and Lyssa descend behind the central door. In the *Orestes* (1625) Apollo (with or without Helen) must use the crane, because Orestes is already on the roof and Menelaos below on the stage. From descriptions, which range in date from Aristophanes through Plato to Pollux, we learn that the crane had a jib which could be raised like a finger and was worked by ropes and pulleys: the actor (or his car) was attached to the rope by a hook. It would seem possible that the Periclean stage-building made the use of the crane more secure, but the Aeschylean uses quoted above, if not also Medea's departure, suggest strongly that it was already known in the pre-Periclean theatre.

A wide central opening, to which were added later two smaller side openings, a rolling platform which can be pushed through the central opening, a roof, and a crane, the whole later flanked by projecting wings—these are the essential structures of the pre-Periclean and Periclean theatre. How far could they show changes of scenery? According to Aristotle 'scene-painting' was introduced by Sophocles, but Vitruvius tells us that the great painter, Agatharchos of Samos, 'made a scene' for a production of Aeschylus. It has been customary to harmonise the two accounts by placing the invention of scene-painting in the period between 468, Sophocles' first victory, and 456, the death of Aeschylus. Recently Professor Rumpf[1] has made

[1] JHS 67 (1947), 13.

a strong case, from the other references to Agatharchos' life and from artistic practice, for dating Agatharchos' activity in the second half and not too early in the second half of the fifth century. If this is true, Vitruvius or his source was interpreting a didascalic notice in some such form as: 'X. produced the Y. of Aeschylus, Agatharchos made the scene', i.e. one of the revivals of Aeschylus in the later fifth century. Vitruvius continues: 'Agatharchos left a commentary on this, which inspired Demokritos and Anaxagoras' to work out the rules of perspective so that buildings painted on scenery could show convincing recession and projection. Demokritos was born about 460 and Anaxagoras died in 428. Perspective on this scale is known to us from art of the late fifth century, and it seems necessary to date Agatharchos' commentary as late as possible, in fact in the thirties. If Agatharchos painted a perspective back-cloth [1] for a revival of Aeschylus in the thirties, this may have been an exploitation of the new possibilities of the Periclean stage-building, which must then have been built by that time. This, as we have seen, is perfectly possible, and our examination has suggested that the *Acharnians*, produced in 425, needed three practicable doors, which were probably a feature of the new stage-building. Aristotle's notice that Sophocles introduced 'scene-painting' remains true. Aristotle was writing a summary history in which he connected inventions with great names. But it is probable that he used 'scene-painting' (*skenographia*) in its technical sense of 'perspective back-cloth' (cf. 'towers which crown the city far away' at the beginning of the *Oedipus Coloneus*) and scenery in a more general sense may well go back to the pre-Periclean theatre: it is difficult to imagine how the *Prometheus* or the *Ajax* could have been produced without some kind of scenery.

The normal palace or temple front, which served for so many tragedies, is easy to imagine; but we have (in addition to several pictures of South Italian sets which will be con-

[1] In the fourth-century a back-cloth seems to have been called *proskenion*. Pickard-Cambridge, *Theatre*, 158.

sidered in the next chapter) an Attic picture of the *Iphigenia in Tauris* dating from the early fourth century (A 8). Here we see a very simple wooden structure, a steep pediment with akroteria, supported by columns which rise from two considerable steps, and sheltering a primitive statue of Artemis, before which a table of offerings stands. The painter undoubtedly thought of Euripides, because Iphigenia is giving the letter to Pylades. But Euripides [1] speaks of 'high-encircling walls', 'doors wrought in bronze', 'triglyphs', 'the gilded cornice of the pillared temple', 'the stone base of the statue', 'the porch'. His conception of the temple is elaborate; is it not likely that the vase-painter, who evidently knew his Euripides, gives us the actual wooden front which was visible? Then Euripides' other elaborate descriptions—the Doric triglyphs in the *Orestes*, the 'painted reliefs in the pediment' of the *Hypsipyle*, the mythological scenes on the Delphic temple in the *Ion*—may be verbal descriptions to which nothing visible corresponded. The determining factor (apart from cost) must have been time. A background giving mythological metopes for the *Ion* or a painted pediment for the *Hypsipyle* was of course within the compass of Agatharchos or any other artist but would not be executed unless it could stay in place for the whole trilogy, or unless there was some other compelling reason for defining the place visibly.

The set illustrated by the Iphigeneia vase is so simple that a similar set can be imagined for the pre-Periclean theatre. It could be a temple or a palace. Verisimilitude could be added by portable statues of relevant gods, which could be changed between plays or even within plays where necessary; in the *Eumenides* the scene changes from Delphi to Athens, a simple switch of Athena for Apollo. Nor would anything more elaborate be needed for the Sicilian audience of Aeschylus' *Aetnaean Women*,[2] in which the scene changed from Etna to Xouthia, back to Etna, then to Leontini, and

[1] *IT.* 96, 99, 113, 128, 997.
[2] *Ox. Pap.* 2257.

finally to Syracuse; these changes must primarily have been made clear by the words. In Euripides' Trojan trilogy the first play was set before the royal palace at Troy, the second and third in the Greek camp. The difference between royal palace and camp is greater than the difference between the temple of Apollo at Delphi and the temple of Athena at Athens in the *Eumenides*. But if we suppose the Iphigenia set with statues of Apollo and some other gods beside it in the first play and bare of statues in the second and third plays, the change of locality would be sufficiently indicated in verbal description and change of costume even without the addition of suitable back-cloths of the towers of Troy by Agatharchos or another. A more striking change is the change from Jason's palace in Corinth to Philoktetes' cave on Lemnos in the Euripidean production of 431 and the change within the *Ajax* from Ajax' quarters to a lonely place on the seashore; the former may, as we have seen, have been an early production in the Periclean theatre; the *Ajax* was probably produced in the forties and therefore in the pre-Periclean theatre.

Dr Hedwig Kenner [1] has recently suggested that the curious habit of half hiding figures behind rocks which is seen on vases of the second quarter of the fifth century B.C. may derive from the Aeschylean theatre and that an Attic black-figure lekythos by the Edinburgh painter of the very early fifth century (A 1), on which Odysseus is tied to a column, two Sirens play to him from rocks on either side, and the background represents the sea, is also inspired by the theatre. This is not the place to examine her further argument that the tradition persisted through Hellenistic times into Byzantine miniature painting, and it is more likely that, as the literary tradition suggests, the habit of half hiding figures behind rocks was invented by the fresco painters; but it is clear that early fifth-century painting suggests the possibility of screens representing rocks and

---

[1] *Ö.Jh.* 39 (1952), 47 f. See now her full study, *Das Theater und der Realismus in der griechischen Kunst.*

possibly of landscape back-cloths. One further Attic vase of the mid-sixth century (F 2) is worth quoting here; both sides are decorated with a row of sweating little men carrying a *phallos* pole; on one side the pole is surmounted by a huge figure of a fat man and on the other by a huge hairy satyr. These are carnival giants, and for the moment interest us because they show that the Athenians were used to monsters made presumably of stiffened canvas or some such material; they would therefore find no difficulty in screens.

We may then assume that screens representing rocks and possibly also a back-cloth representing the sea could be carried on swiftly when desired. Such would be the scenery of the *Philoctetes* of Euripides (and of Sophocles), the second part of the *Ajax*, the *Prometheus* plays of Aeschylus, the *Cyclops* and *Andromeda* of Euripides. In all the central door would remain in its simplest form without statues. On early fifth-century vases the figure is often half-hidden behind rocks. Such a half screen might be an extremely useful property, particularly if used in conjunction with the practicable door. Suitably painted it could be the tomb over the top of which Dareios rises in the *Persae*, the hill out of which Kyllene rises in *Ichneutae* (although I am not entirely convinced that this is not a normal cave as in the *Philoctetes*), and the entrance to the Underworld from which Aeschylus' Sisyphos (fr. 227 N) appeared like an 'overgrown field mouse'. It seems to me very likely that a screen was used in combination with the *ekkyklema* for the *Ajax*, *Prometheus*, and *Netfishers*. These require a little more examination. They could be staged with a screen alone behind the central doorway, but in each case the *ekkyklema* would make the action easier and more readily visible to the audience. We have noticed that the *ekkyklema* would be useful for the early scene in the *Ajax* where the hero appears sitting among the cattle. The second part of the play requires (1) that Ajax should pronounce his last speech near the place where he has planted his sword, (2) that Tekmessa should discover his body, (3) that the actor who has taken Ajax should also play Teucer, (4) that the body should be brought into full view of the audience. If the *ekkyklema* was used, as soon as Tekmessa and the chorus had gone off to search for Ajax, the *ekkyklema* would be pushed forward with a screen in front, representing a bush, behind which the dummy of Ajax is concealed. Ajax himself enters from behind the bush, pronounces his last speech and then goes behind the bush again to commit suicide: the actor can then crawl off unobserved, leaving the dummy to be discovered by Tekmessa (an exact parallel is provided by the last scene of Petrouchka). Tekmessa, like Ajax, comes on through what is normally the house-door and therefore finds Ajax' body, which is hidden from the chorus searching in the *orchestra*.

In the *Prometheus Vinctus* the combination of rock and *ekkyklema* would make it possible for Prometheus to be withdrawn behind the central door at the end of the play, and possibly the chorus would follow him out this way. If, as the title implies, he was freed in the *Prometheus Unbound*, the actor must have been visible through the whole of both plays and cannot, as has been suggested, have played the part from behind a dummy. A tantalising fragment of Aeschylus' satyr play, *Netfishers*,[1] gives two fishermen who have caught something in their nets which they cannot pull ashore. They shout for help and the satyr chorus arrive and pull out of the sea the box containing Danae and Perseus. In a satyr play Aeschylus only uses two actors; therefore at least one of the fishermen must go before Danae can appear. The fishermen pull the seaweed-covered box a certain distance before they shout for help. This may mean that they pull the screen, which is painted to represent the box, upright so that it is visible on the front edge of the *ekkyklema* within the central door. The chorus then pull the *ekkyklema* forward so that it is outside the central door in full view. Meanwhile one of the actors has gone out ostensibly to

---

[1] *PSI* 1209; D. L. Page, *Greek Literary Papyri*, no. 2; Mette, *Supplementum Aeschyleum*. Fragments from the later part of the play, *Ox. Pap.* 2161.

report the discovery but actually to change into female mask and clothing and get on to the *ekkyklema* under cover of the screen, so that he can rise out of the box as Danae.

The summons to the chorus 'All farmers, hither, vine-diggers, herdsmen, and shepherds' is startlingly repeated by Trygaios' summons to the chorus in Aristophanes' *Peace* to drag Peace out of the deep cave in which she has been buried by Polemos. Very similar arrangements are possible here. At the beginning of the play the two slaves feed the beetle through the half-open central door. Trygaios on the beetle is then lifted by the crane from behind the central door (like Medea) and swung over to land on the 'stage', and knocks on one of the side-doors out of which Hermes comes. While Hermes and Trygaios are talking, the central doors are opened and a heap of stones can be seen on the *ekkyklema*. Then Polemos and later Kydoimos appear at the other side door; during their conversation, I suspect, the crane swings the beetle away, so that Trygaios later has to walk home with Opora and Theoria. Then Trygaios summons the chorus and at length with their help and with the help of Hermes they succeed in dragging up Eirene, Opora, and Theoria. Eirene is a statue, to whom later sacrifice is made, and remains on the stage till the end of the play, Opora is later handed over to the prytanis and Theoria is married to Trygaios; they therefore are taken by supernumeraries (they do not speak). Like Danae's chest in the *Netfishers*, I suggest that the figure of Eirene is first pulled upright from where it lies flat under the stones and then is pulled forward on the *ekkyklema*; she is in fact a carnival giant of the same kind of construction as the fat man and hairy satyr on the black-figured cup (F 2), but not so big that Hermes cannot climb up and whisper in her ear.

In the *Ecclesiazusai*, as has been seen, the side-doors represent two houses and the central door is not used, in the *Acharnians* (and with variations in the *Peace*) three houses are needed, in the *Clouds* two houses, one with the central, one with a side-door. The normal tragic set was a palace

front in which only the central door was used; the
front must have appeared as a unity, dominated by the
wide central entrance. How could the separate identity
of the comic houses be established when this was desirable? The answer is suggested by a well-known Roman
relief (C *48*) with a scene from comedy: an elaborate
door on the left is evidently joined to a further door
by an architectural background, but the background is
covered by a curtain, so that the door is isolated. This is of
course much too late for Aristophanes, but with its help we
can interpret a vase of about 425 B.C. and some early texts.
The vase (B *1*) besides giving us, as we have said, the only
picture of the fifth-century stage in Athens also gives the
only picture of the fifth-century curtain, and the curtain is
by the side of the stage so that it isolates the area in which
the comic Perseus dances. Curtains may therefore have been
used already in the fifth century to isolate comic houses. The
Greek for curtain was *parapetasma*, which is often used in
the metaphorical sense of screen or disguise. In the *Ethics* [1]
Aristotle gives as an instance of vulgar extravagance to
'produce a comedy with purple in the *parodos* like the
Megarians'. *Parodos* here means not only the passage up to
the stage, of which little would be visible, but the whole
distance up to the central door. The ancient commentator
notes that curtains in comedy were normally of skin and not
of purple cloth; for this he quotes the Attic comic poet
Myrtilos. This is further evidence for curtains in Attic
comedy as well as Megarian.

In the theatre of Lykourgos, who administered Athens'
finances from 338–326, the orchestra was moved northwards
and the width of the stage was increased from 45 to 66 ft.,
which would give considerably more room for the side-doors,
so that the houses of comedy would be more realistic. The
stage-building was now built of stone for the first time. The
effect of this must have been to emphasise the architectural
features, such as *paraskenia* and doorways, and to give the

[1] *NE* 4, 6, 1123 a 21.

screens representing scenery a marble frame. At the same
time, as we shall see later, the masks of tragedy were changed
to give them a more archaic appearance, and the costume of
comedy also changed before the end of the fourth century:
tragedy became hieratic and comedy respectable.

The next great change was the removal of the action to
the top of the stage-building so that it took place on a stage
66 ft. wide, 9 ft. deep, and about 13 ft. above the level of
the orchestra; at the same time the fronts of the *paraskenia*
were moved back so that they were nearly level with the
front of the high stage.[1] This was a major reconstruction
which is unlikely to have been undertaken soon after the
Lycurgan theatre was completed. The chief advantage was
that the actors could be seen and heard better on the high
stage. On the other hand communication between stage and
orchestra thereby became impossible. This is a fundamental
alteration in the assumptions of drama. The gradation from
actors through chorus to audience no longer exists. Actors
(and chorus) now operate in a private world cut off from the
audience by an architectural setting, a thirteen-foot wall, and
an empty orchestra. It is the beginning of the conventions of
the modern theatre, in which we overhear and observe the
private lives of other people. The essential change is the
removal of the chorus from their physical position in the
orchestra between the audience and the actors. They had
long ceased to perform their original function in tragedy and
comedy. Aristotle notes that from the time of Agathon (who
probably lived into the early fourth century) the tragic
chorus sang interludes, songs which could be transferred
from one play to another, and we may be certain that interludes had become the normal practice before Aristotle came
to Athens in 367. Interludes could not give the poet's

---

[1] The two columns in the foreground of Pl. 1 belong to the western
paraskenion of the Hellenistic theatre; the foundations of the Lycurgan
paraskenion can be seen immediately in front of them. The line of stone to the
left and just behind them marks the front of the Hellenistic stage. The front
of the Lycurgan stage-building lies between this and the Periclean building.

commentary on the action and it would be difficult for the chorus to have a relevant personality if they sang irrelevant songs; interludes could presumably be performed on the narrow raised stage by a reduced chorus. The chief impediment to transferring the action to the high stage must have been continued revivals of Aeschylus and Sophocles and of satyr plays, whose lively choruses needed room. In comedy the chorus sang interludes all through the fourth century from the time of the *Ecclesiazusai,* but we have some traces of special songs by interesting choruses which presumably needed the *orchestra*; the latest in Antiphanes' *Skythai* which can be dated 320/10.[1] In Menander the choruses sing interludes during which the actors withdraw; the solo song and dance of the girl in the *Theophoroumene* is sometimes quoted as evidence of the use of the orchestra but surely could have been performed on a narrow stage. Nevertheless the Antiphanes fragment is evidence that the high stage was not introduced in Athens in the early years of New Comedy. If the *terminus post quem* is 320/10, the *terminus ante quem* is 156–5 when a Stoic philosopher acting as an ambassador for Athens spoke of the removal of dancing from tragedy as something recent;[2] it is reasonable therefore to suppose that the Athenian theatre was reconstructed in the first half of the second century, when the high stage had already been introduced elsewhere, as we shall see.

If this is so, Menander's plays were produced on the low stage of the theatre of Lykourgos and the conventions of New Comedy were formed there. We have no reason to believe that fourth-century tragedy required any other setting than fifth-century tragedy, which was in fact revived every year. It is therefore likely that the central door was still wider than the two side-doors and marked by a columned porch, but that this was now framed in stone instead of wood. This setting would be suitable for those comedies which have two houses and a shrine—the shrine being in the centre.

---

[1] Webster, *Studies in Later Greek Comedy* (=*LGC*), 62.

[2] See Pickard-Cambridge, *Theatre,* 195.

Such were the *Apistos* (=*Aulularia*), *Dyskolos*, *Hiereia* of Menander, and the *Curculio*, which perhaps goes back to an original by Menander. The *Epitrepontes* and *Samia* have two houses; here the central door may have been masked to make the arrangement symmetrical. This seems to me probable even where the contiguity of the houses was essential as in the *Miles*. Three houses are essential for Apollodoros' *Hekyra* and likely in Menander's *Perikeiromene*: that one house had a more splendid door than the other two could not be helped.

We have many pictures of New Comedy but they do not for the most part tell us about the scenery. It is perhaps worth noting that the door of Dioskourides' mosaic with revellers (C 20) has no side columns and therefore is not the central door. The other Dioskourides mosaic (C 19) raises much more complicated questions. Both are accurate copies in mosaic of Greek original paintings which can be dated to the early third century by the use of changing colours and by the proportions of the figures: the cup held by the old woman in the second mosaic has a shape known in the early third century and the two revellers in the first are repeated by late third-century terra-cottas. Whether the originals were in Athens or not we cannot tell, but the strong left light would suit an early morning production in the theatre of Dionysos. The second mosaic is an illustration of the opening scene of Menander's *Women at Breakfast* (*Synaristosai*), adapted by Plautus as the *Cistellaria*. The old procuress and her daughter Gymnasium visit Selenium (seated in the centre), who is keeping house for Alcesimarchus. The old procuress complains of the strength and amount of the drink: the slave has taken away the table and the wine before she has finished.[1] At the end of the conversation Selenium goes home to her mother, Gymnasium keeps house instead of her, the old procuress soliloquises tipsily before going off. The picture shows us an early moment before the table is removed, but the slave is seen on the extreme right, ready to remove it.

[1] Menander 451 K (385 Kö) = *Cist.* 19.

The play has two houses and therefore it is likely that the central door was masked, and this scene plays before or in one of the side houses. It requires couches and a table like the drinking party of the *Mostellaria* (Philemon's *Phasma*), which is hastily moved inside the house when the young man's father is reported to be coming home.

There are two separate problems in such scenes: where did the audience imagine the action to be and where was the action which they saw? Both problems have been much discussed,[1] and the details need not be recapitulated. The Greek house had a courtyard from which its rooms were entered. Drinking parties would normally take place in one of the rooms. But the dramatist can telescope this house plan in any way that suits him. Therefore anything that goes on inside one of the rooms off the courtyard can be, if he wishes, directly accessible to the street. Let us take three cases. In the *Epitrepontes* (563 f. referring back to 510 f.) Charisios overhears from Chairestratos' house the dialogue between Pamphile and Smikrines in Charisios' house. On the stage this is easy: Pamphile and Smikrines converse in front of Charisios' door, and Charisios opens Chairestratos' door to hear. Menander may have expected the audience to imagine that the partition between the inner rooms of the two houses was so thin that such overhearing was possible, but it seems more likely that he is exploiting the actualities of his stage without bothering too much about how such a situation would be possible in real life. In the *Bacchides* (830 f.), an adaptation of Menander's *Dis Exapaton*, the father Nicobulus is led by the slave Chrysalus to look through the door and see his son drinking with his friends, and while they are looking the soldier Cleomachus arrives. Here the courtyard is forgotten and the door on to the street gives immediately into an inner room. In the *Mostellaria* (156–430) the young man Philolaches comes along the street and observes Philematium washing and dressing; they settle down to

---

[1] E.g. Dalman, *De aedibus scaenicis comoediae novae*; Pickard-Cambridge, *Theatre*, 74 f., 174; Beare, *Roman Stage*, 271.

drink; a friend and his girl arrive and the party continues; the slave Tranio comes with the news that Philolaches' father is returning; the whole party is hastily sent inside; Tranio awaits Theopropides outside the front door. Again Philemon exploits the actualities of his stage. At the beginning Philolaches can see into Philematium's room from the street. The drinking party presumably takes place in one of the rooms off the courtyard, but because the audience must be able to see, it can be interrupted from the street and can be removed 'inside'. In fact inside and outside are still as fluid as they have been from the earliest days of Greek drama and the area of stage in front of a house door (called *prothyron* in Greek and *ante aedes* in Latin) can be either the street in front of the house or any room inside the house, but if it is a room inside the house it is at the same time immediately accessible from the street.

The second problem is where drinking parties which were seen by the audience actually took place. There are three possibilities: on the stage, on an *ekkyklema*, inside the doorway. The last seems to me most unlikely if the actors were to be heard. In the *Synaristosai* the slave has removed the table and in the *Mostellaria* (308) Philolaches asks for the table to be brought. If the scene is either on an *ekkyklema* or inside the doorway, there is no need and little room for furniture moving, but if the action takes place on the stage, the furniture must be brought out beforehand and removed afterwards; the instructions for furniture removal rather suggest therefore that the party was held on the stage. It is difficult to interpret the Dioskourides mosaic which illustrates the *Synaristosai*, but Professor Rumpf has shown by contemporary parallels that the coloured strips on the left and at the top are meant to show recession and do not correspond to any architectural feature. Similarly the dark band with the light edge on the right need not be interpreted architecturally. There are two certainties: the artist has not shown a doorway and he has shown three steps along the whole width of his picture. The women are therefore seated on a raised platform with a considerable recession. It is therefore perfectly possible, although it cannot be proved, that we have a picture of the stage and that the couch and table occupy the space between the left *paraskenion* and the left side-door, through which the little servant is going to remove the table.

Such an arrangement would clearly be easier in the Lycurgan theatre, where the stage had a possible depth of 15 ft., than in the Hellenistic theatre, where the high stage was only 9 ft. deep and additional room had to be left for the side entrances from country and town. It would not however be impossible in the late Hellenistic theatre since the total depth of the mosaic scene need not be more than 4 ft. We know extremely little about the late Hellenistic theatre at Athens, and the evidence for scenery in other late Hellenistic theatres will be considered in its place. There were however two developments which are likely to have been universal. Of the first we have an illustration in the cubiculum of the Villa of P. Fannius Synistor at Boscoreale, which corresponds with a description in Vitruvius. Vitruvius[1] distinguishes the scenery of tragic, comic, and satyr plays. Tragic scenery has columns, pediments, statues, and other royal things; this is illustrated on the panels of the alcove of the cubiculum (A 53). The scenery of the satyr play has trees, caves, mountains, and other rustic things, as painted by the landscape-painter (the first recorded landscape painter is dated in the middle of the second century B.C.); this is illustrated on the back wall of the cubiculum. The scenery of comedy shows private houses with balconies and windows. The main panels of the cubiculum (C 23) have a central shrine of Hekate (or Artemis) flanked on either side by fantastic house architecture with balcony and windows above two practicable doors; it has been suggested that broken pots with plants standing above the balconies are gardens of Adonis and that therefore this was the scene for a comedy called *Adoniazusae*. The general scheme of two houses about

---

[1] Vitruvius V, 6, 9; cf. Rumpf, *JHS* 67 (1947), 18.

a shrine we have noted above for several plays of Menander. It is therefore probable that the Boscoreale pictures are copies of painted panels embracing practicable doors which formed the backgrounds for tragedy, satyr play, and comedy in the Hellenistic theatre of the second century. These panels, as we shall find when we consider other theatres, fitted into wide openings in the stage background of the high stage and were known technically as *thyromata*.

Immediately before his account of scenery Vitruvius has mentioned the *periaktoi*.[1] From this passage and various passages in Pollux and other authors, who mention or describe *periaktoi, hemikyklion, stropheion*, and even the *ekkyklema*, it appears that sections of the background near each end of the stage could be revolved. There seem to have been two main types. First, the *periaktoi* were triangular in section and each had therefore three different fronts which could be shown to the audience but no revolving platform; they were used to indicate change of place but also in connection with the thunder and lightning machines to announce the appearance of a god. The second type had a small revolving stage as well as a revolving section of background and was used to display interiors; but it could also be used to display sea gods, heroes who had gone to heaven, people swimming in the sea, and those who had died in battle or at sea. These two uses of the revolving stage are separate: in the first, the small revolving stage is a substitute for the *ekkyklema* or rolling platform. In the second the revolving background is used for the same sort of purpose as the *periaktoi*. We have, I think, no certain evidence that the crane was used in the Hellenistic theatre with its high stage, and a change of background coupled with an appearance of a divine or heroic figure on the roof of the stage-building may have been substituted for it. To explain 'people swimming in the sea' and 'those who had died at battle or at sea' we have two alternatives: either a special background was

[1] See Pickard-Cambridge, *Theatre*, 234 f., 115 f.; Beare, *Roman Stage*, 241 f. for texts.

turned on to illustrate a narrative speech or Pollux (or his source) has imagined it from reading, e.g. the *Rudens* (swimmers) or the *Persae* (corpses). The second alternative is perhaps more likely, as he cheerfully invents for the comic stage a stable with large doors for driving in wagons from a passage of Antiphanes (21 K), which he obligingly quotes; there a character says, 'He has converted the stable used for the farm animals into a work-shop'. Pollux must be used with care, but we must, I think, accept the varied testimony to a small revolving stage and revolving sections of background as part of the same desire for realism which produced the elaborate scenery of the Villa Boscoreale. They can however only have been used in theatres which had more than three openings in the back wall of the stage since three openings were needed for the three practicable doors.

The second development reversed this move towards realism. In the middle of the first century B.C. Scaurus built a background at Rome in three stories with 360 columns. As Rumpf remarks, this became canonical for the future and painting was no more needed. So we see both tragedy (A 52) and comedy (C 22) acted before this kind of background on Roman terra-cottas. Athens itself may have waited until the time of Nero for such an architectural background. If we ask why this change was made, the answer may be that both tragedy and comedy were now felt to belong to a bygone age—classics to be acted before a formal background.

2. COSTUME

(a) *Origins*

If we accept the view that the official beginning of tragedy was in 534, of the satyr play about 500, and of comedy in 486, pictures of tragic, satyric, or comic costume before these dates are pictures of performances from which costumes or elements of costume were taken over into the three forms of drama when they became an official part of

the festivals of Dionysos. It is only in this restricted sense
that we are concerned with the origins of these three forms
of drama. We are interested in early evidence for the wearing
of masks and for the costumes which we associate with
tragedy, comedy, and satyr play in the fifth century. Early
in the sixth century Athens like Corinth, Sparta, Boeotia,
and other parts of the Greek world had choruses of padded
dancers.[1] They were men wearing a kind of jersey which
held in the padding. They danced, often holding drinking
horns. Sometimes they danced with women, padded, naked
or clothed. Sometimes they seem to take part with satyrs in
the Return of Hephaistos. Sometimes they take the place of
satyrs in attendance on Dionysos. On the cup with carnival
giants (F 2) to which we have already alluded the giant fat
man corresponds to the giant hairy satyr and like him holds
an ivy spray, which shows his connection with Dionysos.
These dancers are interesting because their costume clearly
has affinities with the costume of the actors of Old
Comedy.

We must however be more precise. As I hope to show
later, the actor of Old Comedy, when he is to perform a male
part, wears a mask, tights with a phallos sewn to them which
support his padding, and over the tights any other clothing
that suits his part; if he is stripped naked, the audience see
him in mask, tights, and phallos; his tights are his dramatic
skin. There is one important difference between the tights
of the comic actor and the 'jersey' of the padded dancer;
the 'jersey' leaves the legs and arms bare. Full tights are
more realistic but no doubt less comfortable for dancing.
But the dancers' 'jersey' is also their dramatic skin, because
the vase painters often draw them naked. The vase-painter
is never a photographer. He sees a man wearing a mask and
tights; he knows that he represents a naked young man and
he draws him as a naked young man. There are a very few
instances in Corinthian and Attic where the head of a padded

[1] For details and literature see my article in *Rylands Bulletin* 36 (1954),
582 f.

dancer or fat man is stylised in such a way that it looks like a mask; it is therefore probable that some of them wore masks as well as padding. There are some cases also where they are ithyphallic, but whether this means that they sometimes wore phalloi or whether the painter has some other purpose in giving them phalloi is difficult to say. It seems however not unreasonable to suppose that when comedy had a chorus representing men—*Acharnians* etc.—they were the successors of the padded dancers and that the leaders of the padded dancers became the male characters of comedy.

There are however three other questions: what did the padded dancers represent in the sixth century? who are the women who dance with them? and are they women or men dressed up as women? The padded dancers and the naked fat men take part with satyrs (i.e. horse-eared, horse-tailed men) in the Return of Hephaistos, which is a story about Dionysos. They take the place of satyrs as attendants on Dionysos. On the Florence cup (F 2) the naked fat man is the counterpart of the hairy satyr. They are therefore the equivalents of satyrs, and in Corinth, as we shall see, they were probably called satyrs. In Attica it is probably safer, as well as less confusing, to call them Komasts, or Revellers, and this name has the advantage of reminding us that besides this special Komos or Revel there is an everyday komos or revel of ordinary men and women, which is well known on vases and in literature, e.g. the irruption of Alkibiades and his party into the Symposion in Plato. But at the same time it must be remembered that, although satyrs, smooth or hairy, are well known in art in the sixth century, we have no picture of a singing dancer dressed up as a satyr before the fifth century. If therefore in the sixth century men formed a satyr chorus to sing of the Return of Hephaistos, they would presumably dress up as Komasts and the painter might paint them as ithyphallic because satyrs were ithyphallic; this does not however exclude the possibility that their leader always wore the phallos because he was especially endowed with this Dionysiac power and later because he was the leader he became the actor of comedy.

Before comedy was officially recognised in 486, the Komasts had ceased to represent satyrs, because from the beginning of the fifth century Pratinas had won official recognition for the satyr play. As we find all through the fifth century pictures not only of satyrs but also of satyrs wearing drawers which support phallos and tail, it seems reasonable to connect the introduction of these singing dancers dressed as satyrs into the artistic tradition with Pratinas' introduction of the satyr play: one of the earliest of them is on a cup by Makron painted in the second decade of the fifth century (A 2); part of Pratinas' innovation must have been that for the first time he dressed his choruses to look like the lean horse-tailed, horse-eared men, who had been known in painting for about a hundred years. Nor were they only known in art; it is possible that satyr masks were also worn in certain forms of Dionysiac ritual, as seems to have been the case in Ionia. Once established they survive with little change and the essentials of the costume can be seen on the well-known Attic vase (9), which was painted in the late fifth or very early fourth century. It is called the Pronomos vase after the flute-player in the centre, who is known to have performed in Athens in 394. The chorus all wear or carry the same mask with snub-nose, horse-ears, and unkempt hair and beard. The contrasts between the red of these masks and the white or yellow of the masks of the actors corresponds to stage practice, since in Aeschylus' *Netfishers* the baby Perseus is delighted with 'the crimson shining baldness' of Silenos or the satyrs. Our satyrs are not bald. Satyr masks did however vary: the early satyr choreut (2) is bald as satyrs often are said to be, and the bald satyrs on a vase of 470 (3) are drawn as wearing masks, perhaps in Aeschylus' *Thalamopoioi*. Pollux also speaks of a grey-haired satyr mask, which we know from texts and vases. On the Pronomos vase the drawers which support phallos and tail are either shaggy or smooth (top left) and this variation is known also on other vases. Perhaps shaggy drawers means a shaggy satyr, and perhaps they allude to the goat-like quality of satyrs, mentioned in satyr plays. Indubitable goat men appear on a vase of about 460 (5); they have horns and the vase-painter has even given them goat-hooves so that their identity may be certain, but they are performers as their phalloi are attached by loincloths. We should perhaps call them Pans, but it is certainly possible that they are an alternative chorus for a satyr-play rather than a chorus of comedy as some have suggested; they are too thin for comedy and one of them dances the *sikinnis*, the satyr dance. The father of the satyrs, Papposilenos, is clearly distinguished from the chorus (the part was taken by an actor); he is old and covered all over with white hair. He can be seen on the right on the Pronomos vase with his mask in his hand; it has white hair and beard and a wreath of ivy leaves. Arms, body, and legs are covered by tights to which pieces of wool representing white hair have been sewn: this is the *chiton chortaios* (coarse) or *mallotos* (fleecy) of which the ancient authorities speak. He also wears a leopard skin—leopard or panther skins are commonly worn by maenads in art from the sixth century and occasionally by Corinthian Komasts in the late seventh century; [1] they may perhaps give the wearer some authority as the representative of the god. The other characters in the satyr play wore the costumes and masks of tragedy, to which we shall return later.

We have therefore in the padded dancers or Komasts one of the elements which pass over into later Greek drama. We have not yet considered the women who dance with them, sometimes naked, sometimes padded, sometimes clothed. The difficult question is whether they are women or men dressed as women. Clearly the vase-painter who paints a padded masked man as a naked man can also paint a man wearing a female mask and tights as a naked woman. The practice of Greek drama was undoubtedly to give female parts to male actors. In fact there is little evidence for naked

---

[1] Cf. below Ch. III, p. 132.

women in public except solo dancers at symposia.[1] Two vases suggest an answer to this problem. On the first, a little black-figure cup without handles datable about 520 (F 6), a flute-player stands among eight young dancers, one of whom can fairly be called a fat Komast; three of them have a girl's head on the top of their own head. For our present purpose it would be useful to know whether the girl's head is the actual mask that the young man wears or whether it is rather an indication that he is dancing a female part. This is a difficult question on which the other instances of heads above heads do not seem to me to give a clear answer: the painter may mean either 'A behaves like B' or 'A acts B' or 'A becomes B'. There can however be no doubt that these young men are dancing female parts, and as the other young men appear to be Komasts, they must be the women who dance with Komasts. They may have worn female masks or their faces may merely have been whitened; they must have worn white tights, whether they wore clothing or not. The second vase (F 4) is rather earlier: here five young men stand in front of a flute-player, four of them making what can only be described as a come-hither gesture. They are dressed in chitons which come down to their knees and over them a garment said to be a jacket but which I take from its long tail to be a skin. This is the dress of maenads among others, and they are possibly a chorus of maenads, but the painter has not given any indication except their clothing that they are taking female parts. We have here a chorus of maenads in Athens about the middle of the sixth century, the ancestor of the chorus of Euripides' Bacchae and many other Greek tragedies.

If we have a chorus of maenads and if the Komasts are the equivalent of satyrs, should we be justified in describing the women who dance with the Komasts as maenads? Probably we should, but it may be safer to keep the name maenads for the dancing women of Dionysos when they are

---

[1] E.g. red-figure jug in Vienna 1043, Van Hoorn, Choes, fig. 184 cf. fig. 185; Holzinger, Sitzb. Wien. Ak., 208 (1928), 39 f.

either associated with satyrs or distinguished by wearing skins or carrying the thyrsos. Then our women may be given the more general appellation of nymphs. The gain for our main subject is that we know that before the official performances of drama in Athens men dressed up and danced and sang as nymphs and maenads.

Another Attic vase of the middle of the sixth century (F 3) shows choruses with a flute-player. On both sides six bearded dancers are divided by a flautist. Three dancers on each side wear long chitons down to their ankles and pointed caps. Such caps are the normal wear of Amazons, Persians, and Thracians, but on two vases [1] at any rate maenads wear head-cloths (*sakkoi*) which approximate to this shape. On one side the other three dancers wear the same pointed caps but chitons which only reach to their knees. On the other side the remaining three dancers wear ankle-length chitons but their caps are not pointed but have two upright objects in front. These could be interpreted as phalloi and it is tempting to connect this trio with the *ithyphalloi*, to whom we shall return later.[2] The knee-length and ankle-length chitons suggest women rather than men, as do the steps of their dance. We cannot tell whether the painter has omitted their masks or whether they did not wear masks. In spite of the uncertainties, the positive gain is the evidence for choruses of men wearing women's clothing in the mid-sixth century.

To the same date also belongs the well-known Attic vase with a chorus of knights (F 5). A flute-player stands on the left; the three chorus-men in helmets, corslets, and short chitons, are carried on the shoulders of three other men, who wear horses' heads and have horses' tails. This chorus anticipates Aristophanes by a century and a quarter

[1] Cambridge 37.17. Beazley, *ARV*, 104/4. Cf. also the black-figure pelike, Berlin inv. 3228, Pfuhl, *MuZ*, fig. 276.

[2] Sir John Beazley points out that the 'phalloi' are most probably ends of the headband set upright; they must in that case be stiffened, cf. *Annali* 1868, pl. C.

and the official beginning of comedy by some 65 years. Two choruses of cocks cannot be dated so accurately that the possibility of their being comic choruses can be excluded. If however they are comic choruses they belong to the very earliest years of comedy. One (F 7) gives two men in feathered tights with winged sleeves and extra feathers at the knee, and with combs on their heads; they also apparently wear a skin twisted around their waists. On the other (F 8) two men wrapped up in cloaks have cock-masks on their heads.

The results of this survey are meagre. We can however see that there were in Athens in the sixth century various different kinds of chorus in which men represented Komasts, maenads, women, and animals. We can see also that Pratinas made a new start with his chorus of lean horse-eared, horse-tailed satyrs. Comedy had material already to hand for choruses of men (including leaders who could become actors), and choruses of animals. Tragedy found choruses of maenads already existing, but how much else?

(b) *Tragedy*

We are well documented for the costume of tragedy from the end of the fifth century, but for the earlier period we have little to go on. Literary sources are mostly late, confused, and difficult to interpret. The following statements [1] must at least be discussed with such monumental evidence as we have. Thespis first disguised his face with white-lead, then hung purslane over it, then took to plain linen masks (Horace speaks of Thespis' performers with their faces smeared with wine-lees); Phrynichos introduced female masks (or characters); Aeschylus considerably altered costume and footwear and introduced frightening and coloured masks. Most of this we cannot control. Male and female masks had undoubtedly existed in certain contexts, both in Greece generally and in Athens particularly, long

[1] Texts are given in Pickard-Cambridge, *Festivals*, 177 f.

before Thespis, but their introduction into tragedy may yet
have been gradual. In tragedy itself the stages (1) plain
linen, (2) differentiation of sex in characters as well as in
chorus, (3) further developments, may have been historical,
at least in the sense that Phrynichos was known to have
written plays with female characters and Aeschylus was
known to have introduced a chorus of Furies and Lyssa
(Madness) as a character. But the white lead, the wreath
of purslane, and the faces smeared with wine-lees may
contain a reference to other known kinds of performance
which are not wholly irrelevant to tragedy. The wreath and
the wine-lees suggest Dionysiac revels. It is very possible
that the Komasts (even if their leader was masked) had their
faces reddened with wine-lees and that the faces of their
'women' were whitened to match. Thespis may well have
written for them. There is also another possibility. Semos of
Delos in the second century B.C. writes of the *ithyphalloi*:
'they wear the masks of drunkards and are wreathed; they
have embroidered sleeves, chitons with a white stripe, and a
Tarantine robe falling to their feet'. They are Athenian and
surely old. The masks of drunkards and the wreaths give a
possible connection with Thespis; they wear the sleeves and
long chiton later associated with tragedy. Two vases may
possibly be connected with them. One is the cup (F 3) of
which we have already spoken; the three dancers, who may
have phalloi on their caps, wear long chitons with a central
stripe. The other is a red-figure fragment of the early fifth
century (F 9). On this an elderly, ugly man, wearing an
ivy-wreath, a long chiton with ivy leaf pattern, and boots,
holds a phallos-stick, a phallos springs from his forehead and
another from his nose. Here then is another kind of Dionysiac chorus for which Thespis may have written and from
which he or his successors may have taken elements of the
tragic costume, whereas the content of their songs may have
had some influence on comedy.

Sleeved chiton and boots were part of the classical tragic
costume. It is likely that they came from some performance

which was given in honour of Dionysos. A survey of other
wearers does not tell us very much. The sleeved chiton is
worn by Poseidon on a sixth-century Corinthian clay tablet,
by a priestess among the sixth-century ivories from Ephesos,
by a female lyre-player on an Attic cup of about 530, and
by Dionysos on an Attic black-figure amphora of about
500.[1] Boots are more complicated.[2] There are three main
kinds: a cuffed boot of which the top folds over; a loose-
fitting boot with or without a tab at the top; and a laced
boot with or without a tab at the top. Whether the name
kothornos covers all three is not clear. The laced boot is worn
by tragic actors of the late fifth century (A 9 etc.), and earlier
by Thamyras and Lyssa in paintings probably inspired by
tragedy, by an ordinary Athenian rider in a Thracian cloak;
in the mid-sixth century, with wings attached, by Hermes,
Perseus, and the Gorgons; and in the late seventh-early
sixth century by a fat, hairy Corinthian Komast, who also
has a panther skin to suggest his connection with Dionysos
(F 15).[3] The loose-fitting boot is worn by tragic chorus men
in the early fifth century (A 4, 6, 7) and by the man with the
phalloi just described (F 9). The cuffed boot is not connected
with tragedy except in one uncertain instance, but it is worn
sometimes in comedy (B 6) and by satyrs as well as by
revellers, male and female, including Dionysos himself. We
need therefore not look for any origin of tragic costume or

[1] Add to Pickard-Cambridge, *Festivals*, 212 f. the references given by J. D.
Beazley, *JHS*, 51 (1931), 262. A. Alföldi's article, Gewaltherrscher und
Theaterkönig (*Studies in Honor of A. M. Friend*, 15 f.) appeared when this was
already in proof. In brief, he derives the tragic costume from the costume of the
Persian king, as introduced by Aeschylus. The early evidence quoted here for
sleeved chiton and boots makes me unwilling to accept this in general; in particular, he misinterprets the decorated strap, by which the hero on the Pronomos
vase (A 9, see below p. 40) holds his mask, as a tiara.
[2] The instances quoted, other than those in the list of monuments, will be
found in E. Pfuhl, *MuZ*: laced boots—figs. 512 (Thamyras), 515 (Lyssa),
499, 216; loose-fitting boot—figs. 338, 564; cuffed boot—figs. 254, 275, 325,
329, 338, 430, 465, cf. also Pickard-Cambridge, *Festivals*, fig. 202 (*JHS*, 65
(1945), pl. 4a); I do not feel certain that it is an actor.
[3] They are common on these plastic vases which represent Komasts and are
worn occasionally by the padded dancers painted on vases (e.g. F 10).

tragic footwear outside the various kinds of chorus which
were performed in honour of Dionysos in Athens in the
sixth century. But what particular borrowings or developments were due to Thespis, what to Phrynichos, and what
to Aeschylus and what to later producers we have not
enough knowledge to say. We can only note what datable
monuments tell us.

Our first certain picture of tragedy is an Attic oenochoe
painted about 470 B.C. and discovered in the Agora (A 4).
From right to left the fragments show a woman moving to
the right, a boy standing holding a mask, a man standing
facing towards the left wearing a short chiton and probably
pulling on his boot, a woman standing facing left. The boy
with the mask is not part of the play but perhaps a dresser
or a walker on; similar figures can be found at all dates. He
carries the mask by the strap which would fasten it at the
back of the head.[1] The mask is painted white and has short
hair, circled by a wide red band. Pollux describes the mask
of the first shorn maiden as having parted hair cut short, the
colour of the face being pale. Our mask has been compared
with this but I am not convinced that we need conclude that
the girl is in mourning. The man is distinguished from the
women by wearing laced boots instead of loose-fitting boots.
It is probable that he is a character and they are members of
the chorus. The clothing, as far as it can be seen, in no way
differs from the clothing of gods, heroes, and ordinary
Athenians on contemporary vases. Two other vases of the
same date may be mentioned here. On a cup a chorus of
young men wrapped up in cloaks are singing with two
flute-players in front of a colonnade: Dr Bieber has suggested
that they are a tragic chorus rehearsing, but, if so, they are
rehearsing in their ordinary clothes without masks or boots
(one or two of them wear shoes).[2] On the second vase (6)

---

[1] Sir John Beazley suggests rather that it is for carrying or hanging up the
mask.
[2] New York, Metropolitan Museum, 27.74. M. Bieber, *AJA*, 45
(1941), 529. *ARV*, 267/10.

a single maenad with waving hair, himation, close-fitting boots, sword in one hand and a bleeding leg of a fawn in the other, dances in front of a flute-player. The painter has drawn rather the subject of the maenads' song than their actual appearance as a chorus, but flute-player and boots suggest tragedy, and the high fringe and flowing hair may owe something to the mask.

A third running woman in boots is seen on a vase of 440/430 by the Phiale painter (7). Two young men prepare for a tragic female chorus. One is already dressed and is pulling on his loose-fitting boot. His mask lies on the ground. It is like the mask on the Agora oenochoe (4), except that the hair is neater, an earring is shown, and the band round the hair is a sling instead of a bandeau. The second choreut is fully dressed and runs forward with her himation in her hand (her gesture should be compared to the dancers with phalloi in their caps). Here too the clothing is no more elaborate than the clothing of ordinary or heroic young women on other vases.[1]

At the end of the fifth century costume apparently becomes fixed, but it is still rather an elaboration of ordinary costume than a special costume (except in so far as boots and sleeves are worn by all actors). In Aristophanes' *Frogs* (1060) Aeschylus justifies the heroic language of his plays by the heroic robes which tragic heroes wear. The corresponding charge that Euripides dressed his heroes in rags is probably fiction; it was a brilliant comic device for attacking the realism of Euripidean tragedy to show the poet among the rags in which he imagined but did not in fact dress his characters (*Acharnians* 412 ff.). At least we have no evidence that tragic characters were dressed in rags. We can quote Athenian vases, paintings, reliefs, and statues for the end of the fifth and the beginning of the fourth century. It will be convenient to take them together because we have some evidence for an important change in costume

---

[1] Sir John Beazley compares in particular the Thracian women killing Orpheus, *ARV*, 653/1 and 2.

with the rebuilding of the theatre by Lykourgos about 330 B.C. We start with two splendid vases. Besides satyr chorus and Papposilenos, the Pronomos vase (9) shows two actors fully equipped. On the left an adult man with decorated boots (perhaps the close-fitting type), patterned sleeved long chiton with girdle (a very similar chiton is worn by Andromeda on a slightly later vase (10) inspired by Euripides' *Andromeda*), and patterned himation, which covers his left arm. He holds in his right hand by its backstrap a mask with yellow-white face and black hair and beard. On the right, Herakles with decorated laced boots, patterned sleeved short chiton, breast-plate, lion skin and club, holds a mask with shortish hair and beard with the lion's head on the top: the colour is the same yellow white as in the figure on the left but the strands of hair are more clearly separated and this may signify fair as distinct from dark hair. A third mask, dead white, with long black hair, clearly a girl, is held by the woman seated on the end of Dionysos' couch; she wears a sleeved patterned long chiton but her feet are bare; she is not a character but the heroine of the play holding her mask. The painter is so careful that it is reasonable to conclude that satyrs wore reddish masks, men light brown, and women white. The second vase (12), which is contemporary with the Pronomos vase, survives in fragments at Würzburg. It gave the cast and chorus of a tragedy and other figures. On the fragments can be seen above, on the left, member of the chorus holding female mask by the chin, flute-player holding a flute in each hand, member of the chorus seated holding a female mask by the chin, and parts of a female figure in profile to the right (possibly a Muse leaning over the poet, who would be seated as on the Pronomos vase), and below on the left the column supporting the tripod which was erected to celebrate the victory, then a seated goddess, perhaps Aphrodite (she may have been a character and have held a mask in her raised left hand), then the sleeved arm of a character holding a mask (probably male; the hair is short and the hair line is quite different from that of the chorus masks); on the right in the picture, a fragment of elaborate white garment, of embroidered cloak, and sceptre does not belong to this figure (as Professor Möbius informs me) but to another, and farther to the right a figure, probably female, wearing a skin over her clothing is perhaps Artemis; below, another member of the chorus holding a mask upside down by the chin. The chorus are barefoot because the painter wavers between myth and reality. They do not wear sleeves, but this may be a real distinction between chorus and actors. Their hair is short but has not the headband worn on the earlier chorus mask (7). The line of the forehead is flatter than on the masks of the characters on the Pronomos vase and than the mask held by the character already mentioned.

These two vases show us the elaborate costumes of late Euripidean and late Sophoclean tragedy, a short-haired mask for a chorus of women, a long-haired girl's mask, a dark and a fair bearded mask, and a further mask, short-haired and probably male. The sleeved costume with a girdle is worn by the actors on the contemporary relief from Peiraeus (11); the patterns would have been added in paint. The actor nearest to Dionysos' couch carries by its chin a bearded mask, which is also wreathed. The middle actor has a tympanon in his left hand and carries a mask with sharp features and short stiff beard and shortish hair; it looks like an old man's mask and like the other is wreathed. The third actor carries a tympanon and was wearing a mask, which was later deliberately cut out; the prominence of the left breast shows that he took a female part. The temptation is strong to say that we have a dedication made after the performance of Euripides' *Bacchae* with the actors representing (1) Pentheus, (2) Kadmos, and (3) Agave, but other explanations are possible: the tympanon belonged to Kybele before Dionysos, and Sophocles wrote a [*Tympanistai*.

The relief adds an old man's mask and a woman with short hair to the long-haired young woman, two types of bearded men, and possible youth that we have noticed at the turn of the century.[1] If the Peiraeus relief cannot be connected with the *Bacchae*, we have nevertheless evidence of the mask worn by Dionysos in that play; according to Pentheus (455 f.) he has 'long locks, lying along the cheeks, inviting desire' and 'white skin'. Just such a mask is held by the god himself on an Apulian vase (29) of the second quarter of the fourth century, and from this we can recognise also the mask held by the Dionysos child perched on the shoulder of a Papposilenos in stage costume; the original was an Athenian marble group of the same date (13). We can add several further examples, where again style suggests that they belong to the fourth century. A marble mask from near the Dipylon Gate in Athens (15) must be male because the colouring is reddish brown; it is beardless and has short wavy hair round the forehead; two holes show that further locks fell on either side of the face; it may have been like the youth on the Würzburg fragment; possibly it came from the grave relief of a tragic poet. I should like to add here four marble masks from the Small Akropolis Museum, one of which is dated by the lettering of the inscription to the fourth century. The first (16) is an old woman with furrowed brows and short hair, the second (17) is a young woman with eyebrows drawn right up in grief and short hair, the third (18, which has the inscription) and the fourth (19) is a middle-aged woman with long hair. The first, fourth, and possibly third can be recognised on a painting on marble from Herculaneum in the Naples Museum (56). Professor Rumpf has suggested that the style of this shows it to be a copy of an original of about 340. On the left is a heroine, of large size because she is a heroine, wearing the fourth of our masks and chiton and long himation, then an old woman with short grey hair, like our first mask, and finally a woman with long hair not unlike our third mask. It is possible that they are Phaidra, the

---

[1] The mask held by the Muse of Mantua (14), a Roman copy of an Attic statue of the same period, is of the fair short bearded type with an elaborate backstrap.

nurse, and a member of the chorus in a revival of Euripides'
Hippolytus, but many other solutions could be suggested.
Whether the long sleeved chitons and himatia were patterned
or not is impossible to say; such patterns would probably
not be indicated in a drawing which depends on sepia alone,
but the drawing is now too faint for even this to be clear.
Yet another monument belongs to this group, a fragmentary
relief from Athens (*20*). A youth (this is clear from his hair
which may be compared to the actors on the Peiraeus relief
(11)), dressed in sleeved chiton and himation, worn as by
the heroine of the Herculaneum picture, and footwear
which may be kothornoi, holds in his hand by its strap the
mask of a middle-aged distressed woman, which is not
unlike the mask worn by the Herculaneum heroine. The
style, particularly the folds of the himation below the breast,
suggest a date in the middle of the fourth century B.C., and
this relief like the Peiraeus relief would seem to be a dedication after a successful performance.

None of the masks which we have seen has what the
lexicographer Pollux describes as a *lambda*-shaped erection
above the forehead, which is called *onkos*. This can be clearly
seen in many Hellenistic pictures and appears as a kind of
tower of hair. It not only makes the characters look stately;
it also makes them look archaic—for the first time the heroes
of legend are marked as belonging to a bygone time. I have
argued that this change was due to the statesman Lykourgos
in the sense that when the theatre was rebuilt in stone and
adorned with the statues of Aeschylus, Sophocles, and
Euripides, the new masks were also introduced to match
the stately new setting: the earliest instance seems to be the
mask of a bearded man in the hand of a marble statue of a
poet which has been plausibly identified with the Aeschylus
set up in the Lycurgan theatre (21). Another change of the
same kind, which may have come in at the same time is the
substitution of the long for the short chiton, for all heroic
males. Herakles we have seen in short chiton on the
Pronomos vase (*9*); an Apulian polychrome vase of about

350 (34) shows a fair-haired warrior in a short chiton, but in Hellenistic representations both Herakles and young warriors seem always to wear the long chiton—the earliest is the portrait of a tragic actor (57), which goes back to an original of the late fourth or early third century.

After this there is only one important change of costume, the introduction of the high-soled boot. The reason may well have been the removal of the action to a high stage, on which the feet of the actors would have been invisible to the occupants of the special thrones in the lowest rows. By high-soled boot I mean a boot worn by the chief characters which has the sole so thickened that it gives the appearance of stilts; minor characters on quite late monuments may have normal soles. The introduction of this new high-soled boot is likely to have been general if there was, as seems likely, a common dramatic costume over the whole Greek world. It can clearly be seen worn by the personification of tragedy on reliefs of the late second century B.C. from Halikarnassos (79) and Priene (78), and by Herakles on a contemporary terra-cotta statuette from Amisos (75) as well as later (e.g. 73). As it does not appear on some of the best paintings from Pompeii and Herculaneum, for instance the tragic actor (57) and the Achilles and Priam (66), they may be considered to be good copies of an original earlier than the second century B.C. The earliest monuments which show the high-soled boot are later than the supposed date for the introduction of the high stage in Athens, and the new boot may have been introduced in Athens.

The assumption that dramatic costume varied little over the Greek world in the Hellenistic period rests partly on probability and partly on the evidence of the monuments. Even in the early fourth century the influence of Athens was strongly felt, as I shall try to show. Later, Alexandrian scholarship reported and so handed down theatre practice of the early Hellenistic age, and much of this is preserved by Pollux.[1]

---

[1] See Pickard-Cambridge, *Festivals*, 175 f. and my article in the *Festschrift für Andreas Rumpf*, 141 f.

The Guilds of actors [1] which sprang up over the
Greek world in the Hellenistic Age in imitation of the
Athenian Guild, which can reasonably be traced back into
the fourth century, may also have tended to stereotype
practice. The unanimity of the monuments however is in
part illusory. It is true to say that representations of tragic
actors discovered all over the Graeco-Roman world from
the third century B.C. to the sixth century A.D. look extra-
ordinarily alike, but sometimes certainly the likeness is due
to a common artistic source. This is particularly obvious in
Pompeii and Herculaneum. The original of the portrait of
the tragic actor (57) can be dated by style to the late fourth
century, and the originals of the two comedy mosaics of
Dioskourides (C 19, 20) to the early third; they therefore
record both the practice of the early Hellenistic age and the
taste of the owner of the first-century houses in which they
were found. We must consider this problem further in
connection with particular sites, but for the moment we may
use the archaeological evidence of varied dates and places
to establish the common dramatic costume of the Hellenistic
age.

We know that from the early third century classical
tragedy was produced in a special contest at Athens; [2] the
tragedy of Aeschylus, Sophocles, and Euripides now
occupied a greater part of the festival than in the fourth
century when a single classical tragedy was produced every
year at the Greater Dionysia. Hellenistic dramatic costume
must therefore have been adequate for the demands of
classical tragedy, which we can check, as well as the demands
of new tragedy, which we have lost. There is no reason to
think that these demands were different, since we know of
very few authors who strayed from the well trodden paths of
mythology. We can therefore take Pollux' list of tragic
masks, [3] which seems to be derived from a good Alexandrian

---

[1] Cf. Pickard-Cambridge, *Festivals*, 287 f.
[2] Cf. *Athenian Art and Literature in the Fourth Century* B.C., p. 115.
[3] IV, 131 f., cf. my article in *Festschrift für Andreas Rumpf*, 141 f.

source, and ask three questions, (1) does it provide sufficient masks for the tragedies that we know? (2) can the individual masks be illustrated from the monuments? (3) have the individual masks ancestors among the masks of the classical period which we have already discussed?

First, there are six 'old men'. The distinction between 'old' and 'young' is between bearded and beardless, and only the first three of Pollux' 'old men' are really old—(1) the shaven mask, (2) the white mask, and (3) the brindled mask. White is probably the normal mask for old men, actors, and chorus; it has long locks, a low *onkos*, a stiff beard, drooping eyebrows, and off-white complexion. It is worn by Priam with Hecuba and Achilles in the Pompeian paintings (A 66), and the classical version is carried by the middle actor of the Peiraeus relief (11). On the Pompeian paintings Priam wears a long yellow chiton and a purple cloak. The Shaven mask with thin cheeks and beard reduced to stubble has not been recognised; it was worn by Tyndareos in Euripides' *Orestes* (458, with scholiast) and by Priam in some fifth-century play, since 'I will be Priamed' was a comic poet's term for 'I will be shaved'; it may have been a rare mask since Pollux includes Priam among his 'special masks', which are partly tragic and partly comic. This was the mask for an old man in misfortune. The Brindled with hair turning grey and yellowish complexion has also not been recognised; it would be worn by a younger man than the other two. We should probably add a fourth mask for blind old men, since Pollux lists Phineus among his special masks. Thus in Sophocles' *Oedipus Coloneus* Oedipus would wear the blind mask, the stranger and the chorus of old men the white mask, and Kreon the brindled mask.

The middle-aged bearded men are (4) dark, (5) fair, and (6) fairer. The Dark man has dark complexion and presumably dark hair, curly beard and hair, large *onkos*, and is harsh in expression. This is probably the mask held by Aeschylus in the Vatican statue (21) and by the Muse of

tragedy on a late second-century relief from Halikarnassos
(79); an ancestor without *onkos* is carried by the left hand
actor of the Pronomos vase (9). It is the common mask for
the tragic king. The Fair mask has smaller *onkos*, fair hair
and locks, and a healthy complexion. If we were right in
identifying it with the mask worn by Herakles on the
Pronomos vase (9), then we can recognise it later in the
second century statuette of Herakles (75) and in numerous
later monuments. The most interesting example is the actor
on a fragment of an Apulian polychrome[1] vase of about
350 B.C. (34). He comes forward to take his call, carrying
the earlier form of the fair mask without the *onkos*. He wears
a shortish, brown, fringed chiton; a purple cloak hangs over
his arm; he has a sword in his left hand and a golden bracelet
on his right arm; his boots are long, laced *kothornoi* with
normal soles. On a Pompeian wall painting (60) a man in
the same mask wears a long red chiton with violet edges and
a green himation, a sword, and high-soled boots. The Fairer
mask is 'like the fair but yellowish in complexion and
manifestly ill'. It can be seen on a South Italian jug of the
very late fourth or very early third century in Würzburg
(46), and on a curious figure on a Pompeian painting (64);
the interpretation of this is quite uncertain. Herakles,
wreathed, in long chiton, and himation, with his club to the
left; an old man with a young woman moving towards him;
a man with a crook, wearing a mask with wild hair, which
seems to be the 'fairer' mask, reclining on some steps, which
may be the steps of an altar. He wears a white chiton and
a violet cloak. Both Euripides' *Auge* and *Hercules Furens* have
been suggested, but it is not clear why either Aleos or
Lykos should be shown as a sick king. Philoktetes and
Telephos are likely to have worn this mask, and if Herakles
normally wore the Fair mask, he would wear the Fairer in
Sophocles' *Trachiniae*.

[1] Even this vase, which belongs to a group more brightly coloured than
the succeeding Gnathia vases, has a restricted palette and the painter would
not have shown blue, green, or violet, had the actor been wearing them.

The beardless male masks are (7) Admirable, (8) Curly, (9) Younger version of Curly, (10) Delicate, (11) Dirty, (12) Second Dirty, (13) Pale, (14) Second Pale. The Admirable is the oldest of the young men. The mask has thick black hair and a healthy complexion. Achilles wears this mask on a Pompeian painting (66), which also shows long purple chiton and purple cloak over his shoulders, shoes apparently instead of boots, and sword and sceptre. The tragic actor (57)—the original can be dated as early Hellenistic because his features recall the portraits of Alexander's successors—has a similar mask on the table beside him. He wears a long white chiton with a golden sash; a pink cloak lies across his knees; the baldric of his sword is blue, the scabbard and hilt golden; his white sceptre has a golden tip. Achilles would be so dressed in a Hellenistic revival of Euripides' *Iphigenia in Aulis*. It is possible that we should see an earlier version of this mask in the two young male masks which we have already described (12, 15). Among his 'special masks' Pollux lists 'Achilles with his hair shorn in honour of Patroklos', whose death he is mourning.

The Curly mask has fair curly hair attached to a very high *onkos*, raised eyebrows, and is virile in expression. This has been recognised in a mask by the side of Euripides on a relief (22). The relief is a copy of a seated statue of Euripides which can be dated about 330 B.C. The original is likely to have held the Herakles mask; whether the other masks are an addition of the copyist or not we cannot say, but the Curly mask is undoubtedly Lykos in the *Hercules Furens* and the female mask is Megara. The Younger version of the Curly has not been identified. The Delicate mask has fair locks and white complexion; it is cheerful like a god or a beautiful youth. This was the mask worn by Dionysos in Euripides' *Bacchae* (see above p. 42). The later Hellenistic version with *onkos* is common as a decorative mask in Pompeii (e.g. 61), and as it represents Dionysos can be painted among tragic or comic masks. It may have been used

for other gods such as Apollo and perhaps for youths such as
Ion. The Dirty has an *onkos* with wavy fair hair; his colour is
somewhat livid; his expression is downcast and he is squalid.
In Euripides' *Orestes* the hero has 'a squalid, miserable head
of hair' (225) and the mask would have been worn in a
revival. It is perhaps recognisable by the livid colour and
disordered hair in decorative masks in Pompeii (59, 62).
The Second Dirty is younger and thinner but we know
nothing further about him. The Pale has withered flesh,
fairish hair all round his head, and a sickly complexion like
a ghost or a wounded man; the ghost of Polydoros in the
Hecuba comes to mind. The Second Pale is like the Admirable but is pale to show that he is ill or in love. A South
Italian jug of the third quarter of the fourth century (37) is
decorated with the mask of a young man with white face and
light brown wavy hair; the Second Pale presumably had
dark hair; this youth seems to me to have 'wavy hair' rather
than 'hair all round his head' and he may therefore be the
Second Dirty.

The list gives eleven masks for heroic male characters
and this is ample to cover the needs of most plays. The two
plays with the greatest number of male characters are the
Ajax and the *Rhesus*. The *Ajax* could have been produced
with Pollux' set, if Ajax wore No. 6 Fairer as being ill,
Teucer No. 7 Admirable as the younger brother, Agamemnon No. 3 Brindled as the elder brother, Menelaos No. 4
Dark as the tyrant, Odysseus No. 5 Fair. Chorus and
messenger are unheroic and would wear the mask of servants.
Rhesus is more difficult as we do not know whether the
Trojans, distinguished by Phrygian caps, could therefore
wear the same masks as the Greeks; if not, a possible dis-
tribution would be Odysseus and Diomedes, (4) Dark and
(5) Fair; Hektor, Aineias, and Alexandros, (7) Admirable,
(9) Second Curly, (10) Delicate; Rhesos, (8) Curly (he is
boastful like Lykos in the *Hercules Furens*); Dolon (who is
said to be ugly in the tenth *Iliad*), one of the Dirty masks
(11 or 12); Rhesos' wounded charioteer, (13) Pale; and

GTP—D

messenger and chorus servants' masks. In the *Phoenissae*, a popular play for which the standard set should provide, the younger brother Polyneikes has 'blue-black hair' (308). If the producer is to regard this rare mention of hair-colouring other than fair, Polyneikes must wear (7) Admirable, and his elder brother Eteokles one of the bearded masks. In the *Antiope* and *Hypsipyle* twins are contrasted as musical and athletic; if the musical twin wears (10) Delicate, the athletic twin should wear the young Second Curly (11). The only changes of mask which are certain are in the *Oedipus Tyrannus* and *Hecuba* where Oedipus and Poly-mestor both must wear a special blind mask at the end of the play. Hippolytos is carried on at the end of the play 'with his young body and his fair head mangled' (1343); it is possible therefore that he now wore the Pale mask, having worn the Curly mask in the earlier part of the play (the reference to his fairness excludes the Admirable mask and the corresponding Second Pale). Two of Pollux' 'special masks' may be mentioned here: 'Aktaion with horns on his head' and Thamyras with one grey and one black eye. Aktaion appears with horns on classical vase-paintings, but it is perhaps permissible to guess that Pollux or his source is imagining this mask from the text of a messenger speech. The Thamyras mask however must be a theatre mask, and it has been suggested that like some of the comic masks it was double sided; Thamyras turned his bright eye to the audience before he was blinded and his dim eye afterwards.[1]

Pollux lists three servants' masks, (15) Leatherclad, (16) Wedgebeard, (17) Brushed-back. The name of *Leatherclad* comes from the leather jerkin worn by rustics, as for instance the various shepherd messengers in Euripides, but the mask was not confined to rustics nor did rustics necessarily wear it. Varro says (*RR*, 2, 11, 11) 'in tragedy old men are called *diptheriae* because of their skin garment'. He presumably knew a text in which an old rustic was so called. But the

---

[1] A. Lesky, *Anz. Ak. Wien*, 1951, 101 f.   Rumpf in *AJA* 55 (1951), 8 ff. has quoted other evidence for 'two-sided' masks in the late fifth century.

monuments show that it is in fact the mask for old retainers. According to Pollux it has a cap instead of an *onkos*, combed white hair, yellowish-whitish complexion, jutting beard, sharp nose, raised forehead, and frowning eyes. It is surely right to recognise him in the paidagogos of the Medea painting (65) although he apparently does not wear a cap; his sleeved chiton is red and his cloak is green. Another instance also without a cap is the old man in the Herakles scene (64); he wears a yellow cloak but the colour of his chiton is not recorded. An earlier version is seen on an Apulian vase of the third quarter of the fourth century (33); he wears a short white chiton, a brown himation with purple border and laced boots; he has a bundle on his back; he has therefore come from a distance to tell his story and could be the paidagogos in Sophocles' *Electra*. The Wedgebeard is said to be in the prime of life, to have a high wide *onkos* with concave circumference, and to be fair, fierce, and red-complexioned like a messenger. A terra-cotta statuette of the second century from Pergamon (76) in half-length chiton, mantle, and high boots has a mask which might be so described, and should from his gesture be a messenger. The servant on a Pompeian painting (60), who also wears this mask, has a red chiton and a red/yellow chlamys. I think we may add a terra-cotta mask (73 a) of the second century from Thebes with an Oriental cap; perhaps the Phrygian in Euripides' *Orestes* may be imagined like this. The third male servant has hair brushed back, very high *onkos*; is fair and unbearded. He is also a messenger, but no example has been recognised. Euripides' *Electra* would need all three: Wedgebeard for Elektra's husband, Leatherclad for the old man who recognises Orestes, and Brushed-back for the messenger who is the servant of the young Orestes.

The series of women includes three servants, who are placed together, but otherwise seems to be arranged in descending order of age: (18) Grey long-haired, (19) Free old woman, (20) Old housekeeper, (21) Half-shorn house-keeper, (22) Leatherclad girl, (23) Long-haired pale, (24)

Half-shorn pale, (25) Half-shorn fresh, (26) First shorn maiden, (27) Second shorn maiden, (28) Girl. They have a considerable range of complexion: paleish (18, 26, 27), brownish (19), white-paleish (21), pale (23–4), and presumably white for Nos. 25 and 28. The masks of young women on the Agora oenochoe (4) and the Pronomos vase (9) are white and presumably are the ancestors of the Girl (No. 28) and the Long-haired pale (No. 23) in Pollux' list; the chorus-women on the Würzburg fragments (12) with short hair and white faces may be the ancestors of the Half-shorn fresh (No. 25). Aristophanes in the *Wasps* (1413) speaks of Euripides' Ino as 'yellow' and she is the 'tearful Ino' of Horace; so yellow was already used to denote grief in the fifth century. White then is the colour for a healthy woman and the various off-whites indicate distress; thus the brownish old woman's mask is said to 'suggest disaster', the Long-haired pale has an 'expression of grief', and the paleish Second shorn maiden has been 'unhappy for a long time'. We should add the 'livid Tyro' who was beaten by her step-mother Sidero in Sophocles *Tyro*; she is in Pollux' special list.

Hair is white in No. 18, grey in No. 19, not completely grey in No. 21 (presumably therefore the intervening Old housekeeper, No. 20, is grey), black in No. 23; but colour is not otherwise indicated, unless the statement that No. 24 is like No. 23 and No. 25 like No. 24 imply that they also have black hair. These three masks (23–5) cover all the heroines of tragedy who are not either old women or young girls, including the fair-haired Phaidra, Iphigeneia, and Helen; therefore although it is strange that Pollux does not mention colour, which he carefully records for the male masks, it is possible that the two half-shorn masks are fair and only the long-haired mask is dark (the paintings do not help us because they show a brown which might be either dark or fair). Hair is also distinguished by cut: long in Nos. 18, 23, half-shorn (i.e. hair down to the level of the collar-bone) in Nos. 19, 21, 24,

25, and shorn in Nos. 26 and 27 (but with a fringe of short locks in No. 26). The three main variants are very clear in the long-haired mask held by Euripides on a Hellenistic silver cup (54), the half-shorn mask worn by the well-known ivory statuette (73), the shorn mask identified as Lykophron's Kassandra on another Hellenistic silver cup (55). The shorn masks certainly imply mourning or captivity, and the Second shorn maiden is distinguished from the first as having been unhappy for a long time—Elektra as distinguished from Antigone. But these two are essentially young and unmarried; older and married women must have worn the half-shorn masks when in mourning or captivity or more simply when in distress, since Medea certainly wears the half-shorn mask on the Pompeian painting (65). This would give the necessary variation for plays with many female characters. In the *Trojan Women* Kassandra's mask would be the Second shorn maiden, Andromache's the Half-shorn pale, Helen's the Half-shorn fresh, and Hekabe's the Free old woman. On various occasions characters cut off locks of hair during the course of the play;[1] it would be easy to arrange that locks should be detachable, but I do not feel certain that the audience did not imagine the action and the change.

The Grey long-haired has not been recognised in the monuments; Pollux describes her as the senior in age and rank; Aithra in Euripides' *Supplices* is an example. Hekabe in a Pompeian painting (67) wears the Free old woman's mask with green chiton and green himation. I am inclined to see an ancestor of this mask in the old woman in the Small Akropolis Museum (16). The Old housekeeper with a lambskin cap and wrinkled cheeks is the nurse in the *Hippolytus* and other plays—we have noticed a possible example (56). The Half-shorn housekeeper is perhaps the mask for Hekabe's servant in the *Hecuba* and for the chorus

---

[1] S. *Aj.* 1173; *El.* 448; E. *Hel.* 1087. Helen goes into the house and her shorn hair is noted on her return (1187); in the other two plays the action, if performed, must be performed before the eyes of the audience.

in the *Hecuba* and *Trojan Women*. The Leatherclad girl is younger; the name seems simply to be a feminine of the Leatherclad male and therefore means nothing more than young attendant: perhaps the chorus of the *Ion* would wear this mask. The Long-haired pale is often represented, and would be worn by heroines who were neither old nor young nor fair nor excessively distressed: Deianeira in the *Trachiniae* and Kreousa in the *Ion* seem to me likely instances. On a Pompeian painting (63) a woman carrying a child wears this mask; she has a violet sleeved chiton with a green border, a yellow belt, and high-soled boots. It is difficult in the archaeological material to distinguish the two half-shorn masks; the face of Medea (65) is too much shaded to show whether the complexion was yellow or white; she wears a green, sleeved chiton. The mask on a South Italian vase (47) is dead white and this is presumably the Half-shorn fresh, as worn by Helen in the *Trojan Women* and *Helen*. Phaidra on the other hand who is wasted away with sickness would wear the Half-shorn pale. Only one example has been plausibly suggested of the First shorn maiden, with no *onkos* and parted smooth hair cut short round her head— on a South Italian vase (45); this, as we have said, would be the mask for Antigone. It is possible that the young woman in the Small Akropolis Museum is an early example (17). The mask of the Second shorn maiden, who has been unhappy for a long time, like Elektra and Kassandra, can be seen on a South Italian vase (48) as well as a Hellenistic silver cup (55); it is in fact like the Long-haired pale and the Half-shorn masks stripped of all their locks. Lastly, the Girl is described as young like Danae or any other young girl; it has not been recognised—Ismene and Chrysothemis in Sophocles and Iphigeneia in the *Iphigenia in Aulis* of Euripides are probably examples.

Pollux in his list of special masks adds Madness (Lyssa) and Fury (Erinys). We know that these masks were worn but we have no examples; they are easy to imagine —women with wild hair—from the pictures which show Lyssa in the Actaeon scene and the Furies with Orestes.

The chief value of this survey is to give some idea of the theatre practice at different stages. We can however now say in addition that we know most of Pollux' masks, that they would be adequate for revivals of the surviving plays, and that we can in four or five instances see how earlier Attic masks were varied in Hellenistic practice. Most of the examples are not Attic in the strict sense of 'found in Attica' —we can indeed quote a bronze soldier of early Imperial date (23) and a half-shorn mask of the fourth century A.D. (24)—but this lack of Attic material does not matter, since it is clear that there was a common tragic costume in the Hellenistic age which is likely to have originated in Athens, and many of the monuments derive from the early Hellenistic Attic tradition.

(c) *Old and Middle Comedy*

For Old and Middle Comedy there is no lack of Attic material, and only Attic material will be used in this section except where a new development can only be demonstrated from some other monument. Attic comedies are undoubtedly illustrated on South Italian vases, but they will in the main be reserved till the next chapter, in which an attempt will be made to give some picture of the theatrical life of Tarentum and other Greek cities in the West. For our purposes Old and Middle Comedy can be taken to mean Comedy from the first official production in the early fifth century to the first production of Menander in 321. The boundary between Old and Middle Comedy may be taken as the year 400, since the last two plays of Aristophanes have long been accepted as belonging to Middle Comedy rather than Old, but the costume was not changed in essentials; some new masks were however introduced in the fourth century to supply the needs of new dramatic situations and characters.

The material comprises first the early vases which have

been discussed under origins, secondly twelve Attic vases dated on style from about 420 to not later than 380 (the period of Aristophanes), thirdly a marble relief of a comic poet with two masks, which can be dated on style about 380, fourthly more than one hundred and fifty different types of Attic terra-cotta statuettes dating from about 400 to not later than 325 (most of them seem on stylistic grounds to have originated before the middle of the century), fifthly a marble relief with comic masks erected in the Attic deme of Aixone in the year 340. The Aixone relief (B *31*) honours two men who had produced a Comedy and therefore the five masks are undoubtedly comic masks; the other relief (*10*) is the grave monument of a comic poet (he holds a roll in his hand) and again the relevance of the masks is undoubted. The reason for accepting the terra-cottas and vases as illustrations of comedy is threefold. First, their masks either repeat the seven certain masks of the two marble reliefs or belong to the same general kind. Secondly, the figures wear the padded obscene costume which is indicated in the texts of comedy. Thirdly, it is difficult to imagine any other performance which was so popular that statuettes of it were exported all over the Greek world and locally copied.[1]

One further monument can now be added: a marble base from the Athenian Agora which can be dated stylistically and epigraphically to the fourth century (*31a*).[2] The base has reliefs and the preserved fragments show padded dancers wearing masks with pointed beards, short chitons, caps, cloaks, and tights, and carrying spears over their shoulders. The caps, cloaks, and spears are so like those worn by the soldier in a Pompeian wall painting (C 2 5) that these men must be soldiers. Three are preserved from head to knee

---

[1] I have argued this at length in *Eph. Arch.* 1954 (forthcoming) and I have given some of the evidence for this diffusion in *Rylands Bulletin*, 36 (1954), 566 f. Add replicas of the statuettes, Nos. 11*c*, 12*b*, 12*f*, in the Museum at Paestum. Cf. also *CQ*, 49 (1955), 94.

[2] This is to be published by Miss E. Harrison in the Catalogue of Sculpture from the Agora Excavations, and I am grateful to her and to Professor Homer Thompson for permission to describe and illustrate it here.

and five from knee to foot; the former are not phallic. They are led by a figure with long chiton and himation who might be either a flute-player or Dionysos himself. A separate fragment gives the upper part of a similarly clothed figure with a full round beard. The parallels in costume and masks with the reliefs and terra-cottas mentioned above make it highly probable that the relief commemorated a victory won with a comedy and illustrated the final procession when chorus and actors danced off together; the non-phallic soldiers with pointed beards are chorus-men, the round-bearded soldier is an actor. Strattis' *Macedonians* is perhaps too early; Mnesimachos' *Philip* may well have had a chorus of Macedonian soldiers, but many other plays are possible. This relief seems to provide our only illustration of a comic chorus impersonating men as distinct from women and animals.

When comedy started officially in the early fifth century, the poets had various existing performances as models. We have spoken of the padded dancers, who may have had a phallic and masked leader, the men dressed up as women who dance with them, other choruses of women, a chorus of knights, and a chorus of cocks. We shall see when we come to speak of the Peloponnese and Asia Minor that there is also evidence for men dressed up as ugly old women. The choruses of feathered men (F 7) and knights (F 5) give us some idea of the special choruses of comedy such as Aristophanes *Knights*, *Wasps*, and *Birds*. On a polychrome oenochoe in the British Museum (B 5) a little fat man is rowing an enormous blue fish with very long oars; so perhaps one should imagine the entry of the chorus in Archippos' *Fish*, in which the fish made war on the Athenians and later came to terms and were addressed as 'Gentlemen Fish'. Perhaps the long oars were stilts with the fish swinging between them, but the fish may rather have been on wheels like Charon's boat in the *Frogs*.

Pollux' list of special masks, to which reference has already been made, includes some which we can connect with Old and Middle Comedies of various dates, but it is always possible that he (or his source) deduced them from the plays. The Argos mask covered with eyes may have been used in the *Panoptai* of Kratinos. The Centaur mask was needed for various plays entitled *Centaur* or *Cheiron* (in the singular and plural). This can be illustrated from an Athenian vase (B 2) of about 410 B.C.: four Centaurs draw Herakles and winged Nike in a chariot; their bodies are more beautiful than they would be on the stage, but their faces are stylised in the manner of comic masks to look remarkably like slaves. The Titan in Pollux' list, which would be used for the *Ploutoi* of Kratinos, and the Giant, which would be used for the *Giants* of the younger Kratinos, would not look very different. The City mask for the *Cities* of Eupolis, Philyllios, Anaxandrides, and Heniochos would be feminine, so also the Islands [1] (Plato and Pseudo-Aristophanes) and Arkas (or Arkadia), probably the prologue figure of Antiphanes' play. The Demes of Eupolis and the Laws of Kratinos, neither of which are mentioned by Pollux, must have been male; we can add the mountain Lykabettos from Theopompos' *Mede* (Pollux lists a mountain mask) and the hill Knoithideus (Antiphanes); both presumably spoke the prologue. Pollux also lists masks for the Muses (who formed the chorus of comedies by Phrynichos and others) and the Seasons (Aristophanes and Anaxilas, and presumably Peace and Autumn in Aristophanes' *Peace*), and finally Drunkenness, who appeared as Kratinos' mistress in his *Pytine*. To these we can add similar figures who probably spoke the prologue in the Middle Comedies named after them—Dorpia (Philyllios), Kalligeneia (Aristophanes), Echo (Euboulos), Pannychis (Euboulos and Alexis), Lethe (Timokles), and Poiesis (Antiphanes). But here we must call a halt and note that of this whole list the first, Argos, is the only one which must have a special mask and even he could wear his extra eyes on his clothes, as he does sometimes on

----

[1] A vase-painter of the late fifth century imagined the Islands as Maenads (cf. J. D. Beazley, *Vases in Poland*, 63).

Greek vases. All the rest could wear ordinary male or female masks and be distinguished by what they said and wore and sometimes by what they carried; Peace would carry a horn of plenty, a city might wear a mural crown. Their masks might be more or less comic according to their parts; less comic for prologue speakers and more comic for members of the chorus and characters in the play; this agrees with what Aristophanes says about the Clouds, who are 'like mortal women' and 'have noses' (341, 394) and about Poverty in the *Plutus* (423 ff.), who is a cross between a tragic fury and a landlady; she has the clothes and attributes of a fury but the face of a landlady. We may therefore doubt whether Pollux' list of special masks is not largely inferred from the text of the plays. One other class which Pollux does not mention is satyrs; satyr choruses occurred in comedies by Ekphantides, Kratinos, Phrynichos, and Timokles. They must have been distinguished from the satyrs of the satyr-play; on an Apulian vase (35) a little fat hairy satyr, apparently without a tail, wears a slave mask and I suspect the satyrs of comedy may have been fat and hairy (like some of their ancestors among the padded dancers) to distinguish them from the lean smooth satyrs of the satyr play.[1] This may also have been the costume of some of the prologue figures of Middle Comedy: Dithyrambos (Amphis) and Hybris (Anaxandrides)[2] are satyr names; Tychon (Antiphanes), Orthanes (Euboulos), and Konisalos (Timokles) are names of fertility spirits, who may well have been portrayed as satyrs.

Two other kinds of character might be expected to have special masks—historical personages and the gods. Aristophanes tells us in the *Knights* (230) that the Paphlagonian does not wear a portrait mask of Kleon; for this play it was funnier to have him appear as a slave; but Aristophanes'

[1] Satyrs on Attic vases are sometimes caricatured and it is possible that they are inspired by comedy, e.g. F. Brommer, *Satyrspiele*, Nos. 35, 116, 155.

[2] Hybris could alternatively be a fury-like figure, cf. Lyssa. Pollux lists a hybris mask.

apology at least suggests that the audience expected a
portrait mask, and this is corroborated not only by the
suspect Pollux but by the story of Sokrates standing up
during the *Clouds* so that the audience could see his likeness
to the actor. Perikles appeared as Zeus in the *Thracian
Women* and *Nemesis*, and as Dionysos in the *Dionysalexandros*
of Kratinos. The actor presumably wore a portrait mask of
Perikles and the attributes of the god with whom he was
identified, just as Pheidias is said to have introduced Perikles
in the character of Theseus in the Amazonomachy on the
shield of the Athena Parthenos.[1] We know that in the *Dionysalexandros* Perikles had the saffron robe, the coloured cloak,
the drinking cup, and the thyrsos of Dionysos. But although
portrait masks would be possible and likely for people known
in Athens during the fifth century, since even when they
were dead their portraits could be copied, they seem much
less likely for Hesiod, Archilochos, Sappho, and Alkaios;
moreover the natural explanation of the plural titles *Archi-
lochoi*, *Hesiodoi*, etc. is that the chief actor and the chorus
wore the same masks. Twenty-five men wearing portrait-
masks of Archilochos would be unlikely, but twenty-five
bitter ancients led by one named Archilochos would be
feasible. Portrait masks may sometimes have survived as
standard masks, but we lack conclusive evidence. It is
tempting to say that we can see the beginning of clean-
shaven masks for young men (as distinct from boys) in the
portrait masks of Kleisthenes and Agathon in the *Thesmophoriazousai* (191, 575). Twenty years later in the *Ekklesiazousai* Praxagora and her friends put on beards to disguise
themselves as men and she is described as a 'good-looking
fair young man like Nikias' (428), which shows that respectable young men in the early fourth century still normally
wore beards. The earliest clean-shaven man among the terra-
cottas is the fat man (12*d*) in a set found in a tomb in Athens,
which can be dated before 348 because replicas were discovered at Olynthos. The general fashion changed when all

[1] Cf. T. Dohrn, *Symbola Coloniensia*, 82.

the young men wanted to look like Alexander, but the Aixone
relief (*31*) shows that the young lover might be clean-shaven
in 340, and a very similar terra-cotta mask was found at
Olynthos (80).[1]

Special masks might have been expected for the gods,
but such evidence as we have is against it. It is true that
Herakles has a special mask, which he wears in the Centaur
picture (2) and in many other representations (e.g. 13); it
has goggling eyes, shortish fat nose, an enormous mouth,
and a shortish beard; it does not seem to be worn by anyone
else except Herakles. In the Centaur picture winged Nike,
who drives Herakles, wears a snub-nosed dark-haired mask
very like that worn by the female chorus on another Attic
vase (9). On the Leningrad oenochoe (4) a standing actor,
wearing a chiton and a large himation over his tights, holds
a mask with scanty white hair, hooked nose, and considerable
beard. The mask has a small crown and the actor holds a
sceptre. He is therefore playing Zeus, but the same mask
is used indiscriminately for gods and men in South Italy.
Dionysos on an oenochoe recently discovered in the Athenian
Agora (7) has nothing to distinguish him from the other fat
phallic men of Old Comedy; this might very well be the god
as he appeared when doing his military service under
Phormio in Eupolis' *Taxiarchs*. The only other evidence
which comes ultimately from Athens is a terra-cotta group
(78), known from several replicas and imitations, of a man
riding on a mule, which has been interpreted as Hephaistos.[2]
If this is right (and the Return of Hephaistos is a very likely
subject for a comedy), Hephaistos wears a mask which is
commonly worn by slaves, as he also does on a South
Italian vase (37). In South Italy, as we shall see, with the
exception of Herakles, gods and men wore the same masks;
the slight evidence quoted from Attica suggests that the
same was true there, that in fact it was part of the fun of this

[1] There are also a few clean-shaven masks on South Italian vases, see below
Ch. II, p. 112 ff.
[2] N. Breitenstein, *Act. Arch.* 9 (1938), 127.

kind of comedy that the highest gods should be indistinguishable from men 'worse than ourselves'. Gods are
distinguished only by their attributes, just as Priam is
only distinguished from any other old man by his Eastern
head-dress (36).

Study of the Attic vases and terra-cottas suggests that
about twenty-four masks of Old and Middle Comedy can
be distinguished; I propose to mention these very briefly
and then consider what the plays tell us about masks. The
following list only gives the best examples; others will be
found in the catalogue, where the masks are denoted by the
capital letters prefixed to them in my account here. There
are two old men: G, the Zeus mask already mentioned, and
E, mild old man with smooth eyebrows and a short nose.
On the Leningrad oenochoe (4) it is held by a man sitting
on a bundle and therefore should be a slave mask but in
other instances (8, *14*) this is not clear. As we shall see, the
boundary between slave and free man is not rigid. The
contrast between short nosed and long nosed is found in the
Birds (805/6) where Peisthetairos, 'a plucked blackbird',
is contrasted with Euelpides, 'a caricature of a goose', and
they may well have worn these two masks. Later, when the
gods arrive in Cloudcuckooland, Peisthetairos must be
distinguished from Poseidon, who would wear the long-
nosed mask like Zeus on the Leningrad oenochoe (4);
Herakles would wear his special mask and Triballos a slave
mask.

Then four masks are perhaps middle-aged rather than old.
The first (A) can be seen in the background of the Lyme
Park relief (*10*), a man with a good head of hair and a short
spade beard (it is possible that this is the Wedge-beard of
Pollux' list of comic masks since we seem to have no good
evidence for him in New Comedy). The second (M) is the
man on the left of the Aixone relief (*31*) with a good head
of hair and a short square beard. These two are worn by the
chorus and the actor respectively on the new Agora relief
(*31a*). The third (L) has a good head of hair and a longish

beard; this mask is very common on terra-cottas and is worn by the distressed traveller (*11d*) in the New York set, to which we shall return. It may be the first Hermonian of Pollux' list, which has receding hair, a good beard, raised eyebrows, and an energetic expression; Hermon was an actor of Aristophanes' time. On a Campanian vase (66) an old man in this mask looks at a colossal figure with a horn of plenty; he may be Trygaios in a revival of the *Peace*. We can then think of Dikaiopolis, the other peace-loving countryman, wearing the same mask in the *Acharnians* and the chorus of Acharnians could wear the wedge-beard mask (A), which Pollux characterises as 'rather embittered'. It is also worn by an elderly man who has espied a girl (*15*). The fourth (F) is bald with a tuft of hair on the back of his head, a little turn-up nose and a scrubby beard. He can be seen on an Attic oenochoe (3), dancing along with a torch like Blepyros at the end of the *Ekklesiazousai*. This may be the second Hermonian of Pollux' list 'with bald pate, meeting brows, and a goat-like beard'.

Then two men who seem to be younger. One (H) has neat hair and beard; his mask is lying on the ground on the right of the Leningrad oenochoe (4). The other (D) has a hooked nose and a straggly beard, very like Sokrates' description of Meletos in Plato's *Euthyphro* (*2b*) as 'stringy-haired, scrubby-bearded, and hook-nosed'; as a terra-cotta in Munich (16) with this mask has a large torch, he is probably a wild young man like Pheidippides in the *Clouds* or the debauched son of the *Banqueters*, whereas the sober youth in that play would wear (H). It seems to me possible that this is the mask for the *alazon*, of whom the rake is one type; then it would also be worn by the braggart soldier when he becomes a stock character in the fourth century.

Five other masks are sometimes worn by slaves, but it seems to be impossible to draw a hard and fast line between slaves and the poorer members of the free population: the author of the *Constitution of the Athenians* (1, 10) says that *demos* and slaves are indistinguishable in clothing and

appearance, and the Maison mask, which according to
Festus was worn by cooks and sailors—normally free men—
is listed among the slave masks by Pollux. A glance at the
dramatis personæ of Aristophanes shows the need for a
variety of such masks—in the *Acharnians* the sycophant,
Nikarchos, the servant of Lamachos, and two messengers,
or in the *Peace* Kydoimos and the arms manufacturers. Of
these five masks the first (B) has a trumpet mouth like the
New Comedy slaves—it can be seen on the knee of the poet
on the Lyme Park relief (*10*) and is held by the man on the
right on the Leningrad oenochoe (4). The second (K) has
a good deal of hair and a wide beard; many of the slaves of
the New York set wear it (e.g. 11*e*, *f*, *g*). The third (N) has
fuzzy hair and a wide beard with a small point; this is the
centre mask of the Aixone relief (*31*) and is worn by the
torch-bearer in the Centaur picture (2). The fourth (P) is
bald with a very short spade beard (this may be the Maison
mask noted above); it is worn by a man carrying a basket,
who may be a cook (17). The Sausage-seller in the *Knights*
would presumably wear this mask. The fifth (C) has peaked
hair, brows flying upwards, and a longish beard: one
terra-cotta on which it occurs (12*e*)—a seated man with a
purse—was very popular. He is very like the 'meddlesome'
Lycomedian of New Comedy, and such a mask would suit the
interfering Blepsidemos in the *Ploutos* (335).

The three clean-shaven masks are the worried young man
(O) who looks like a distressed lover on the Aixone relief
(*31*), a variant (Z) with raised eyebrows from Olynthos (81),
and the disgustingly fat young man (Q) in the second New
York set (12*d*) whom I take to be a parasite—he also is
unique but very popular. Parasites only became stock
characters in the fourth century and there was certainly at
least one other mask which they wore.[1] These clean-shaven
masks I suspect belong to Middle Comedy rather than
Aristophanes.

We can distinguish eight female masks. We have already

---

[1] See below p. 112; *Studies in Later Greek Comedy*, 64 f.

noticed the snub-nosed black-haired mask (T) worn by winged Nike (2) and by the choreuts on the Heidelberg vase (9). In the *Lysistrata* three masks are needed for Lysistrata, who has raised brows (8, 707),[1] Lampito, and the chorus who are older (637); I take Kalonike and Myrrhine in the first scene and the three women who appear later to be members of the chorus. A straight-nosed mask with a mop of hair (R), which can be seen on the Aixone relief (*31*) and on a popular figure from the second New York set of terra-cottas (12*b*), could be worn by Lampito, and the chorus could wear one of the old women's masks. Of these two can be distinguished, a little old snub-nosed wizened mask (U), worn by the nurse in the first New York set (11*a*) and by the procuress in the Würzburg group (18), and a fat woman (Y) known from several terra-cottas (e.g. 19). We have to postulate a third old woman for the parade of uglies in the *Ekklesiazousai*: the first (940) is snub-nosed (U) the third is like a toad and a monkey (1072, 1101) and should be the fat woman (Y). As monkeys are snub-nosed, the second should be a long-nosed woman, like the Clouds and Poverty in the *Ploutos*; an admirable mask of this kind can be seen on South Italian vases (e.g. 42). Two of the uglies presumably appeared as Plathane and Pandokeutria in the *Frogs*. A woman with very elaborate hair-dressing (X, e.g. 20) is presumably a rich hetaira and therefore belongs to Middle Comedy. I think it is extremely likely that three other hetaira masks and a young hetaira's maid were already known in Middle Comedy. They appear on South Italian vases [2] of the third quarter of the fourth century and one on a doubtful Attic terra-cotta (21). It is just this period which is badly represented in the Attic evidence apart from the Aixone relief, because the terra-cottas, whenever they were actually

---

[1] An Apulian vase (37) shows Leda wearing a variant of mask (T) with raised brows. I have assumed that the mask for a wife with long hair which appears on two local imitations of Attic terra-cottas (59, 84) had not been introduced in the fifth century. It appears also on a fourth century Attic terra-cotta in the National Museum at Athens (16268).

[2] Cf. below p. 90 ff.

made, seem to belong stylistically to the second quarter of
the century rather than the third. Finally, there are three
younger women; (S), a girl with simple hair-dressing, who
appears on the right hand side of the Aixone relief (*31*), (V), a
girl with her hair bunched on the forehead in a clasp, who
plays the part of Auge in the first New York set (*11b*), and
(W), a girl with her hair tied in a bow over her forehead (22).
These three also belong to Middle Comedy and were the
heroines of the various adventures which can be classed
under the general headings of rape and rescue, found
particularly in intrigue and recognition plays.[1]

In spite of the very considerable variety of masks they
are not enough for Aristophanes' larger casts, and as I have
suggested, about six of them are likely to have been introduced after the death of Aristophanes. The *Acharnians* has
some twenty-seven characters (counting plural characters
like Pseudartabas as one). Let us try to allot their masks and
say what we can about their costume. The comic actor or
chorusman wears tights, which can be clearly seen on vases
and terra-cottas because they wrinkle at the knees and
elbows. I suspect but cannot prove that if the actor represents a man, the tights are pink/brown and if a woman,
white; Praxagora is described as 'white' when she is dressed
as a man in the *Ekklesiazousai* (428), and the First woman
tried to brown herself by sunbathing (64), but too much
emphasis must not be placed on these passages. If the actor
is playing a male part, he has a phallos stitched on to his
tights; it may be tied up, or it may dangle if obscene jokes
are to be made; the two positions can be seen clearly on the
Leningrad oenochoe (4), and Aristophanes refers to them
in the *Clouds* (538).[2] The tights are in fact the skin of the
character and if he is stripped like Mnesilochos in the
Thesmophoriazousai (213 f.), he appears in tights and *phallos*,
as for instance the seated man on the Leningrad oenochoe
(4). Over this skin he may wear various garments alone or in

---

[1] Cf. *Studies in Later Greek Comedy*, 74 f.
[2] Cf. *CQ*, 49 (1955), 94.

combination: short chiton (which leaves the phallos uncovered), short himation with chiton or alone (so apparently Mnesilochos before he is stripped), long himation with chiton (like the Zeus of the Leningrad oenochoe, 4). A felt hat, *pilos*, is worn by travellers and countrymen (e.g. *11d*). The himation (with or without chiton) may be worn in various different ways, slung over the arm (2, the man with a torch), round the shoulders (*11d*), round the body and over one shoulder (*14*), or over the head (*11f*). The countryman of the second New York set (*12f*) wears a skin cloak (*diphthera*). When Mnesilochos is dressed up as a woman, he wears a long chiton (*krokotos*), himation, veil, headband, and shoes. The chiton and himation can be seen clearly on the Heidelberg vase (*9*) and on many of the terra-cottas; the veil cannot be easily distinguished in terra-cottas from a himation worn over the head.

We can then return to the *Acharnians*. We have suggested mask L for Dikaiopolis and mask A for the chorus; they would probably wear short chiton and himation. We can suppose that Euripides, Kephisophon, and Lamachos had portrait masks and Pseudartabas (and his colleague) and the Megarian's daughters special masks. Pseudartabas' beard (97) is so remarkable that Dikaiopolis suggests that he is the clean-shaven Kleisthenes with a false beard (117).[1] Euripides would wear nothing but a himation and Lamachos a military cloak. We can picture him and his servant from the new Agora relief (*31a*) and from a very popular figure of the soldier/traveller/porter class who has flask and basket hanging in front of him (*23*).[2] Dikaiopolis' wife would look like the women on the Heidelberg vase (*9*) with mask T; his daughter would wear the girl's mask S. The only other women are the *paranympheutria*, probably an elderly woman, for instance U, and the two *hetairai* at the finish (perhaps V). We can provide a parallel to the Megarian in the various

---

[1] I am not clear whether Pseudartabas is accompanied by one man or two, or whether they are distinguished from him (see Rennie on 119).

[2] On figures of this kind cf. *Studies in Later Greek Comedy*, 152.

figures carrying animals, if they are to be interpreted as countrymen rather than cooks (one in the Louvre (24) wears a short chiton only and mask K), and to the Boeotian pipers, e.g. 25, who wears a skin only and mask K. Another country-man is the Farmer in the second part of the play. We are still left with (in order of appearance) prytaneis, heralds, Amphitheos, archers (54), ambassador, Theoros, Ody-mantians, Xanthias, Sykophant, Nikarchos, Herald, Par-anymphos, Messenger A, Messenger B. Either standard masks are an illusion or several characters wore the same mask. The argument for standard masks rests partly on the practice of New Comedy but more on the monumental evidence; we have more than 160 different Attic monuments, reliefs, vases, and terra-cottas dated between 425 and 339, and when due allowance is made for the individualism of the artist, they seem to fall into 26 types; again, as we have so many monuments, it seems unlikely that we have lost many additional types of mask; the long-nosed woman which we added to the list is in fact attested on South Italian vases. It is possible that non-speakers did not wear masks, but that would only cut out prytaneis, archers, Odymantians, Xanthias, and we should then have to suppose that the Odymantians wore costumes but not masks and that the *paranympheutria* and *hetairai* were taken by women. The other solution seems more probable and there is some further evidence which can be considered later. It would obviously be convenient if in the earlier part of the play the Ambassador wore the same mask as Theoros since the parts are taken by the same actor, and Theoros comes on ten lines after the Ambassador goes off—he would then only have had to redrape his cloak, but it must be remembered that in the *Ekklesiazousai* the actor who takes the first old woman goes off at line 1044 and comes on again as the yet more hideous second old woman at line 1049. The principle may have been merely the negative one that two characters who have a considerable conversation together should not wear the same mask and the same costume.

Then, to go through the *Acharnians* from the beginning,
Dikaiopolis wears mask L, the prytaneis (40) presumably
one of the old masks, E or G, the herald (who reappears
later) one of the masks which can also be worn by a slave,
let us say P; Amphitheos as a good young man can wear
H, the archers (54) who presumably wear a parody of
Scythian costume are perhaps clean shaven and wear a form
of Z;[1] the Ambassador and Theoros could both wear D,
the rake's mask, as that is what Aristophanes thinks of them
(if they are rather older, F, who is also rakish, is a possibility);
Pseudartabas and his colleague wear a special mask; the
Odomantians one of the masks which can be worn by slaves,
let us say N and reserve this for low military characters;
the chorus wear A; Xanthias wears the slave mask B,
Dikaiopolis' daughter and wife S and T; Kephisophon,
Euripides, and Lamachos wear portrait masks; the
Megarian's daughters wear a special piglet mask; the
Megarian comes on later as the Boeotian and both can wear
K, as the terra-cottas suggest—they are distinguished by
what they carry. The Sycophant and Nikarchos in Aristophanes' opinion belong to the rake class and can wear either
F or D. The servant of Lamachos as a soldier wears N. The
herald again wears P. The farmer, who is not received with
sympathy, should perhaps be distinguished from the
Megarian and the Boeotian and could wear C. The *para-
nymphos* is young and good; so he may again wear H and
the *pronympheutria* U. The messenger from the generals
(1071) like Lamachos' servant wears N. The messenger
who comes to Dikaiopolis need not be distinguished from
the herald. The hetairai may wear V.

This is clearly a conjectural allocation, but it shows how
the masks which we know could be used for producing the
Acharnians without confusion. If some such allocation is
right, then, some masks are confined to a single character,
others tell the audience something about the character, that
he is a soldier, or that he belongs to the class of citizen whom

[1] See next chapter for evidence of kalyx krater in New York (33).

the aristocratic pseudo-Xenophon cannot distinguish from slaves, or that he is a worthy person or a valueless person in the poet's eye; and provided that the chief characters are kept clear by their masks this is all we need to know in Old Comedy. New Comedy with its small cast can have a mask for each character, and the aims of New Comedy are different.

One other piece of evidence for the sharing of masks has already been quoted. The natural explanation of the plural titles *Hesiodoi*, etc., is that the chief actor and the chorus wore the same mask. Another such title is the *Odysses* of Kratinos, and there the fragments show that the chorus were composed of sailors of Odysseus and Odysseus himself took the chief part. It is difficult to think of any other explanation for the plural title here except that chief actor and the chorus wore the same mask. In fact the boundary between chorus and actors was not always rigid. If in the plays with plural titles the actor merges with the chorus, in other plays members of the chorus may themselves have some individuality. Thus in the *Lysistrata* (see above), in the *Thesmophoriazousai* (760 f.), and in the *Ekklesiazousai* (opening scene) members of the chorus have parts in the dialogue, a number of special birds come on singly before the main body of the chorus in the *Birds* (267 f.), and in Ameipsias' *Konnos* some at least of the chorus of Sophists seem to have worn portrait masks.

If then it is highly probable that several characters wore the same mask, the first New York set of terra-cottas (11) becomes easier to understand. The figures are: (*a*) nurse in long chiton and himation pulled over her head, mask U, and carrying baby, (*b*) young woman in long chiton and himation, which covers her head but which she is pulling aside from her face, mask V, (*c*) Herakles in his usual mask wearing short chiton, lion-skin cap; the lion skin falls down his left side where it has another head; he also has a bow and a club, (*d*) man in felt hat, mask L, himation draped over his shoulders and short chiton, lamenting, and then three men (*e, f, g*) wearing mask K, one in short chiton and himation over his left shoulder carrying a basket, one with himation over his head carrying a pitcher, and the third in a short chiton, sitting cross-legged with his hands round his knees on a seat which he has covered with a himation. The last three might be one man at different moments but it seems to me more likely that they are different men. The unwanted baby we know from a fragment of Alexis' *Stratiotes* (209 K) which can be dated 350/40, and from several terra-cottas of men standing with children; a man in a felt hat taking refuge on an altar with a baby (26) may be Telephos with the infant Orestes. The baby in the New York set is presumably the child of Herakles and the young woman. The story may therefore well be the Auge story; Euboulos wrote a Middle Comedy with this name. The baby will then be Telephos and the old man is presumably the father, Aleos. Herakles is having a feast prepared: one slave is being sent out to market and the other is fetching water. A third is sitting down, trying to think of a scheme to outwit Aleos, an early intriguing slave like the parallel figure in the second New York set (12*g*). This intriguing slave in the second set has his chin pillared by his hand, the *os columnatum* of Roman comedy.[1] In these two cases we cannot say what the seat is; very often it is an altar, either the round altar which may belong to a private house or the square altar belonging to a temple, if this distinction is valid.[2] Thus in the second New York set the man with a purse sits on a square altar (presumably it is a safe place to count his swag), but the man with a felt hat and a skin round his shoulders is sitting on a round altar for thought but presumably also for safety, since there could be no other reason for choosing an altar as a seat.

The man with the water jar has his himation over his head (11*f*). Professor Rumpf[3] lists it with other figures similarly draped as an example of men dressed up as women in Old Comedy. I think we may be rather more precise.

---

[1] *Miles Gloriosus* 200 f. where Plautus describes the gestures of the thinking slave, many of which can be paralleled in the terra-cottas. Cf. also 27.

[2] Cf. on round altars E. Bielefeld, *Wissenschaftliche Zeitschrift der Universität Greifswald*, 1 (1951) 14 f.

[3] In *Mimus und Logos; Festgabe für Carl Niessen*, 168.

First, men could carry water-pots in comedy without dressing up as women (28). Secondly, the *hydriaphoros* (water-pot carrier) was a woman, as Pollux says (3, 55) and as appears from many vases and terra-cottas; but the pitcher-bearers of the Parthenon frieze are men. Is our comic actor then performing a momentary parody? The man sent to fetch water puts his cloak over his head like a female *hydriaphoros*; a possible text for this is given in the *Ekklesiazousai* 738, where the man arranging his belongings outside his door says: 'Bring hither the hydria, O water-pot carrier'; I should like to think that he puts his cloak over his head and the hydria on it. But although it seems probable that the water-carriers are at least for the moment pretending to be women, other explanations may be easier for the not infrequent standing men with cloaks over their heads (e.g. 29). Ancient Greeks put their cloaks over their heads to promote thought, to escape detection, to disassociate themselves with what was going on, or in grief or shame.[1] The little men of comedy are for the most part frightened and/or ashamed and this is sufficient explanation. Male characters of comedy did however dress up as women, and we have discussed what was done with Mnesilochos in the *Thesmophoriazousai* (220 f.). Presumably he had a special mask which could be shaved on the stage. The terra-cotta maker could not show this but he could do a man wearing woman's clothes, and we are justified in regarding a figure in the Louvre (30), wearing the rake's mask, but, like Mnesilochos, a headband, a long chiton, and a himation, as a male character dressed up as a woman.

The evidence for different characters wearing the same mask has been discussed. This was only necessary in plays with a large number of characters. The whole point of the Comedy of Errors depends on two chief characters (or as in the *Amphitruo* two pairs of characters) wearing the same mask, and would be less easy to appreciate if it was usual

---

[1] Typical texts: thought, *Clouds* 735; detection, *Birds* 1495; disassociation, Aeschines 2, 107; grief, *Frogs* 911; shame, E. *HF* 1159, *Or.* 459 ff.

for characters to wear the same mask. The earliest play that
we can suggest was a Comedy of Errors is Ephippos'
Homoioi, produced 380/70.[1] From that date the audience
must have become more ready to demand that in other kinds
of play all characters should be distinguished by mask, and
as the intrigue comedy with its small cast became popular
the demand became easy to answer. If, as I believe, *Menaechmi*, *Persa*, and *Amphitruo* all reproduce originals of
Middle Comedy, we know three Middle Comedies with
small casts which would not be difficult to equip. *Menaechmi*
has identical twins (H), slave (B), hetaira (X), hetaira's maid
(U), cook (P), old man (A), wife (T), doctor (? Z or D);
Persa has three slaves (B, C, K), parasite (Q), hetaira (V ?),
hetaira's maid (U), girl (S), *leno* (F); *Amphitruo* has elderly
twins (G), slave twins (N), wife (T), wife's servant (U),
pilot (P). These allocations are not necessarily right but are
certainly possible. The second New York set of terra-cottas
(12) and the Aixone relief also probably give the casts of
intrigue comedies. The terra-cottas (not later than 350 B.C.,
because replicas of some were found at Olynthos) give an
intriguing slave (mask N), an old countryman in a skin cloak
(mask L), who is probably his master. The man seated with
a purse (mask C) suggests that agricultural money was
diverted as in the *Persa*, *Truculentus*, and *Asinaria*. There
remain a young man (mask D ?) with a cloak over his head
to escape detection (?), a hetaira (mask V) and perhaps her
mother (mask R), and the fat parasite (mask Q). The five
masks of the Aixone relief (*31*) could be fitted into a similar
scheme—mask M, father; R, mother (of boy or girl ?);
N, slave; O, young lover; S, girl. These intrigue comedies
with small casts are clearly a late stage before New Comedy.

(d) *New Comedy*

New Comedy is the comedy of Menander, his contemporaries and successors. What we mean by the costume

---

[1] See *Studies in Later Greek Comedy*, 67 f.

of New Comedy is the costume that we know from countless monuments dating from the third century B.C. to the end of antiquity. The striking contrast of this costume with the costume of Middle and Old Comedy is that it is no longer obscene. The padding has gone and male characters all wear chitons which reach at least to their knees and free men, unless they are soldiers, wear long chitons. New Comedy also has a number of new masks, notably for fathers and sons, who are important in these plays. We do not know whether this was a gradual change or a sudden change. We could imagine that such a change to respectability was made either when the new masks for tragedy were introduced under Lykourgos (about 330) or when Demetrios of Phaleron was dictator (317–07). But our only evidence is the monuments, and among them the earliest that can be dated with something like certainty are the original of the Menander relief (C 49) in the lifetime of Menander (before 292) and the originals of the two Dioskourides mosaics (19, 20) in the first quarter of the third century. If, as I shall suggest later, one of the advantages of the new masks was that families could be recognised by their hairdressing, some of them may have been introduced at a single moment to make this possible, and the idea may have been due to a single man who was interested in family comedy; and who is more likely than Menander himself? But we must remember that we are comparatively badly off for illustrations of comedy which can be dated with any certainty in the last thirty years of the fourth century, and therefore the change may have been more gradual than we suppose; the texts show that obscene jokes were still occasionally made in New Comedy and that the phallos was sometimes visible.[1]

Nevertheless New Comedy like Hellenistic tragedy had a standard costume and standard masks for which we have

---

[1] E.g. *Rudens* 429 (cf. Prehn, *Quaestiones Plautinae*, 79). When the terracottas from the Athenian Agora are published, they will provide some evidence for New Comedy types in Athens in the late fourth century. Cf. also below on Larisa and Alexandria.

evidence in a multitude of monuments from all over the
Greek world. They may be used in the same way and with
the same reservations as the monuments of Hellenistic
tragedy discussed above. There is however one difference;
for the majority of the forty-four masks in Pollux' list we
can provide examples either from Athens or of Athenian
origin. I shall therefore first consider Pollux' list and note
good examples of masks which can reasonably be identified
with his types, describing also costumes where relevant;
secondly, I shall point out which of these masks are identical
with or obviously derive from earlier masks; thirdly, I shall
suggest what characters in the Greek fragments and Roman
adaptations of New Comedy wore these masks.

We have one valuable link between Menander and the
pictorial tradition, a marble relief in the Lateran (49), which
Studniczka dates in the first century A.D. Much here is
uncertain, but it is clear at least that we have Menander
inspecting three masks, a young man, a girl, and an old
man; they are not the complete cast of the play, but perhaps
the three speaking characters in a particular scene; they
have been identified with three masks in Pollux' catalogue—
No. 11 the dark youth, 34 first pseudokore, and 4 the old
man with wavy hair.[1] Let us consider these masks further.

The old man with wavy hair, according to Pollux, has a
long fine beard, smooth brows, and looks lethargic (νωθρός).
He is contrasted with No. 3 the leading old man, who has a
hooked nose (presumably, therefore, the old man with wavy
hair has a straight or snub nose), and one brow raised.
These two are new masks for which no earlier parallels can
be found. Of the other old men's masks in Pollux Nos. 1, 2,
5, 6 do not appear in the New Comedy but were common
in Middle Comedy; they were the masks labelled, G, E, L,
A. Pollux No. 9, our F, called 2nd Hermonian after a fifth
century actor, appears once on a silver cup of the early third
century (8). The two new masks are seen together on a
marble relief in Naples (48) where the leading old man

[1] See Simon, *Comicae Tabellae*, 59, 119, 92 n. 59.

restrains the old man with wavy hair from attacking his son, who is dancing drunkenly, supported by his slave; a rough parallel is afforded by the scene in the *Heautontimoroumenos* (1045) where Menedemus restrains Chremes from attacking Clitipho. The same pair appear also on a terra-cotta relief known in various versions (22); here the slave of the wavy-haired old man has taken refuge on an altar like Daos in the papyrus fragment of the *Perinthia*. Have we then here the masks of the pairs of fathers who are so common in Menander's plays? Let us consider how far they meet the requirements. There are four chief differences between them: hair, nose, brows, shape of face. Hair does not help much here except that, as we shall see later, wavy hair belongs also to the soldier and can therefore be a sign of irascibility; in the *Physiognomonika*[1] the man of fierce temper has a great beard and his hair shows a vigorous growth (808 *a* 22). According to the same authority (811 *a* 22 f.) straight noses are a sign of stupidity, snub noses of sensuality, and hooked noses of shamelessness or greatness of soul. Raised brows are a sign of conceit according to many texts and therefore in old men of a readiness to criticise their juniors. A long face signified lack of sensibility and a round face shamelessness (*Physiognomonika*, 807 *b* 27, 32). Finally, Pollux' description of the old man with wavy hair as lethargic is glossed by the author of the *Physiognomonika*: 'lethargic movements betray softness of character' (816 *b* 25). We have therefore two basic types: an energetic old man who can, however be calm (only one eyebrow is raised), and a normally calm old man, who may be subject to fits of anger, and these types can be varied further by minor alterations. Take, for instance, Nikeratos and Demeas in Menander's *Samia*: Nikeratos is a straightforward, energetic old man and can wear the leading old man's mask; Demeas combines moments of fury with moments of idealism, which makes Nikeratos describe him as 'soft' (197), and he may

[1] Ascribed to Aristotle but dated by Ross (*Aristotle*, 12) to the third century.

therefore be the old man with wavy hair. Professor Rumpf[1]
has suggested that a bronze statuette (76) of a man
wearing the mask of the old man with wavy hair but the
short tunic of a slave (down to the knee) and openwork
stockings is an old man, masquerading as a eunuch, presumably in one of those disastrous love adventures which
fathers of New Comedy occasionally undertake.

Pollux also describes other old men's masks. The Lycomedian (18) is curly-haired, long-bearded, with one
eyebrow raised, and 'suggests interference' (*polyprag-
mosyne*); on a Pompeian painting (42) he has a brown chiton
and a darker brown himation. The mask is not unlike the
mask C worn by the seated man with the purse from the
New York terra-cottas (B 12*e*), and this may be its ancestor.
Megaronides in the *Trinummus* is an obvious candidate,
perhaps also Smikrines in the *Epitrepontes*. The *leno* or
procurer (No. 8) is 'generally like the Lycomedian, but has
a slight smile on his lips and connected brows; he has
receding hair or is bald'. He is described in the *Rudens* and
in the *Pseudolus*: in the *Rudens* he is 'curly, grey' (125),
'bald like Silenus . . . twisted eyebrows, frowning forehead' (317 f., cf. 1303 *inraso capite*) and 'bearded' (769).
Ballio in the *Pseudolus* differs in having a goat's beard (957).
The *leno* has been recognised in a terra-cotta from Myrina
(C 65); he has a large wreath on his head and an elaborately
draped himation; this may be the flowery wrap which
Pollux (4, 120) gives him to wear with a dyed chiton. Ballio
with his goatbeard according to Dr Simon[2] was wearing
the 2nd Hermonian mask, No. 9, and this description
admirably fits the instances which we have discussed above
(mask F); if this is right, the 2nd Hermonian was taken over
by the *leno* when he first appeared in Middle Comedy and
later a new mask was introduced for him in New Comedy.
Dr Simon[3] also suggests that the *eikonikos* (No. 19),

[1] *Mimus und Logos: Festgabe Carl Niessen*, 167 f.
[2] *Op. cit.*, 84.
[3] *Op. cit.*, 94; cf. also Navarre, *R.E.A.*, xvi, 20 f. for relevant texts.

described by Pollux at the end of the young men as 'sprinkled with grey, shaven, richly dressed, and a foreigner', was used for rich bankers, who were usually foreigners; she quotes Lyco in the *Curculio* and Misargyrides in the *Mostellaria*. The same mask may have been used for other elderly foreigners like Crito in the *Andria*, Hanno in the *Poenulus*, and Demeas in the *Misoumenos*. This mask has no ancestor. Two identifications have been proposed: a strange and foreign looking mask in the Louvre (77), and a terra-cotta statuette of a man in an elaborate himation, who is clean shaven but appears older than most of the youths of comedy (66).

On the Lateran relief (*49*) Menander holds the mask of a youth. It is difficult to decide whether it is the 'dark youth' or the 'delicate youth', because the main distinction between them is colour, which of course is missing on the relief. The first four youths in Pollux' catalogue are arranged in order of age, but also differ in character. The oldest, the *panchrestos* (No. 10), is an athlete and is contrasted with the 'cultured' dark youth (No. 11), who is younger: his darkness may correspond to 'the dull dark eye which betokens moderation' in the *Physiognomonika* (807 *b* 36); the slight redness of the *panchrestos* is a sign of health and possible hastiness (806 *b* 4, 808 *a* 22), and his wrinkled forehead is a sign of courage (807 *b* 4); these characteristics are repeated in the third young man, 'the curly-haired' (No. 12) who like the *panchrestos* has raised brows, a sign, as we have seen, of energy, contrasting with the smooth brows of the 'dark youth' and presumably of the 'delicate youth' (No. 13), the youngest of the quartette, whose 'whiteness' is not only due to his studies in the shade, but also perhaps betokens a certain lack of courage (812 *a* 13). We have descriptions of two of these young men: Plesidippus (*Rudens*, 314), who is 'energetic-looking, ruddy, and strong', is clearly the *panchrestos*; Philocrates in the *Captivi* (647) is described as 'thin-faced, sharp-nosed, pale, dark-eyed, reddish hair, curly' and will be the 'curly-haired youth', who is rare in

Comedy. The surest pointer to the delicate boy in Menander is the presence of his pedagogue, e.g. in the *Dis Exapaton* (= *Bacchides*, Pistoclerus and Lydus), *Phasma*, and *Kolax*. The 'dark youth' is 'cultured rather than addicted to physical exercise'; Robert seems therefore justified in giving this mask to Charisios in the *Epitrepontes*.[1] The curly-headed youth (No. 12) is clearly distinguished by his hair from the other three. He is not very common among the monuments, but curly hair seems to be indicated by the short carefully twisted locks on a terra-cotta head (67), which pairs with a head of a hetaira, and on a marble head from Ephesos (78). The admirable *panchrestos*, the dark boy, and the delicate boy have the same hairdressing but differ in colour. The dark boy, as we have said, may be recognised on the Menander relief (49); the other two appear together on the Dioskourides mosaic of revellers (20). There the *panchrestos* wears a blue chiton and a red himation and beats a tambourine; he is *tympanotriba* like Diniarchus in the *Truculentus* (611), while the delicate youth in violet chiton and white himation dances with clappers. A flute girl accompanies them, wearing a blue chiton and a yellow wrap. The small figure on the left is possibly a slave, but he is not a speaking character, as he does not wear a mask. The general situation is not unlike the arrival of Callidamates and Delphium in the *Mostellaria*, but here the two youths are brothers, if my theory about hairdressing is correct. All these four young men are, as far as we know, an invention for New Comedy.

The 'rustic' (No. 14) has a snub nose, flat lips, a dark complexion, and a crown of hair; he should therefore be sensual and cowardly according to the *Physiognomonika*. We have Donatus' authority that Chremes in the *Eunuch* is a rustic, and he shows himself a coward as well as getting drunk (another certain instance is Strabax in the *Truculentus*, who is clearly sensual). The rustic wears a skin according to Pollux (4, 119), and Varro (*RR*, 2, 11, 11) tells us that the young man in Caecilius' *Hypobolimaius*, based on Menander's

[1] *Die Masken der neueren attischen Komödie*, 65.

Hypobolimaios or Rustic, wore a skin; he was no doubt the true-born country son, Charippos, who is contrasted with the supposititious town son, Moschion.[1] It seems difficult to avoid the conclusion that this mask was also worn by the country son, Ctesipho, in the *Adelphi,* who is both cowardly (537 f.) and sensual. Two other characters, who presumably wear this mask because of their occupation, are quite different, Gorgias in Menander's *Heros* and his namesake in the *Georgos.* On a Hellenistic silver cup (24), one of a pair which also has tragic masks, the skeleton of Menander holds a mask with flat nose, wide lips, and a wreath, which seems to be the rustic at a party, perhaps the rustic who gave its alternative title to the famous *Hypobolimaios.* Professor Rumpf has also recognised him with a girl and an old woman on a terra-cotta brazier, which was probably made in Athens (5). He seems to have a Middle Comedy ancestry; on a Paestan vase of the mid-fourth century (B 60) Hermes, conducting Zeus on a nocturnal adventure, has turned up nose and thick lips, which look very like the Rustic.

Pollux then describes a contrasted pair of masks with wavy hair, which we have suggested is a sign of irascibility. The first is 'a soldier and a braggart with dark skin and hair' (No. 15); the second is 'more delicate and has yellow hair' (No. 16). Identification of the braggart soldier has been confused by the assumption that he appeared on a wall-painting in Pompeii (C 25), which we know only from drawings. The figure there with Macedonian cap (*kausia*), chlamys, short chiton, and spear is undoubtedly a soldier, but the stylisation of the mouth and beard shows that he is man, not officer; it may very well be an illustration of the Harpax scene in the *Pseudolus* (594 ff.). The braggart soldier himself is beardless and we know him in various versions, striding forward in his military cloak (62), standing over his girl while his rival stands on the other side (57), wrapped in a civilian himation, looking lovesick (68) like Polemon in Menander's *Perikeiromene* (58f.), and looking cheerful with

---

[1] See *Studies in Menander,* 100, n. 1.

a wreath round his head (1) like Polemon at the end of the
Perikeiromene (421). The last is a terra-cotta mask of the
early third century which is believed to be Athenian because
of its clay. The younger version, No. 16, is worn by the
young man who is dancing tipsily on the Naples relief (*48*).
In the Middle Comedy material we have seen two masks
(Z and O) which may perhaps be the ancestors of these two
masks, the former (B 81) with raised brows on a terra-cotta
from Olynthos, the latter on the Aixone relief (B *31*), but
they only became common when the young men wanted to
look like Alexander. In Menander, Bias in the *Kolax* is the
traditional type of the braggart soldier; Polemon in the
Perikeiromene is an idealisation and the mask might be
somewhat softened, but Menander may have wanted to
contrast appearance and character. The second young man
(No. 16) has yellow hair, which denotes courage according
to the *Physiognomonika* (812 *a* 16).   As he is also 'delicate',
he is presumably the same age as the 'delicate boy' (No. 13),
but shares the soldier's wildness and irascibility and may
have sometimes some connection with military service,
which the delicate boy lacks. Dr Simon [1] has suggested that
Chairea in the *Eunuch* wore this mask because he was doing
his ephebe service (296) and his character fits admirably;
we can add Moschion of the *Samia* and Alcesimarchus of the
Synaristosai (= *Cistellaria*) since they both call for arms (*Sam.*
346; *Cist.* 284 ff.), and Clinias of the *Heautontimoroumenos*,
who has been on military service (100 f.), but is still very
young (113). The Naples relief (C *48*) suggests that the
connection with soldiers is not essential, but that the mask
could be used for any wild young man about town, e.g.
Moschion of the *Perikeiromene*, who is 'rich and always
drunk' (22 f.). Then we may also follow Dr Simon [2] in
attributing this mask to Diniarchus in the *Truculentus* (610 f.),
'the soft, long-locked adulterer, lover of the shade, player
of the tambourine'. This mask, with its yellow hair, pale face

---

[1] *Op. cit.*, 68.
[2] *Loc. cit.*

and straight nose, is the obvious contrast for the dark-haired, dark-complexioned, snub-nosed rustic in Menander's *Hypobolimaios* (Moschion/Charippos), *Heros* (Pheidias/Gorgias), and *Georgos* (X/Gorgias).

Pollux mentions three parasite masks. There is no trace of the Sicilian parasite (No. 20) in Menander, but Dr Simon has detected him in a fragment of Diphilos,[1] where someone is said to be 'stuffed fat with Sicilian lard'. The other two are both dark, hook-nosed (probably cowardly therefore and certainly shameless according to the *Physiognomonika*), and fat; the parasite (No. 18) is distinguished from the flatterer (No. 17) because his ears are more damaged and he looks more cheerful, the flatterer's brows are raised more maliciously. Gelasimus in the *Stichus* (Menander's *First Adelphoi*) and Gnatho in the *Kolax* are obvious examples of the two types in Menander. Gelasimus carries strigil and lekythos (*Stich.* 230), which Pollux notes as the equipment of parasites. All three have been identified (69, 54, 12). If we want to find ancestors, the fat man in the second New York set (B12*d* with mask Q) provides an Attic ancestor for the Sicilian parasite. For the other two we have to go to South Italy to find examples from the middle of the fourth century: the flatterer with curly, receding hair and raised brows is extremely like one of a pair of youths on a Paestan vase (B 61) who are dragging an old man off his money chest, and the parasite appears both on an Apulian vase (B 42) pursued by a woman and as a terra-cotta statuette in the Temple of Ceres at Paestum (B 58).

Pollux lists six masks for slaves. The old slave's mask (No. 21), who may also be a freedman according to Pollux, would be used for *paidagogoi* in the *Dis Exapaton*, *Phasma*, and *Kolax*, and for old men like Geta in the *Adelphi*. Two masks are assigned by Pollux to leading slaves: 'the leading slave has a roll of red hair' (a sign of hastiness and shamelessness according to the *Physiognomonika*), 'raised eyebrows, knitted brows; takes the same position among the slaves

[1] Simon, 54; Diphilos, 119 K, cf. also 133 K.

as the leading old man among the free . . . the leading
slave with wavy hair (No. 27) is like the leading slave
except for his hair'. The descriptions in the *Pseudolus*
(1217 ff.) and the *Asinaria* (400 ff.) would fit either. Masks
of these slaves are very common in all materials and media,
and they were extremely popular at all times and places.
We may notice two examples in which the colours of the
costumes are also preserved. In a wall-painting from
Herculaneum (C 26) the Old Slave (No. 21) stands on the
left with his stick, wearing a yellow chiton, a short himation,
yellow sleeves, yellow stockings, and red shoes. He looks at
a younger slave seated with his arm round the neck of a flute-
player. The younger man is the Leading Slave (No. 22) and
wears a short white chiton and a small green himation, green
sleeves and stockings; the flute-player wears a long yellow
chiton and a violet jacket; her brown hair is parted and she
has a wreath entwined with a yellow fillet. These are the
kind of revels which occur at the end of the *Stichus* and
which Grumio criticises in the *Mostellaria*. We should
perhaps notice that one wall-painting (34) has two white-
haired slaves, one with a roll of hair, as normally; if the other
had wavy hair (but unfortunately it is too badly preserved for
this to be clear), we should have also an old wavy-haired
slave, who is needed as the pedagogue of wavy-haired young
men like Chairestratos in the *Epitrepontes*, Charinus in the
Mercator, and probably Epidicus wears this mask, since
Epidicus is evidently older than Thesprio, who has gone
to the wars with his master. The wavy-haired Leading Slave
(No. 27), whom we have already seen on the Naples relief
(*48*) supporting his young master, stands in a Pompeian
painting (36) with his hand to his beard while his master,
the wavy-haired old man (No. 4), interrogates him; the slave
wears yellow short chiton, sleeves, and stockings, and violet
himation, the master long yellow-white chiton and sleeves,
and yellow-green himation. This could, as Robert says, be
an illustration of the scene between Demeas and Parmenon
in Menander's *Samia* (91 f.). Ancestors for the Leading

Slave and the wavy-haired Leading Slave can be found in the Middle Comedy masks which we labelled B and N; we also noted that the white-haired mask E was sometimes used for a slave.

Of the other slaves the 'straight-haired' (No. 23) has receding red hair and raised eyebrows; the curly-haired (No. 24) has receding red hair and squints; Maison (No. 25) is bald and red; Tettix (No. 26) is bald and black with two or three locks on his forehead and two or three to form his beard. The last two are cooks and, according to Athenaeus (XIV, 659a) Maison was the citizen cook and Tettix the foreign cook; according to Festus (134 M.) the Maison mask was used for 'cooks, sailors, and such like'. It is interesting that these two masks are included among the slave masks, although cooks were usually free in New Comedy; the distinction in external appearance between poor citizen and slave was very small in Athens; the cook might be a citizen or a foreigner or a freed man or a slave. We are only concerned to note that Menander had two cooks to use, and the red-haired Maison is more energetic and courageous than the black-haired Tettix. Robert[1] seems to me therefore to be right in giving the Maison mask to Congrio and the Tettix mask to Anthrax in the *Aulularia* (Menander's *Apistos*). The first two of these masks (Nos. 23 and 24) cannot be clearly recognised in the Middle Comedy material, and I am not clear whether K is the ancestor of either of them. They are not very common in the New Comedy material, but both have been recognised in terra-cottas (70, 71). If my suggestion about hairdressing is right, the curly-haired slave would be needed when the third household had a slave; for instance, if Charinus and Byrrhia in Terence's *Andria* come from Menander's *Perinthia* they would in that play have worn the masks of Curly youth and Curly slave; Charinus and Simia are a similar pair in the *Pseudolus*. There remain a few extras for the straight-haired slave: Daos in the *Epitrepontes*, Olympio in the *Casina*,

---

[1] *Op. cit.*, 73, cf. however, Simon, *op. cit.*, 74.

Lurcio in the *Miles* (if he is not a Plautine addition). The
two cooks are common enough. A very fine Maison from
Megara is shown carrying his basket (56); the Middle
Comedy mask is P. A good Tettix can be seen on the
Pergamon frieze (72); he is anticipated by the little satyr
fluting on an Apulian vase of the third quarter of the fourth
century (B 35).

Pollux' list of female masks starts with three old women.
The first (No. 28) is the withered, long-faced, wolfish woman
with many thin wrinkles, a yellow complexion, and a roving
eye (in the *Physiognomonika* (808 *a* 18) the outward signs
of bitterness are a withered skin and a wrinkled, fleshless
face). The Fat old woman (No. 29) has fat wrinkles in a fat
face and a ribbon round her hair (it may be relevant to
remember that the 'dissembler' in the *Physiognomonika*
(808 *a* 27) has fat surrounding his face and wrinkles round
the eyes). The third (No. 30) is the Little old housekeeper
with a snub-nose and two teeth in each jaw. We may take
Staphyla in the *Aulularia* or Sophrone in the *Epitrepontes* as
the typical wearer of the Little housekeeper mask and the
lena of the *Cistellaria* as the typical wearer of the fat woman's
mask. Many examples in literature can be given of both.
The Wolfish old woman still eludes us; Dr Simon,[1] following
Robert, divides the *lenae* between the 'wolfish old woman'
and the 'fat old woman', because of the associations of the
word 'wolf' in Greek and Latin. If, however, as 'wolfish'
suggests, the long nose is the distinguishing feature of the
mask, it may rather have been worn by the more domineering
kind of wife, like Menander's Krobyle, whose nose is a cubit
long (fr. 402 K, 333 Kö.). We have seen all three in Middle
Comedy (long-nosed, U, and Y). I know no New Comedy
example of the Wolfish old woman, unless perhaps an Attic
terra-cotta in Bonn (C 2), but Dr Luschey objects that it looks
too soft for her. Of the Little housekeeper the British
Museum has a fine example (73). The Fat woman is seen on
the right of the Dioskourides mosaic (*19*), which illustrates

---

[1] *Op. cit.* 131 and 129, n. 7, cf. also Navarre, *R.E.A.*, xvi, 27.

the first scene of Menander's *Synaristosai*; [1] she wears a grey chiton and a yellow wrap. She wears a yellow chiton and a yellow wrap in the picture (37) which may illustrate a later scene from the same play—then she is observed by a slave as she takes her daughter away from the house.

The next group of masks are all classed together by Pollux as young women. Three are going to be married: the Maiden (No. 33) and the two False-maidens (Nos. 34 and 35). Dr Simon [2] has given a convincing explanation of the term false-maiden, pseudokore; she is a maiden because her parents will be discovered before the end of the play, but she is a false-maiden because she has already lived with the man whom she will marry. The obvious examples are Selenium in the *Synaristosai* (= *Cistellaria*), Antiphila in the *Heautonti-moroumenos*, and Glykera in the *Perikeiromene*. It is difficult to see why there should be two such masks. Dr Simon thinks that a distinction can be drawn between the gentle Antiphila and the stronger Glykera and Selenium, but this is too fine a distinction to warrant a different mask. There is another possible class of characters who could be called false-maidens —the women who have been raped in youth, who have brought up their children, and who certainly (or probably) marry at the end of the play; they are the priestess in the *Hiereia*, Myrrhine in the *Georgos*, and Dorippa in the *Epidicus*. The only other possible mask for them (they are not wives, they are hardly 'little old women' if they are going to marry) is the 'concubine', but a 'concubine' should surely be living with a man when the play opens and is not married off at the end. As Pollux' list places the oldest of each kind first, these women presumably wore the first of the two 'false-maiden' masks. The 'maiden' knows her citizen origin and has not yet lived with a man, but is in some misfortune like Palaestra in the *Rudens*, Krateia in the *Misou-menos*, the girl in the *Kolax*, or Adelphasium in the *Poenulus*

---

[1] Cf. above p. 23.
[2] *Op. cit.*, 101.

(we must suppose that her sister Anterastilis wore the same mask with slight variation).

The maiden has straight dark brows, parted hair, and a white face. The false-maiden has her hair bound about the front of her head and looks like a bride; the second version differs only in having her hair parted. These masks were taken over from Middle Comedy masks S, W, V. For New Comedy the large terra-cotta statuette from Pompeii (27), which pairs with a *panchrestos*, is a very fine Maiden, wearing a blue chiton and red himation; her mask also occurs with others on a gold necklace (4) from Thessaly, which is probably of Athenian workmanship, and in the surrounds of Pompeian mosaics (21). The first False-maiden is joined with the Dark Youth and the Wavy-haired old man on the Menander relief (49). If Menander were writing a scene of the *Hiereia*, which we know from a summary,[1] the first pseudokore would be the priestess herself; the old man would be the chief character, who raped her in her youth and now discovers his children and marries her; the youth is the son of her neighbour who wants to marry her daughter. The second pseudokore mask is worn by one of the young women in the Dioskourides mosaic (C *19*); she faces the audience, dressed in a yellow chiton and wrap, her parted hair held in a silver clasp above her forehead (this curious formation is very clear on the Middle Comedy terra-cottas). If the identification with the *Synaristosai* is right, she is the woman whom Plautus calls Selenium.

There are two masks for wives: the garrulous with a wreath of hair (No. 31) and the curly-haired (No. 32); Dr Simon[2] suggests that the main distinction is between the garrulous wife who bullies her husband—Menander's Krobyle, the heiress wife of the *Plokion*, whose nose is a cubit long (402 K) and who is more talkative than a dove (416 K, 346 Kö.), is the perfect example[3]—and the curly-haired

---

[1] Cf. *Studies in Menander*, 149.

[2] *Op. cit.*, 104, 107.

[3] Cf. also Artemona in *Asinaria*, Nausistrata in *Phormio*, Dorippa in *Mercator*.

wife, who is for some reason or other distressed, e.g. Pamphile in the *Epitrepontes*. This distinction is not maintained in the plays where two wives appear (e.g. *Casina*, *Hecyra*, *Stichus*) and Myrrhine in the *Perikeiromene* and Eunomia in the *Aulularia* do not fit into either category. We may therefore prefer to think that the 'garrulous' is the normal mask for the wife, and that the 'curly-haired' was introduced for the second wife, when a second wife was needed; Menander's Krobyle and her like might, as we have suggested, more suitably wear the mask of the 'wolfish old woman'. But there is a real difficulty here because we need two old wives for the *Hecyra* and two young wives for the *Stichus*.

Pollux' list of hetairai is introduced by two which are not hetairai in the normal sense. The 'Greying garrulous (No. 36) declares her looks in her name, and signifies a hetaira who has ceased her trade; the concubine (No. 37) is like her but has a wreath of hair'. The concubine's mask was worn by Chrysis in the *Samia*.[1] There are three candidates for the 'Greying garrulous'; Melaenis in the *Cistellaria*, Scapha in the *Mostellaria*, Syra in the *Hecyra*. Melaenis was a hetaira and must be distinguished from the *lena*; she therefore seems likely. Scapha and Syra are more doubtful; Scapha has been a concubine rather than a hetaira (*Most.* 199 f.); Syra shows a similar realism based perhaps on similar experience (*Hec.* 63 f.); they are not *lenae* and they are too old to wear the mask of the hetaira's maid; they may then be 'Greying garrulous'. Pollux' assertion that this mask 'signifies a hetaira who has ceased her trade' excludes its use for the elderly wife, for whom it would have been useful. It has always been assumed, as far as I know, that the text of Pollux is correct in this passage. If however the sentence 'and signifies a hetaira who has left her profession' were transferred from the 'Greying garrulous', it would be an accurate description of the concubine and would leave 'Greying garrulous' as a possible mask for the old wife.

[1] I assume that Chrysis was not finally recognised as an Athenian citizen and married to Demeas. Cf. *Studies in Menander*, 46.

This would solve our problem since we have still got the Wolfish old woman when we need a second old wife. Melaenis, Scapha, and Syra could wear other masks; Melaenis perhaps the Concubine and the two maids the Little housekeeper.

The wives of Middle Comedy were mostly snub-nosed (T) but there are two terra-cottas,[1] one from Cyrene (B 84) and one from Paestum (B 59), which show another type, a woman with long locks of hair falling over her shoulders, and this is not unlike the New Comedy terra-cotta which has been recognised as the Garrulous wife (C 11). She appears again on a wall-painting (28), where she wears a green chiton and a long white wrap; she has a *sakkos* over her head and brown hair falling in long locks over her shoulders. An old man, presumably her father, with the Leading old man's mask (No. 3), yellow chiton, and yellow himation is walking away from her in fury; the scene is overheard by a Wavy-haired slave (No. 27) in yellow chiton and red chlamys; he is presumably the slave of her husband. The general situation is not unlike the beginning of the *Stichus* or the scene between Smikrines and Pamphile in Menander's *Epitrepontes*.

The Curly-haired wife is unknown to Middle Comedy and very rare among the New Comedy monuments (50). The Greying garrulous is also unknown to Middle Comedy and rare in New Comedy (13). The concubine is not uncommon in Middle Comedy, if, as I think, she develops out of the straight-nosed mask with a mop of hair (R); in New Comedy however I only find a single example, on a South Italian jug of the first quarter of the third century (7). A very fine terra-cotta in Copenhagen (3), which is probably Attic, is the mask of a fat elderly woman with a considerable nose, raised eyebrows, and a large bow on the forehead. Dr Luschey calls her the Fat woman, but the Fat woman has fat wrinkles and (if the identifications are right) a short nose; this woman has neither, and I am inclined to think that she must be either the Greying garrulous or the concubine.

[1] Add also the Attic terra-cotta mentioned above, p. 65 n. 1.

Of the hetaira masks it is clear that the 'fullgrown' (No. 38) with red cheeks and locks round her ears is older than the 'blooming' hetaira (No. 39) who uses no makeup, and the masks might be used for a pair of sisters like the Bacchides in their name play (Menander's *Dis Exapaton*). The 'golden' hetaira (No. 40), who has much gold on her hair, must be a rich and independent hetaira; the 'blooming' hetaira and 'little torch' (No. 42), called after her streaming tail of hair, both appear as musicians and therefore are likely to be owned by a *leno* or to be under the control of their mothers. We have no evidence of the status of the wimpled hetaira (No. 41), whose hair is held in a coloured scarf, except that on the monuments she generally looks young. We have, therefore, probably two masks for the independent hetairai and three for the dependent hetairai.

All of these have been recognised in the New Comedy material. The 'fullgrown' hetaira appears in a wall-painting (29) wearing a yellow chiton and a white wrap as she sends her slave to market. The woman on the left of the Dioskourides mosaic (*19*), Gymnasium in the *Cistellaria* and daughter of the old *lena*, wearing a yellow chiton and a yellow wrap with a red fringe, has earrings and a yellow fillet wound three times round her hair; she may be the Blooming little hetaira; the same mask is worn by the flute-girl with the revellers in the other Dioskourides mosaic (*20*). The Golden hetaira is known from a marble bust in the Vatican (*51*); the Wimpled hetaira is common, and a pretty mask (67), which pairs with a Curly youth may be mentioned. Little Torch can be seen on a painting (30); she wears a violet chiton, yellow wrap, and red shoes; the *panchrestos* in white chiton and brown himation stands beside her, and together they overhear an old slave in yellow chiton and yellow himation deliver a tirade; we think of Tranio reporting the return of the father in the *Mostellaria*, although he is not old.

In Middle Comedy the hetaira with the elaborately dressed hair (X) may well be the ancestress of the Golden hetaira. A terra-cotta, which comes from Athens (B 21), is undoubtedly Little Torch; as there is nothing in the style to preclude a date in the fourth century and as it is heavily padded, I believe it to belong to Middle Comedy, and the existence of the mask is shown by South Italian vases of the mid-fourth century (B 46). Hetaira masks with 'wimples' and various arrangements of hair or unwimpled and with melon hair are common on South Italian vases of the third quarter of the fourth century,[1] and it is just this late period of Middle Comedy where our Attic evidence is weakest. The hetaira mask with melon hair is not uncommon in New Comedy (e.g. C 74) and is perhaps a slightly earlier version of the Blooming hetaira as it often has a fillet tied round the hair.

In the plays we find the Independent hetaira who may be either voracious (Thais in her name play, Phronesium in the *Truculentus*) or good-hearted (Thais in the *Eunuch*, Bacchis and perhaps Philotis in the *Hecyra*), and the Dependent hetaira maintained by a *leno* (the harpist in the *Adelphi*, Habrotonon in the *Perikeiromene* and *Epitrepontes*, the two harpists in the *Epidicus*, Phoenicium in the *Pseudolus*, Philematium and presumably Delphium in the *Mostellaria*) or by her mother (Gymnasium in the *Cistellaria*, Philaenium in the *Asinaria*) or by a citizen (Pasicompsa in the *Mercator*, Acroteleutium in the *Miles*).[2]

Pollux finally describes the masks of the wife's maid (No. 43) and the hetaira's maid (No. 44). The former would be worn by Stephanium in the *Stichus* and by the disguised Milphidippa in the *Miles*, perhaps also by Doris in the *Perikeiromene* who is Polemon's slave, and the latter by Mysis in the *Andria*, Pythias in the *Eunuch*, and Astaphium

---

[1] Cf. J.H.S. 71 (1951), 223, nos. 14, 20, 21, 29, 36a.

[2] Perhaps, however, when Acroteleutium and Milphidippa appear, they wear the masks suitable to the parts that they play: wife and wife's maid. It is true that Philematium in the *Mostellaria* has been liberated, but there is no sign that she will be recognised as a citizen nor that she will be taken over by Theopropides.

in the *Truculentus*.[1] The wife's maid may be an attractive little girl with whom either the husband or the son becomes involved. She has short hair and wears a white chiton with a girdle (but no himation). Dr Simon suggests that she may be recognised in a smiling, snub-nosed mask with short hair in Naples (31). The hetaira's maid has parted and combed hair and a turned-up nose and wears a scarlet chiton with a girdle. A terra-cotta in Athens (75) may represent her. Among the hetaira masks on South Italian vases of the third quarter of the fourth century which we have mentioned some look remarkably like this terra-cotta, and here again we have evidence for an anticipation in Middle Comedy (B 47).

This completes our survey of Pollux' list, and we can answer one of our questions: how far were the masks of New Comedy traditional? The answer appears to be that the pictorial material gives no evidence before the New Comedy period for the following masks: leading old man, old man with wavy hair, *leno, eikonikos, panchrestos*, dark youth, curly youth, delicate youth, curly-haired wife, greying garrulous, wife's maid, fullgrown and blooming hetairai. If we consider the characters to which we have allocated these masks, they include many that would naturally be regarded as typical creations of the New Comedy, such as Demea and Micio of the *Adelphi* (Menander), Plesidippus of the *Rudens* (Diphilos), Charisios of the *Epitrepontes* (Menander), Philocrates of the *Captivi*, the terror- and love-stricken boy of the *Phasma* (Menander), and Philematium of the *Mostellaria* (Philemon). We can see them as the outcome of two strains in New Comedy: the two old men, the dark youth, and the delicate youth spring from the character comedy of Menander; the *panchrestos*, the curly-haired youth, the *leno*, and the little hetaira belong rather to the adventurous comedy of Philemon and Diphilos.

To answer the question on what principle poets allotted masks to plays, we must consider whether the assumption

[1] Oeri, *Typ der komischen Alten*, Basel, 1949, 58 f. makes Pythias in the *Eunuch* and Astaphium in the *Truculentus* old. I see no reason to follow this.

that hairdressing marked families is justified. It has so far enabled us to give a sensible interpretation of a considerable number of monuments. Two of the new masks are the masks of fathers of families, who are distinguished by their hair (Quintilian,[1] describing the leading old man, calls him *pater ille*). Pollux says that the leading slave, who has the same hairdressing as the leading old man, 'stands in the same relation to the slaves as the leading old man to the free' and then that 'the wavy-haired leading slave is in all respects like the leading slave except for his hair'. He (or rather his source) seems to indicate a distinction of two households by hairdressing, and this is made possible by introducing the two old men's masks to correspond to the two traditional slave masks. The *panchrestos*, 'dark youth', and 'tender youth' are added as possible sons for the leading old man; the rustic, who has a similar 'wreath of hair', already existed. The first and second youths with wavy hair already existed as possible sons for the new 'father with wavy hair'— we do in fact know of one case where a soldier's father appeared, the *Misoumenos* of Menander. Finally, the introduction of the 'curly-haired youth' made a third household possible with the curly-haired old man (the Lycomedian) and the curly-haired slave.

If the characters of the surviving plays are allotted masks on this principle, no difficulties arise. It would be tedious to go through them all,[2] but it may be useful to consider the two best preserved plays of Menander. For the *Epitrepontes* Robert's suggestion that Charisios is the dark youth is likely; Onesimos will then be the Leading slave; Chairestratos is the wild young man about town and therefore the second young man with wavy hair; Syriskos, as his slave, will be the wavy-haired leading slave and, if I am right[3] in supposing Simias to be his pedagogue, he will be the wavy-haired old slave. Smikrines is the curly-haired old Lycomedian; we may

[1] xi, 3, 74.
[2] Cf. *Rylands Bulletin* 32 (1949), 124 ff.
[3] Cf. *Studies in Menander*, 36.

suppose if we like that his daughter Pamphile is the curly-haired wife but that may be pushing the principle too far. Daos can wear the straight-haired slave mask as he is outside all the families. The cook Karion can be either Maison or Tettix. Sophrone is the Little Housekeeper and Habrotonon one of the younger hetairai. In the *Perikeiromene* we meet an apparent difficulty; Polemon must be the soldier, the first young man with wavy hair (and his servant Sosias will therefore be the wavy-haired leader); but Moschion is clearly the wild young man about town and therefore should be second young man with wavy hair. This is, I think, right. There is no possibility of confusion; Polemon in the earlier part of the play appears in uniform, and the two masks are distinguished also by colouring, dark and fair. Then Pataikos as the father of Moschion will be the wavy-haired old man. Daos belongs to the household of Myrrhine and is therefore the leading slave; if as I think,[1] Myrrhine's husband appears in the course of the play, he is the leading old man. Habrotonon is a young hetaira. Doris as Polemon's slave may wear the mask of the wife's maid, as we have said. Glykera would wear the mask of the second pseudokore because she has been living with Polemon but will be recognised as Pataikos' daughter.

If this is right, and that Moschion should be the second young man with wavy hair and Glykera the second pseudokore seems to me as nearly certain as any such attribution can be, then any character who is going to be recognised wears a mask which is appropriate for the state in which he or she will end the play rather than for the state in which he or she is when the play begins. This solves the difficulties of the *Captivi*, a Plautine adaptation of an original probably by Philemon. The captives are all slaves but they are all set free at the end, therefore they all wear young men's masks; we have seen that Philocrates is in fact described as if he were the Curly-haired youth. Tyndarus, who is the slave of Philocrates at the beginning, is recognised at the end as

[1] Cf. *Studies in Menander*, 9 ff.

Hegio's son; therefore he wears the mask of Hegio's son. Hegio then is the Leading old man, Philopolemus is the *panchrestos*, Tyndarus either the dark or the delicate, and the irresponsible Aristophontes is the Second young man with wavy hair.

There is no clear difference in character between the two leading slaves, with and without wavy hair, and the masks were allotted to fit the household to which the slave belonged. But where father and son wore masks with the same hair-dressing, this could signify more than community of house-hold. In Menander particularly fathers got the sons that they deserved. The sons of the leading old men have three masks available; for the sons of the old man with the wavy hair there is normally only one mask, since the soldier son, as far as we know, was extremely rare. There is, however, a common quality, perhaps best described as emotionalism and often expressed in a momentary desire to go to war, which unites the youths with wavy hair. In their fathers this quality shows itself in various ways; one form is mildness, or a refusal to act consistently by conventional standards; clear cases are Demeas in the *Samia*, Micio in the *Adelphi*, Chremes in the *Phormio*, and Daemones in the *Rudens*. A rather different form is seen in the anxiety and troubles which Menedemus in the *Heautontimoroumenos* and Char-mides in the *Trinummus* give themselves on behalf of their sons. A less pleasant form of emotionalism is the prurience of Nicobulus in the *Bacchides*, Lysidamus in the *Casina*, and Demipho in the *Mercator*. I think it quite possible that these three types were all given the same mask on the ground that they were all deviations from the strictness of the severe father, the leading old man.

The developed system of New Comedy masks emphasises the contrasts which the poet wants to point between characters differing in age, household, position, or sex. Menander perhaps makes the fullest use of this technique; for instance, in the *Epitrepontes*, Charisios is contrasted with Chairestratos, but also with Pamphile, Onesimos, and

Smikrines; Pamphile is contrasted with Habrotonon as well as with her father; Onesimos is contrasted with Habrotonon as well as with Charisios and Smikrines; Syriskos is contrasted with Daos. But we can see the same technique in the other poets—in Diphilos' *Rudens* Palaestra and Ampelisca, in Philemon's *Mostellaria* Grumio and Tranio, or Lysiteles and Lesbonicus in his *Trinummus*.

There is another kind of contrast which is important. It is generally accepted that Menander gave an entirely new and sympathetic interpretation of certain traditionally satiric characters, notably the soldier (Polemon in the *Perikeiromene*), the rich hetaira (Chrysis in the *Eunuch*), and probably also the flatterer (Gnatho in the *Kolax*). He does not seem to have invented new masks for these, but rather to have played on the contrast between the original mask and the new conception of the character. We may perhaps therefore explain the use of the rustic mask for such differing characters as Chremes in the *Eunuch* and Gorgias in the *Georgos* in the same way; Gorgias is the sympathetic new edition of the traditional rustic. The audience (like the other characters in the play) have to learn that external appearance is not necessarily a sound indication of character. This was a dangerous game to play with theatrical conventions, but Menander could use the prologue spoken by a god or by a personification to give a hint: thus in the prologue of the *Perikeiromene* personified Misunderstanding tells us, 'I led him (Polemon, the soldier) into anger, although by nature he is not such'.

II. SICILY AND ITALY

I. INTRODUCTION

T H E reason for considering next the Greek Cities of South Italy and Sicily is that the evidence from this area is much fuller than the evidence from mainland Greece and from other parts of the Greek world. From literary sources we know that Epicharmos was writing his comedy in Syracuse in the early fifth century, and that Aeschylus visited the court of Hiero and produced the *Persae* and the *Women of Aetna* in Syracuse; the story of the prisoners singing choruses of Euripides after the Sicilian disaster is evidence that Euripides was well known in Syracuse before the end of the fifth century; in the early fourth century Dionysios, the tyrant of Syracuse, invited Attic tragic poets to his court and himself wrote tragedies; two later comic poets, who were popular in Athens, came from the West, Alexis from Thourioi and Philemon from Syracuse; early in the third century an actor from Tarentum called Drakon was victorious at Delphi and Delos; shortly after the middle of this century Livius Andronicus from Tarentum produced translations of Greek comedy and tragedy in Rome; in 44 B.C. according to Plutarch,[1] Brutus on a visit to Naples found very large numbers of Artists of Dionysos there—actors and their various assistants.

This long history of drama in the West is reflected in the monuments. I do not propose to deal in detail with the theatres of the West. The remains are difficult to interpret and have been explained in many conflicting ways. I do not think there is any evidence that the relative positions of actors, chorus, and audience in Western theatres was essentially different from those obtaining in corresponding periods in Athens, and this is the essential point for our

[1] *Life of Brutus*, 21.

study. It is possible that the long trench in the theatre at Syracuse [1] was used for manipulating scenery and that therefore scenery was more elaborate there than in Athens, but we have no contemporary pictures of productions in Syracuse. It is possible also that more time was allowed in the festivals for changes of scenery than in Athens but again we have no evidence for their arrangements, unless it be significant that on one South Italian vase (B 33) a tragic actor watches a comedy; this may imply that comedies were produced immediately after tragedies as in Athens. The theatre in Syracuse can be convincingly traced back to the time of Hiero. The evidence of theatre-building from South Italy has been conveniently summarised by Pace; [2] it is interesting to note that in Rhegium, Locri, Pompeii, Cumae, Poseidonia (Paestum) we have evidence for theatres as early as the fourth century B.C. Unfortunately we know nothing of Tarentum, but besides literary references from the time of Polybius (in the second century B.C.) abundant vases and terra-cottas show that there must have been a flourishing theatre from the end of the fifth century.

The two chief masses of evidence which we have to consider are fourth century vases from Apulia (the chief centre being undoubtedly Tarentum), Campania, and Paestum, and the various dramatic monuments of Pompeii, mostly dating from the last century B.C. and the first century A.D. There are many other dramatic monuments from different places in Italy and Sicily which are contemporary with, between, and later than these two main masses; these will be discussed in so far as they are relevant to our theme. We must however first ask whether we know anything about the earliest Sicilian drama of Epicharmos and his successors. We have pieces of a story which starts in Corinth in the seventh century and ends in Tarentum in the third. In chronological order these are the pieces. In Corinth, as we

---

[1] Cf. C. Anti, *Teatri Greci arcaici*, 85 f., 251 f., 294 f.
[2] *Dioniso* 10 (1945), 266 f. On Segesta and Tyndaris see most recently von Gerkan in *Festschrift Andreas Rumpf*, 82 f.

shall see in the next chapter, the dances of padded men were extremely popular at least as early as the late seventh century; among other themes they sang of the Return of Hephaistos, and it is possible that when they were dressed up they represented satyrs. Some sort of form was given to their performance by the lyric poet Arion from Lesbos, and Arion made a tour of Sicily and South Italy in the late seventh century. In essentials, although not in all details, the costume of these early padded dancers recurs on numerous Apulian, Campanian, and Paestan vases of the fourth century. Many of these vases represent stage scenes (to which we shall return later). But the padded men do not only occur in stage scenes. They often appear with Dionysos in the company of maenads or by themselves.[1] This suggests that they have a history which goes back before the fourth century and that they were, like satyrs, regular attendants on Dionysos. Athenaeus (621d), quoting Sosibios, a writer of the third century B.C., mentions an ancient form of comic entertainment provided by the Spartan *deikeliktai* (to whom we shall return) and then quotes as a parallel the Italian *phlyakes*. This suggests that in the third century Sosibios knew an ancient form of Italian entertainment provided by performers who were called *phlyakes*, and it is natural to give this name to the performers on the fourth-century South Italian vases, which show them in the preceding century. If Sosibios regarded them as ancient and if they appear on fourth-century vases as attendants of Dionysos, their history would seem to go back before the fourth century, and it is not unreasonable to suppose that the Greek colonies of Sicily and South Italy brought with them to the West the dances of padded men which were common in early times in most Greek cities. Syracuse itself was colonised from Corinth about a hundred years before Arion's tour. The padded dancers were therefore probably established in Syracuse long before the time of Epicharmos. One of their subjects in Corinth was the Return

[1] E.g. Apulian, B 38; Paestan, B 65.

of Hephaistos. Epicharmos wrote a play called *Komastai or Hephaistos* and we are told that the subject was the return of Hephaistos. One of the Corinthian padded dancers (F *12*) has the name Komios (reveller), and we have seen that the safest name for the padded dancers in Athens is Komasts (revellers). It is therefore at least possible that the Komastai of Epicharmos were padded dancers and that in his other comedies he used them for his chorus and actors; his comedy certainly admitted dancing and singing (fr. 127, probably also fr. 123 Kaibel). As the Komastai must almost have been a chorus, presumably the *Choreuontes* and the *Bakchai* were also the names of choruses, and it is tempting to explain the curious title *Dionysoi* on the analogy of similar titles in Attic comedy,[1] as a chorus of padded dancers with a leader Dionysos, marked out by special attributes, perhaps panther skins, boots, and phallos.

Epicharmos' actors also were presumably padded, and perhaps male characters wore the phallos like their successors in the fourth century. A difficult note in the tenth-century 'Suda' lexicon (commonly known as 'Suidas') seems to say that Epicharmos' contemporary and compatriot Phormis introduced clothes stretching to the feet and a scene decorated with purple instead of skins. If we are right in supposing that Epicharmos' male characters looked like the Corinthian padded dancers and the actors on fourth-century South Italian vases, they did not wear long clothes. If however we are also right in supposing that the naked women shown dancing with the padded dancers were men wearing white tights over their padding (and we have considered the evidence in Attica),[2] at some time between the early sixth century, when the women dancing with padded men on Corinthian vases are naked, and the early fourth century, when the female characters in the South Italian comic scenes wear ordinary clothes, long clothes for female characters must have been introduced, and this may have

----

[1] Cf. above p. 60.
[2] Cf. above p. 32.

been the new step which 'Suidas' recorded for Phormis. What the change from a background of skins to a background of purple curtains means is unclear, quite apart from the corruption of the text. A possible explanation is that skins were a legacy from the time when these dances were danced after a sacrifice and to enhance the effect of a sacrifice, and the introduction of purple curtains marked the change to comedy, to a performance less obviously and directly connected with religious ritual. But perhaps all that we can say safely is that curtains formed part of the background of Syracusan comedy as of Megarian and Attic comedy.

2. SCENERY IN THE FOURTH CENTURY

The chief South Italian vase fabrics of the fourth century can be dated with a considerable degree of accuracy thanks to the work of Mrs Oakeshott and Professor A. D. Trendall. We are concerned with the following: (*a*) early South Italian, which lasts from about 440 B.C. to about 370 B.C.; (*b*) Apulian red-figure, which carries on part of the early South Italian tradition till near the end of the fourth century; (*c*) Gnathia, which I am using as a generic term for all vases with the decoration painted in polychrome on the black ground; the best of these are Apulian (and I do not think that I have included any that are not Apulian) and the series runs from rather before the middle of the fourth century until about 270; (*d*) Campanian: the vases which concern us belong to the third quarter of the fourth century; (*e*) Paestan: chiefly, for our purposes, the work of Assteas and his successors, roughly 360–330 B.C. A considerable number of vases in all these fabrics have some relation to the theatre, and they can be used to sketch a history of the production of Attic tragedies and satyr plays in South Italy, starting with a production of Euripides' *Cyclops* before the end of the fifth century (A 25).[1] Similarly with the comic vases, for the

[1] Cf. my article in *Hermes* 82 (1954), 294.

majority of the mythological scenes we can suggest an Attic comedy which could chronologically have been the inspiration of the vase painting, and where they give comic representations of everyday scenes they are scenes which we can parallel in Attic comedy. I need not repeat the evidence which suggests to me that Attic comedy from the time of Aristophanes' *Frogs* (cf. B 34) was as popular as Attic tragedy in South Italy, because here these vases are only of interest to us in so far as they tell us something about staging and costumes in the Greek theatres of South Italy.[1] We are not here concerned with the plays themselves but with their production.

In the comic scenes (as distinct from pictures of masks alone) we always see actors and sometimes the stage and sometimes even the background. We have a certain number of pictures of tragic masks and a very few pictures of tragic actors; but where tragic scenes are represented the characters show at most a faint reminiscence of the actors in their elaborate costumes; most often only some architectural features suggest the theatre. In an admirable picture (A 30), inspired by Euripides' *Iphigeneia in Tauris* (725 f.), an Apulian painter has painted the temple in perspective, separated by rising ground from the altar on which Iphigeneia finds Orestes sitting when she brings him the letter. This picture, although obviously inspired by a particular scene of Euripides' play, tells us nothing about staging or costume, since we must assume that in any production of the *Iphigeneia in Tauris* the door of the temple would be the main central door of the stage-building as we saw it on an Attic vase of the early fourth century (A 8). We have several other South Italian pictures of the *Iphigeneia in Tauris*; two of them are interesting. For whatever reason the general scheme of

[1] Cf. *CQ*. 42 (1948), 19 ff.; *Rylands Bulletin*, 36 (1954), 568 f. Add now the striking likeness of subject between two late fifth-century Attic polychrome oinochoai (B 5, 6) and two Apulian vases (B 40, 39) with subjects man riding on fish and men carrying off meat on a spit (? cf. Ephippos *Obeliaphoroi*); add also the likeness of an Attic terra-cotta in the British Museum to Priam on an Apulian vase (B 36).

the Attic vase, building with figures grouped round it, was commonly used for pictures inspired by tragedy in Apulia in the fourth century. On an Apulian krater of the last third of the century (A 41) Iphigeneia steps out of the building, which also contains the altar with the statue of Artemis on it. The building is wooden, has a low pediment with palmette akroteria; two columns in front and two behind are drawn in such a way as to show a section of the roof in perspective and are themselves mounted on a single low step. This building is often called an *aedicula*, a name which is both conventional and confusing. I suggest that what the audience saw in the theatre at Tarentum was a wooden doorway with two columns supporting a pediment with akroteria, but that the vase painter has completed the building as an independent unit to house the statue and the altar. The simplest representation of this doorway is seen on an early South Italian bell-krater (A 26), which has been already quoted as possible evidence for the *mechane* or crane. Moreover a similar doorway with columns and pediment is combined with a stage on another early South Italian vase which gives a scene from comedy (B 33).

In the *Iphigeneia in Tauris* Iphigeneia came out of the door, as we see her in the painting, and to this extent we are looking at an actual stage scene. But the vase painters play variations on this theme, which are sometimes confusing. The completed building may be used to show an event which goes on inside it. About the middle of the fourth century the beginning of the *Eumenides* is so illustrated (A 36). The wooden doorway with columns and pediment is completed into an *aedicula* in which Orestes sits holding the omphalos while the Furies lie on its steps; to the right of the temple the priestess runs away. Much of this was in fact seen by the audience as we have said,[1] but on the rather later Medea vase (A 42) the painter has shown the death of the Corinthian king and his daughter inside the *aedicula*; this was an event which happened inside the palace out of view of the audience

[1] See above p. 8.

but was undoubtedly related by a messenger in this fourth-century tragedy, as in Euripides. On the contemporary Hypsipyle vase (A 43) Hypsipyle pleads with Eurydike and Amphiaraos intervenes to save her; this is an actual stage scene (preserved in the Euripides papyrus) and the *aedicula* has been extended to a width of four columns instead of two to cover it. Perhaps in the epic these events too took place inside the palace, but in the theatre of Dionysos they took place outside the palace door where chorus could participate and audience see. The long step of the *aedicula* is decorated with a very similar pattern to that decorating the long step on the Dioskourides mosaic with a scene from Menander's *Women at Breakfast* (C 19) and this may be a reminiscence of the theatre. Similar decoration is seen on the step of Niobe's *aedicula* on another vase (A 44), but here the *aedicula* with its step stands on a high base, of which two sides are drawn, decorated with winged women who grow out of scrolls; in Aeschylus' *Niobe*, as in his *Persae*, the stage-building represented a tomb, the tomb of Niobe's children, and this is the allusion which the painter of the Apulian vase makes. Some change of this sort to show that the con-ventional palace/temple front represented a tomb may also have been made in the theatre.[1]

These vases then give us some idea of the central door. The other interesting picture of the *Iphigeneia in Tauris* (A 38) may with interpretation take us a little further. We see at each end double doors in a framework comprising pediment with akroteria, square wooden pillars or pilasters, and steps. They are connected by a roof which hangs in the air. The Tauric Artemis stands in front of the left-hand door and Iphigeneia issues from the right-hand door; the centre

[1] A parenthetic word of caution is needed here; the monuments which appear on Apulian vases (e.g. Pickard-Cambridge, *Theatre*, figs. 25, 32) and are often compared with the *aedicula* are not, as they are often called, *heroa* (shrines of departed heroes) but grave-reliefs of the men at whose funeral feasts these big vases were used; they are always quite shallow and the figures are white, i.e. marble. Cf. Richter, *Greek Sculptures in the Metropolitan Museum*, 48.

is occupied by Orestes and Pylades, who are spying out the temple. The painter was more interested in exposition than visual impression, and so has shown both Artemis and Iphigeneia; whereas in the play Iphigeneia lives in the temple of Artemis, and both Iphigeneia and the statue of Artemis are inside the temple when Orestes and Pylades enter (67). It is therefore quite unjustifiable to say that this is a stage-building with no central door but two side doors; the painter has duplicated the central doors at the sides, because only so could he leave the centre clear for Orestes and Pylades. This vase shows us a slightly different kind of door (a Campanian set would naturally differ from an Apulian set) and suggests the possibility of a roof in the background; what is more important is the clue that it gives to the interpretation of a rather earlier vase from Tarentum (A 35). Here we see a building with double doors at each end, through each of which a girl listens; at both ends the doors are set between the two back columns of a projecting porch, which has pediment and akroteria; the two porches are connected at the back by a roof with gutter tiles supported by a single column in line with the four back columns of the porches; in front of this centre section a young traveller stands beside an old man, who holds a phiale for a libation. Professor Rumpf has recently suggested that this vase has nothing to do with the theatre; I am however still inclined to think that the wooden palace derives from a theatre set, but that the Campanian vase must be used to interpret it. Whatever this play was, a girl overheard a conversation between an old hero and a young hero, and the girl had a sister, who differed from her as Ismene from Antigone or Chrysothemis from Elektra in Sophocles' plays. The painter wanted to show all these four characters, just as the Campanian painter had to show Artemis and Iphigeneia as well as Orestes and Pylades; and he has adopted the same method. We can then only say that this set at Tarentum had an elaborate central door, and in time it is intermediate between the early simple doorway in the Death of Sarpedon (A 26) and the elaborate *aedicula* vases. We can guess that the back wall of the stage-building was decorated with columns supporting architrave and roof tiles. If in fact the theatres in Tarentum and Campania had projecting wings like the theatre of Dionysos, then the painters may allude to this in the shape of the building which they have drawn, but it is, I think, no more than an allusion; the wings could not have been used like this.

The question remains whether the roof supported by columns was a normal part of the stage set. There is a good deal of evidence for columns, and I suspect that the multiplication of columns in the larger *aediculae* (e.g. *Medea* and *Hypsipyle*, A 42–3) is a reminiscence of the row of columns on either side of the columned central door. These columns must have had some sort of architecture over them, and the roof which we see on the Campanian vase and which we can assume behind the roof-tiles of the Tarentum fragments seems reasonable enough. There are however two questions which must be asked, whether we can answer them or not. How do we provide for the *theologeion* (or high platform) in tragedy, and how do we provide for an upper story when one is needed in comedy. Some vases seem to show a roof projecting outwards from the back wall which could be so used, but I am inclined to suppose, as we have supposed with the *aedicula*, that although the artist is inspired by a tragedy and alludes to the theatre by making the architecture of wood, he is completing the building so as to show an interior. Thus the building in which Meleager dies on an Apulian vase of the mid-fourth century (A 32) is simply a large six-column *aedicula* without a pediment; Althaia rushes out horror-struck (out, I think, rather than in; the only indication of the door is the doorstep beneath her feet). The building in which Oinomaos and Hippodameia receive Pelops on a slightly earlier vase (A 31) is the same with variations to the backwall; on the left the backwall is absent; on the right the backwall is three-quarter height so that the horses' heads can be seen over the top. This is convenient because the artist

wants to show the horses, but some sort of loggia of this kind
was probably an architectural feature in South Italian houses.
It appears again in a more elaborate form in the Paestan
Madness of Herakles (A 39). The backwall has an engaged
column, and the space above it is divided by three columns.
They are tied by a roof to the two long columns in front.
On the right is a door. Essentially this building is the same
as the right half of Oinomaos' palace. We need not discuss
what tragedy inspired the painter—not Euripides, because
he has substituted Mania for Euripides' Lyssa. Mania,
Iolaos, and Alkmene look through the windows because they
are in their different ways concerned (like the various divine
and human figures who appear outside the *aedicula* on
Apulian vases). The easiest interpretation seems to me to be
that Herakles went mad and threw his children on the fire
inside the house, and Megara rushed out to report it and
was then herself caught by Herakles, who pursued her. The
figure of Megara at the door is remarkably like the Apulian
Althaia, whom we have just discussed, and like the priestess
in the Apulian *Eumenides* (A 36); in each case the painter is
struck by the spectacle of a woman storming out from a
scene of horror inside.

These vases seem to me to suggest that a row of columns
along the backwall between the central door and the wings
were not uncommon in the palace/temple sets of South
Italian theatres about the middle of the fourth century, and
we see columns also in the background of five comedy
scenes from Campania (e.g. B 67). The Paestan Madness of
Herakles (A 39) adds a form of doorway which we have not
seen before. Besides the double doorway and the door-step
we see a cross-strut carrying a beam which projects almost
as far as the doorstep. The natural explanation is that the
painter has drawn the strut in profile instead of full face
so as to make its function clear and that it supported a porch
over the door. Porches can also be seen in comedy pictures.
The same Paestan painter, Assteas, painted Herakles and
Apollo at Delphi (B 62). Apollo has taken refuge from

Herakles on the roof of his temple. The strut and the beam which it carries are again painted in profile. This structure is repeated on a Campanian vase (B 68) and on an Apulian vase (B 41); on both it is the porch of a door with an Ionic column, and the strut ends in a swanhead; it is therefore found in all the three great centres in which vases with dramatic pictures were produced. Most of the doors in the comedy scenes (e.g. B 34, 37 Apulian; 61 Paestan) do not show this porch or any other adornment, but three other Apulian examples should be mentioned. One (in New York; B 33) has a doorway with Ionic columns and a pediment, but the pediment has a flat surface on the top; it looks as if the pediment was not structural but was merely painted on the beam which formed the front of the flat roof. The two others seem at first sight to show the porch, one with a simple strut (B 32), the other with Ionic column and swanhead strut (B 43); but both of them have a sloping roof which would be useless for sitting or standing; another possibility, which should perhaps be mentioned, is that in these last two the painter has again made a right-angled turn and shown us one of the outer corners of a pediment. The vase painter and his client knew what the structure was, and the vase painter was more concerned to remind his client of essentials than to give a photographic impression.

However this may be, Apollo is undoubtedly sitting on the roof in the Paestan comedy (B 62), and the flat porch could provide the roof of the house in comedy. If, as we have suggested in discussing Athens, the two houses which were common in fourth century comedy were on either side of the elaborate central doors, the doors with flat porches were side doors; they could have been used for the high platform in tragedy, but we cannot know whether this was so or not. Besides doors the backwalls of comic scenes occasionally had windows, e.g. for Zeus to visit his beloved (B 60, cf. 37). In the Cheiron scene (B 32) two nymphs sit in a grotto, like landladies in their window watching for custom; perhaps we may assume screens painted to look like rocks and set on either side of the opening which could be a window. Other properties are portable: a palm to signify the sanctuary of Zeus Ammon (B 44), statues, altars, tables, and seats (e.g. B 67).

These comedies were acted on a stage. This was supported by posts, which might be either simple or elaborated into columns (e.g. B 61 Paestan; 44 Apulian). The spaces between them might either be left bare or filled with curtains (e.g. B 44 Apulian). The stage was approached by a short flight of steps (e.g. B 67 Campanian, 32 Apulian). The vase painter cannot tell us the width of this stage because he is restricted by the space available on his vase. He sometimes puts the door at the extreme end (e.g. B 61 Paestan; 37 Apulian), which suggests that the stage runs the whole width of the theatre, but this may be a false inference. The supposition that these were special stages for comedy, erected in the theatre in front of the stage-building, has its own difficulties. This would imply that tragedy and comedy were not played in close succession; but we have the tragic actor watching a comedy on an Apulian vase (B 33), and we have our one picture of a similar comic stage from Athens (B 1), where we know that comedy was performed immediately after tragedy. Until more certain evidence is found, I think we may assume that the same low stage was used for tragedy and comedy and that a single flight of steps was set in front of the central door for tragedy, while for the normal two-house comedy of the fourth century each of the side doors would have its own flight of steps.

The evidence so far examined does not take us beyond 325 at the outside. The *aedicula* vases may be a little later, but only tell us that the central door had columns. For the first three quarters of the fourth century Apulian, Campanian, and Paestan theatres seem to have had a wooden set representing a single-storey building with a row of columns along the back, a central door ornamented with a pediment and side doors sometimes at any rate with a flat-topped porch, which could represent the roof of the house

or be used as a high platform for gods. When the Athenians
built their stage-building in stone, the South Italians
probably followed suit. Apart from the remains of theatres,
which are extremely difficult to interpret, one curious
terra-cotta survives at Naples (A 49); it seems to be a model
of a theatre front, and on the low stage traces can be seen
where figures have stood. The main building is flanked by
narrow projecting wings with doors in front (we may doubt
whether the doors did not really open inwards towards the
stage if the wings took the place of *parodoi*). Between the
wings is a two-storied stage-building crowned by a pediment;
the lower storey has two small side doors and one large
central door between columns; the upper storey has four
columns; whether roof scenes could be played between these
upper columns is not clear. The terra-cotta has been dated
on technical grounds in the late fourth or early third century.
This would give us a South Italian theatre with an elaborate
stage-building, which appears from its solid forms to be
constructed in stone, not much later than the theatre of
Lycurgus and earlier than the late Hellenistic developments
described in the first chapter. Such a theatre would be
suitable for the production of Menander's plays when they
were brought to South Italy.

3. COSTUME IN THE FOURTH CENTURY

The vases which we have used as evidence for the scenery
of tragedy in South Italy tell us nothing about masks and
only a little about costume. The painters prefer to draw the
characters as they imagine them, the young men in heroic
nudity and the women in the normal costume of the day.
But most of the pictures inspired by tragedy have some
allusion to tragic costume not only in Apulian but also in
Campanian and Paestan. The costume is the costume which
we know from the Attic red-figure vases of the early fourth
century, elaborate sleeved robe and *kothornoi*. Thus in the
Hypsipyle picture (A 43) Amphiaraos wears an embroidered

chiton down to his knees, breastplate, chlamys, and *kothornoi*;
if he had had sleeves he would have been in stage clothes.
In the Medea picture (A 42) Medea, Kreon, and the
paidagogos all wear red, embroidered sleeves; Medea and
Kreon wear elaborately embroidered chitons and himatia;
the *paidagogos* wears a chiton to his knees, a himation with
a broad red border, and *kothornoi*. Two other vases which
show costume are the fragments from Tarentum with the
tragic actor dressed in *kothornoi*, brown chiton down to his
knees, sleeves, and purple cloak, and carrying the fair-haired
mask (A 34), and the Apulian kantharos with an elderly
messenger (A 33). Both of these have been already described,
and we have also mentioned the male and female masks
which appear on Gnathia vases of the later fourth and early
third centuries (A 37, *45–8*). We can add an early South
Italian vase (A 27) of the very beginning of the fourth
century with a satyr chorus; the masks are very like those of
the Pronomos vase (A 9), and tails and phalloi are secured
by drawers ornamented with a rosette such as are also found
on Attic vases; the shaggy white Silenos of the Pronomos
vase appears on a Paestan vase, which may illustrate a
revival of Aeschylus' *Sphinx* (A 40). All this suggests that
costumes and masks of tragedy and satyr plays in South
Italy ran parallel to costumes and masks in Athens; the
onkos also seems to have come in about the same time in both
areas: the two Gnathia vases (A 47, *48*) which show the
onkos clearly can be dated by shape and style to the beginning
of the third century, whereas the tragic actor, datable soon
after 350, holds a fair-haired mask without *onkos* (A 34).

For comic masks and costumes in the fourth century the
South Italian vases give us abundant evidence. The main
bulk of the vases cover the period from 390 to 330; they are
therefore later than all except one of the Attic red-figure
comic vases and contemporary with the Attic terra-cottas.
The essentials of the costume are the same, tights which
support padding and phallos, short chitons, and himatia for
males; female characters usually wear long chitons and

himatia. But the vases show us figures in scenes, and so we can say what characters wear what masks and costumes. Sometimes they are gods and heroes, sometimes they are ordinary men and women, but we can only tell the difference because gods can often be recognised by their attributes and the painters have often added names to guide us. We must not expect too great uniformity in the masks; the vases show us productions in three different areas over a considerable period of time, and the painter may always give a mask a particular expression for the particular moment which he is depicting; thus even a statue may smile delightedly at an untoward event (B 63). Nevertheless a strong likeness can be seen between the masks in different centres and, as I have said, I am inclined to see here the influence of Attic comic practice. The popularity of Attic comedy is further attested by imported Attic terra-cottas and local imitations of them,[1] but by the side of these other terra-cottas survive which have no Attic parallels. This does not of itself show that they are a native invention: for the later period of Middle Comedy (350–20) we have less Attic evidence, and we may perhaps assume that two terra-cottas found at Paestum, the parasite with bald clean-shaven mask and longish chiton and the wife with flowing locks, are imitations of Attic. The wife (B 59) is very like a terra-cotta from Cyrene (B 84), and this in itself suggests a common origin in Athens.[2] The parasite (B 58) recurs on an Apulian vase (B 42); he wears an elaborately embroidered chiton and is eating a cake as he runs away with a jar of wine, hotly pursued by a fierce female with a very long nose, whom we have identified as the wolfish woman. Certain terra-cottas (e.g. B 70) belong to the general class of slaves but differ from Attic comic slaves; they, I think, may represent a kind of dance and song which goes right back to the time of Epicharmos and probably beyond; the bearded faces of these are rather differently stylised: the eyebrows are more exaggerated, the mouths wider, the beard juts out

[1] Cf. above p. 56 n. 1.
[2] Cf. above p. 65 n. 1 for an Attic terra-cotta which shows this mask.

horizontally and turns up; on the bodies the nipples are more emphasised. These characteristics can often be seen on the vases too, and they are a local trait in a comedy which was, I believe, largely Attic in inspiration.

A full study of the vases with comic scenes, which number more than one hundred and twenty, must await the publication of Professor A. D. Trendall's *Phlyax Vases*. Here I can only describe certain examples which are interesting from the point of view of costume. Two early Apulian vases have staging which has been described.[1] The kalyx krater by the Tarporley painter (B 33) has an elaborate door with columns and painted pediment on a stage supported by simple pillars. The comic scene (marked as such by the slave mask (B) hanging in the background) is watched by *tragoidos*, a tragic actor after his play is over. The central figure is naked; tights and padding are clearly visible; he wears the mask of an old man (E); he stands on tiptoe with his hands above his head, saying 'She (or he) has bound my hands above'; Sir John Beazley has suggested that he is bound by a spell, as there is nothing to tie his hands or feet. On the left a man stands with a rod; he says 'Noraretteblo', which is gibberish for something like 'Now I will put you in prison'; he also is naked; his mask is clean-shaven with long hair; he is perhaps a Scythian policeman. On the stage is an old woman wearing himation and long chiton, which shows the padding; the mask is the snub-nosed wrinkled white-haired mask (U); she says 'I will hand (him over)'. The old man has been caught stealing food; on the stage is a bird, and a basket, in which a kid's head can be seen, rests on his cloak, which he dropped when he was surprised. The old woman has caught him and 'fixed' him until the policeman arrives. Presumably the whole action took place on the stage, but the painter has made an amusing and intelligible arrangement which gives him a clear ground for figures and inscription. On the early bell krater (B 32) also the stage has an elaborate door and the movable flight of steps from the orchestra is shown:

[1] Types of masks are indicated by the same capital letters as above p. 62.

the old Centaur Cheiron is being pulled and pushed up the
stairs. For this moment he looks like a Centaur, because the
slave pushing behind gives him an extra pair of legs. His
tights and those of the two slaves can be clearly seen; he
wears a cloak draped round his shoulders; the pushing slave
has his tied round his middle; the slave in front wears a short
chiton fastened on his left shoulder; he has put down the
luggage on the stage; it is wrapped up in an embroidered
blanket tied with straps, and a felt hat rests on the top. He
wears the bald Maison mask (P), the other slave the old
mask (E), and Cheiron a coarsened variant of the old mask
with a hooked nose (G). Two nymphs in chiton and himation,
one with the mask of the snub-nosed wife (T), the other
with the straight-nosed mask (R) gossip in their grotto. The
nice young man in carefully arranged himation who watches
the procession has been interpreted as Achilles, the pupil
of Cheiron; but if Achilles appeared in this play, he would
surely have been caricatured like the rest; he is therefore
an onlooker, but whether poet, producer, or (as on the kalyx-
krater) tragic actor, the painter has left no inscription to
tell us.

The Paestan painter Assteas (whose work covers roughly
the period 360–340) has left several excellent comic scenes
—a harridan Kassandra belabouring a bearded hook-nosed
Ajax as he takes refuge at the amused statue of Athena
(B 63), Apollo sitting on the roof of his temple at Delphi
while Herakles steals his offerings (B 62), Zeus and Hermes
on a nocturnal love adventure (B 60), a miser being robbed
(B 61). The last two may be described in detail. The Paestan
costume has two peculiarities: the padding is held by and the
phallos attached to a red jerkin with patches of lighter pink
for the area round the nipples and navel, whereas the arms
and legs show the ordinary tights. I suspect that this
differentiation of colour is a local survival. Attic Komasts in
the sixth century often have red chests, and Corinthian
padded dancers often had red padding; this indicated, I
think, the hairy vitality of the spirits whom they originally

represented. In Paestum in the middle of the fourth century the red padding is traditional and meaningless, but it suggests that these Paestan actors have a long ancestry of padded dancers behind them. The other peculiarity is a white line running down the arms and legs; this has been interpreted as a white seam, but I should prefer to regard it as a high-light to emphasise the dark on either side, like the white on the space between the brow and the eye. Highlights were a new discovery in fourth-century painting, and as such were at first used to excess. Zeus wears this costume on the bell-krater in the Vatican (B 60) and is naked except for the absurd crown which appears against the ladder carried on his shoulders; crown and hook-nosed mask (G) both recall the Attic oenochoe in Leningrad (B 4). Hermes has an orange cloak and an orange hat; he carries his herald's staff and a small lamp; his mask is clean shaven, snub-nosed, and thick-lipped, like Pollux' description of the rustic mask of New Comedy. Alkmena in her window wears a kerchief round her hair; the kerchief is red with white dots which may be gold brooches like those on the sleeves of her red chiton; she also has a necklace; her head is modelled on the mask of the rich hetaira (X). On the Berlin kalyx krater (B 61) two young men are trying to drag an old man off a chest while his slave looks on in horror. The young men are called Gymnilos and Kosilos; the old man Charinos, and the slave Karion. Charinos and Karion are names known from Attic comedy. For the scene it is tempting to remember Julian's remark (*Or.* 1, 19*d*) about 'old misers dragged on to the stage by the comic poets'. The object is presumably to secure money for the two hetairai whose masks hang in the background— masks of young women with a kerchief round their hair, younger than the rich hetaira pursued by Zeus, forerunners of the 'wimpled hetaira' of Pollux' list (No. 41); it is of course possible that the painter has put in two to make the background symmetrical and that only one young woman is involved. The old man wears tights, a white chiton, and a long himation; the mask is, I think, the common mask with a good beard (L) but the beard is crumpled up in his contortions; his slave (mask B) wears a white chiton and tights; Gymnilos and Kosilos both have the red jerkins and tights of Paestan nakedness; Gymnilos has a short himation over his left arm; Kosilos has white shoes. Both have clean shaven masks, Gymnilos has receding curly hair like the later flatterer (Pollux, No. 17), Kosilos long locks like the later young man about town (Pollux, No. 16). In New Comedy the flatterer is distinguished from the parasite as an active intriguer on his patron's behalf, and it looks as if this is already the relation of Gymnilos to Kosilos here.

A kalyx-krater of the third quarter of the fourth century (B 67) shows Herakles unveiling and perhaps abducting a woman from a shrine while an old woman and a man look on: it is possible that this painting illustrates the same Auge comedy which inspired one set of New York terra-cottas (B 11). The women wear long chitons and himatia; like her Attic terra-cotta counterpart, the young woman has long hair which is held in a clasp over the forehead (mask V); the old woman has a fat face with fat wrinkles and scanty hair (mask Y); the men wear tights and white chitons, the onlooker a himation and Herakles his lionskin; the jerkin which holds Herakles' padding can be seen below his chiton but it is not distinguished in colour from his tights; Herakles has the usual goggling broad-mouthed short-bearded mask, the onlooker has dark scrubby hair and a small uneven point to his beard (mask N). This vase and other comedy vases by the same painter were found in Sicily; although they are closely connected stylistically with Campanian vase-painting (and I have therefore left the description Campanian), Professor Trendall tells me that a kiln containing similar pottery has been found in Gela; it is likely therefore that they were made in Sicily.

Gnathia vases (the best, as we have said, are Apulian and run from the middle of the fourth until early in the third century) tell us more about colour than the comic scenes on

Apulian redfigure. A cook running with a cake on a three-legged table (B 48) has brown tights on which the white lines are certainly highlights and not seams: he has the bald Maison mask (P) with highlights on his cheeks and nose and with red hair. A reveller (B 49) in brown tights and a white himation with a battlement pattern, with a flaming torch over his shoulder, has the hook-nosed, wavy-haired, straggle-bearded rake's mask with a little white crown (D); he is yet another Zeus on a nocturnal adventure. Another reveller (B 50) with neater beard and hair (perhaps mask H) also carries a torch; he wears an elaborate white wreath, a white chiton, red himation over his arm, and black sandals; his tights are a paler yellow than the jerkin which just appears under his chiton.

Gnathia vases are often decorated with hanging masks, and for some of these provide our only South Italian evidence. Thus the female mask with the hair tied over the forehead (mask W) is seen on a bowl (B 51) of the third quarter of the fourth century, and the male mask with raised eyebrows and longish fair hair (mask O) on a bell-krater (B 52) of the same period. These are both interesting because they both belong to the later period of Middle Comedy and to the comedy of intrigue and recognition: W is known from a single Attic terra-cotta (B 22) and O from the Aixone relief (B 31) and a terra-cotta in Olynthos (B 80). These masks show little of the comic distortion seen in the masks of slaves, old women, and old men. They anticipate the more solemn masks of New Comedy. In fact, about two of these hanging masks on Gnathia vases we may ask whether they belong to tragedy or comedy. The vases in question were made in the third quarter of the fourth century, and our first tragic masks with the *onkos* on Gnathia vases belong to the very early third century (e.g. A 47). One of these masks is a young and beautiful Pan known in two examples (B 53, 54); the other is a smiling youth with pale complexion, like Pan, and shortish fair hair (B 55, 56); the hair is not long enough for the tragic hapalos mask worn by

Dionysos, and I think that he may be a Hermes or a Hero. Gods or heroes were caricatures, as we have seen, when they were characters in Middle Comedy, but we have no evidence that they were caricatured when they spoke the prologue, and these masks may therefore have belonged to the prologue figures of comedy.

The hanging masks on Gnathia vases might be regarded as the beginning of the decorative use of masks which is common in the Hellenistic age. I must however try to make the meaning of decorative more precise. What we want to know is whether a given mask is illustrative of contemporary dramatic practice or belongs to a decorative tradition out of touch with the theatre. For the Gnathia masks there is no reason to doubt the connection with the theatre; they can be paralleled, as we have seen, on other contemporary works. If we cannot assume that these mixing-bowls and cups and jugs were specially made for celebrations of dramatic victories, they must at least have been produced to catch the eye of theatre-lovers. The tragic actor coming forward to take his call (A 34) must surely have been painted for the party which celebrated his successful performance, and Professor Trendall has suggested that the wreath between the two female masks in Assteas' 'Robbing the Miser' (B 61) is 'perhaps an indication that the play was a prize-winner'; if so, the vase was presumably painted for the party after the victory. The party itself is shown on a bell-krater by another Paestan painter Python (B 64); three young men are playing kottabos on a couch; below, a flute-girl, a sleeping papposilenos, and a young satyr; above, hanging on an ivy-trail the masks of a slave (B), a girl (S), and an old man (A). The three actors sit beneath the masks of the chief characters in the play; Dionysos (who is seen with satyrs and maenads on the back of the vase) has sent some of his followers, Papposilenos, and the young satyr, to join in their celebrations. Campanian (B 69) and Apulian (A 28) parallels can be cited. It is more difficult to explain the presence of the mask hanging in the background of grave reliefs depicted

on two Apulian vases (B 45); one is the mask interpreted
above as Hermes, and the other the wedge-bearded old man
(A), who recurs on a Gnathia bowl (B 57). On the Attic
relief in Lyme Park (B 10) with the same mask in the background the dead man is shown to be a poet by the rolled
manuscript in his hand; but nothing characterises the young
men on the Apulian grave reliefs as poet or actor; they are
richly dressed and one has a slave with a lyre and a mixing
bowl, the other a dog. They seem more likely to have been
lovers of the theatre than poets or actors. It is reasonable
to suppose that lovers of the theatre also sometimes had
masks hanging on the walls at their drinking parties and
liked tableware decorated with masks, and this is the probable
explanation of the numerous Gnathia vases with masks
(eighty are known to me and there are no doubt many more
surviving).

4. POMPEII AND HERCULANEUM

From the third century onwards masks as distinct from
figures wearing or carrying masks become increasingly
common in all materials—stone, metal, clay, glass, mosaic,
and paint. They may be alone, in pairs, or in quantity. We
can seldom say that the artist is thinking of the cast of the
play; sometimes even love of the theatre or association with
Dionysos does not satisfy as an explanation. Why for
instance should a mosaic (C 21) of doves drinking or of
seven sages (or philosophers) be surrounded by a border of
comic masks set in a garland of fruit? The answer must be
that they are a pleasant decoration. But if they are simply
decorative, then they may be part of a decorative tradition
and tell us nothing of contemporary practice. This may very
well be true in some cases, but three things may be said.
First, we can often check these decorative masks by cross-
reference to complete figures, painted or moulded. Secondly,
the theatrical masks themselves seem to have changed little
after the introduction of the *onkos* for tragedy and the

standard masks of New Comedy; costume also seems to have been standardised for New Comedy and for tragedy in the late fourth century, and the only major development was the introduction of the high-soled boot which can be used, as we have seen, for dating the originals of some of the Pompeian pictures.[1] Thirdly it may be doubted whether the decorative tradition would have been allowed to depart far from the contemporary dramatic tradition, whether in fact the citizens of Pompeii with its excellent theatre would have had painted masks on their walls, marble masks in their gardens, or bronze masks on the handles of their jugs, which differed widely from the masks which they saw in the theatre.

The practice of Hellenistic tragedy and comedy has already been described in the last chapter. My purpose here is restricted and highly selective—to give some idea of the spread of dramatic monuments over Italy in the third and second century and to describe certain houses in Pompeii whose owners seem to have had a particular taste for the theatre. The best of the Gnathia vases were made in Apulia, and some of those with hanging masks are as late as the first quarter of the third century: typical examples are a pair of jugs (C 6–7), both with masks of New Comedy—one a hetaira, the other a concubine. From Tarentum also comes a very fine silver cup of the third century (C 8) decorated with masks; the leading old man, the second Hermonian, the dark youth, the leading slave, the Maison, and the maiden. Two excellent terra-cotta statuettes were found in a single grave at Tarentum, probably dating from the third century (C 9–10): one is a cook, wearing a himation, with a basket (from which an animal's head looks out) in one hand and in the other a purse, he has the bald-headed Maison mask; the other is a leading slave wearing a short chiton (but considerably longer than those worn in Middle Comedy) and carrying a baby, which presumably has been or will be saved from being exposed. Terra-cottas of this general

---

[1] Cf. above p. 44.

kind, dramatic figures and masks of the third and second century, have been found in many sites in Italy and Sicily, and there is no reason to suppose that most of them are not of local manufacture. Thus very fine examples of the garrulous wife and of the fat Sicilian parasite come from Capua (C 11–12), and a mask of the 'greying garrulous' from Corneto (C 13). The excavations of the area near Paestum have produced masks of the admirable youth, the delicate youth, a hetaira with melon hair, and a wreathed slave (C 14–17), as well as two bearded tragic masks, one with an elaborate wreath which is probably the dark tyrant, and the other with wild hair which is probably the Fairer man (A 50, 51). In Pompeii itself many terra-cotta comic masks of the same period have been found, old men, young men, slaves, young women and old women (e.g. C 18); two statuettes of two-thirds life size, the hero and heroine of a New Comedy, the admirable youth and the maiden (C 27) were probably however not made before the first century A.D.

In discussing tragedy and comedy we have had occasion to mention many of the paintings and mosaics and some of the other objects, bronzes, silver cups, marble reliefs, and masks, which were found in the excavations of Pompeii, Herculaneum, and Boscoreale. Here I propose to describe briefly the theatrical illustrations in four houses in Pompeii, whose owners seem to have had a particular interest in drama.

The House of the Centenary in Pompeii (Region 9, Insula viii, No. 3) was decorated in the first century A.D. and was excavated in 1879. The decoration has now largely perished but we know from early reproductions three pictures from the atrium and a remarkable frieze from the triclinium. Two of the pictures in the atrium are comic and one tragic; a fourth was presumably also tragic, but it has been destroyed beyond recognition. The tragic picture which survives in reproductions is the curious scene already discussed, with Herakles on the left, then an old man and a young woman, then a man with a crook seated on the ground (A 64). One of the two comic scenes is clear enough (C 33); a young man is walking about with two smaller figures while an old slave watches him through the door. The young man is night-walking because he is in love, and the old slave, his paidagogos, will duly chide him or help; such opening scenes are known in comedy. The two smaller figures are difficult to interpret; the young man and the slave are undoubtedly masked, but these two figures wear no masks; I am inclined to suppose that boys who wanted to act may have been allowed to 'walk on', and to see 'walkers-on' also in the little figures in both the Dioskourides mosaics (C *19, 20*).[1] In the other comic picture (C 34) a girl stands on the right and is apparently addressed by an old slave, who comes towards her from an altar, on which there is a body of a bird; the two are watched critically by another old slave wearing a green hat. Here we can only guess: it seems to me possible that the girl is a priestess of some kind (cf. Menander's *Hiereia* and *Theophoroumene*) and that the first slave is trying to persuade her to do something (presumably his young master is involved) and that the other slave who belongs to another household is critical.

The triclinium is surrounded by a small frieze, high on the wall, in which tragic and comic scenes alternate. Of the tragic scenes Medea (A 65), Achilles, and Priam (A 66), Priam and Hekabe (A 67) have already been described. The other tragic scenes show (*a*) a heroine with a little slave 'walking on' behind her, (*b*) a bearded man with a spear talking to an old man seated on a square block which may be an altar, (*c*) a young man with a spear and a small 'walker-on', (*d*) a young man with a spear, (*e*) a bearded man receiving an old slave who arrives in haste. These, like those described, illustrated known scenes, but we have lost the clue; all of them show masks with the high *onkos*, none of

[1] These figures are not masked; they are not therefore speaking characters or characters who have spoken earlier or will speak later; they may however perform some function e.g. in C *20* the 'walkers on' will remove the table; for C 33 E. W. Handley refers me to Plautus, *Curc.* 75.

them high-soled boots; they go back therefore to early Hellenistic originals. The comic scenes show (a) a young man, probably the admirable youth, urging on an old slave, who turns his back and draws in the sand with his stick; I take it that he is thinking out an elaborate plan (C 35); it is remarkable how like the mask of the young man is to the mask of Achilles in the tragic scene; this treatment of the hair, particularly in the young male masks of comedy, is a frequent and very real source of confusion to modern interpreters, (b) wavy-haired old man interrogates wavy-haired slave, who rather uncomfortably turns aside to collect his thoughts (C 36), (c) slave watches departure of fat old woman and girl, perhaps a scene from the *Synaristosai* (C 37), (d) fat old woman with 'walker-on' (C 38), (e) leading old man talks to old slave, who leans pensively on an altar (C 39); he seems almost to be goading the slave on to further plans like Chremes in the *Heautontimoroumenos*.

This house is peculiarly rich in dramatic paintings. Another house in Pompeii (Region 1, Insula vi, No. 11) also has large pictures of tragedy and comedy decorating the walls of the atrium; these pictures also belong to the first century A.D. The picture of Herakles, with a young woman, an old man, and a man with a crook seated on the ground, which we noticed in the atrium of the Casa del Centenario, appears in a variant on the east wall of this atrium, a variant which omits Herakles (A 68). To the right of the tragic picture three comic masks (delicate youth, admirable youth, and maiden) can be seen, ornamenting an elaborate candelabrum painted on a black ground (C 40). Further on is a comic picture with the old slave delivering a tirade while a young man and a young woman look on (C 41): this also is known in another copy from Herculaneum (C 30). It is unfortunate that these two known pictures are also the best preserved. On the same east wall fragments of another tragic picture (A 69) can be seen: a young man with a mask with high *onkos* and curly hair faces a heroine (only the long hair falling on her shoulder is preserved) and a little maid (an unmasked 'walker-on'). From the west wall the upper part of a single comic figure survives; he is an old man leaning forward (presumably on his stick) but turning his head to address the public; the mask is the 'meddling Lycomedian' (C 42). Finally, the North West corner of the atrium also had a comic picture (C 43): a cook wearing the Maison mask sits beside a cauldron on a tripod stand; a parasite addresses the public, one arm stretched out towards the cook, a little 'walker-on' can be seen in the corner; whether the cook is at home waiting to be hired, or whether he has brought his cooking pot with him to the party which he is going to serve we cannot say, but we can appreciate the juxtaposition of the ever-hungry parasite with the often long-winded provider of food.

A house decorated in the earlier part of the first century A.D. (Region 1, Insula ii, No. 6) has groups of dramatic masks alternating with small landscapes on the walls of its peristyle; the groups of masks are alternately tragic and comic, tragic on the right, comic on the left as you look at the wall. The best known of these is a curious group from the East wall (A 70*a*) inspired by Euripides' *Andromeda*. On the left the mask of Perseus, a dark-haired youth with high *onkos*, and on the top of it his cap of darkness with wings and a griffin-head, is posed on a ledge of a cliff with his scimitar and a bag (for the Gorgon's head); then comes a small monster rising from the sea, and on the right three masks, one high on the rocks with long fair hair, and two together on a lower rock, a bearded man with dark hair and *onkos* (certainly Kepheus wearing the dark mask) and a woman with long dark hair and *onkos*. The two female masks were interpreted by Robert as Andromeda and Kassiopeia, and this is probably right, although Echo and Andromeda would be also possible. The comic picture is lost, and a further group of tragic masks (*b*) was badly damaged by the time that Robert had them drawn in 1874. They are in two rows; of the pair and trio at either end of the top row nothing can be said, but in the middle a mask of a long-haired youth

with *onkos* is set in a frame with a 'staff or thyrsos' crossing
behind; I take him to be Dionysos, and think this may be
the explanation of the young seemingly tragic mask which
is sometimes found with comic masks at Pompeii and
Herculaneum (for instance in marble between two marble
masks of old men of comedy in the House of Neptune and
Amphitrite (C 32)). In the lower row are two youths both
with high *onkos*, one with wild hair (perhaps one of the
Dirties) and the other with neat hair, probably the Curly;
an open basket in the centre may perhaps mean that this was
a recognition play; it will be remembered that Ion was
exposed in a basket with wheels. Groups of tragic masks
also survive from the West wall (*c*) and from the South wall
(*d*). The former has two bearded masks, one with grey and
the other with fair hair, the White and the Fair, and three
women's masks of which little can be seen. The latter has
first a bearded mask with brown face and hair, probably the
Dark man again; a sword and a travelling sack below the
mask indicate that he has come on a journey. In the middle a
pair of masks, one male and apparently beardless with dark
curly hair, the other female; a sceptre beneath them suggests
that they are royal. On the right a bearded male mask with
wild hair and yellow face, the Paler man. These two walls
also have sets of comic masks. Those surviving from the
West wall (C 44*a*) are the Second Pseudokore with her hair
held in a clasp over her forehead, and an old slave; another
female mask has vanished except for the end of her long hair
(perhaps one of the two masks for a wife); the mask on the
right with a wreath, short hair, and smooth brows I think
may be the delicate youth. The South wall (C 44*b*) has a
pair of young lovers and a dark-haired slave on the left with
a kithara and a wine-jug near by, in the centre an old man
with short nose and long beard, whom Dr Simon rightly
takes as the Lycomedian, and on the right a pair, of old man
(leading old man) and middle-aged woman (probably the
garrulous wife). The young man on the left with dark hair and
raised brows is probably rightly identified as the admirable

youth and will be the son of the old pair on the left.
The young woman is identified by Dr Simon as a maiden;
if this is right, and it is perhaps the most likely identification,
she was presumably exposed and is now employed as a
harpist but will in due course be recognised as the daughter
of the old man in the middle.

The House of the Golden Cupids (Region 6, Insula xvi,
No. 7) has a different kind of theatrical decoration. The
peristyle surrounds a garden, and peristyle and garden are
decorated with marble masks in relief and in the round.[1]
Marble masks and marble reliefs with masks have been
found in quantity in Pompeii and elsewhere in Italy; here
however we have a collection which decorated a single house;
we can see how they were used and consider them as an
indication of the taste of a wealthy man in the Neronian
period. The walls of the peristyle are painted and divided
into quadrilaterals by painted candelabra. In them are set,
without much regard for the painted decoration, marble
reliefs of which the following show masks: on the South wall
(a) a wavy-haired comic slave mask with a wreath, standing
on rocky ground against which a lighted torch leans (C 45a),
(b) in front, mask of comic leading slave and mask of leading
old man with a curtain beneath them, between them mask of
admirable young man with elaborate wreath, in front of the
curtain a lyre to the left and a blazing altar and torch to the
right (i.e. the young man has fallen in love with a lyre-player
during a night festival); at the back, in low relief an old and
young satyr with Pan pipes and crook to show that comedy
belongs to Dionysos (C 45b), (c) three tragic masks with
high *onkos*, on the left two women (or perhaps an admirable
youth and a woman), on the right a bearded man wreathed, in
the foreground a shield and a sword, and between them a

---

[1] The possibility that such masks and reliefs were sometimes imported from
Attica (and therefore the local examples may have been copied from Attic
imports) is shown by the recent discovery in the Agora in Athens of a disk of
Pentelic marble decorated with a young satyr in low relief (Agora Museum,
S 934; Homer A. Thompson, *Hesperia*, 18 (1949), 222 pl. 44/2). Similar
disks decorated the House of the Golden Cupids and other houses in Italy.

little satyr head, which is rather an allusion to drama in general than to a satyr play in particular (A 71); on the West wall, (*d*) a youth with curly hair, probably the curly youth of comedy rather than of tragedy (A 72). Marble masks also hung between the columns of the peristyle: on the South side, (*e*) a second wavy-haired youth with an elaborate wreath (C 46*a*); on the West side (*f*) a delicate youth (C 46*b*); on the North side (*g*) a maiden (C 46*c*). In the garden were herms, statuettes, and low pilasters carrying rectangular double-sided reliefs; one of these last (*h*) has on one side three comic masks, a wimpled hetaira facing a young and an old wavy-haired man (C 47*a*), and on the other side a young satyr in low relief, and another (*i*) a leading slave in front of a curtain facing a wimpled hetaira and a leading old man; the reverse has in low relief a young Dionysos and an old satyr (C 47*b*).

These are sufficient examples of the theatrical tastes of the people of Pompeii. Many more could be given and the story could be extended to cover many more sites and could be continued down to the Byzantine period. But for our purpose it may be ended here; in Pompeii the tradition of Hellenistic tragedy and New Comedy is still alive, sometimes at first hand and sometimes at several further removes. It is this connection with living Greek drama which makes Pompeii relevant to our present subject.

III. MAINLAND GREECE

I. SPARTA

THE evidence for the rest of Greece is not nearly so full as for Athens itself and for Italy and Sicily, but we can say something about theatres, festivals, and guilds in the Hellenistic age, and we have other fragments of knowledge about drama or the prehistory of drama in Sparta, Corinth, Boeotia, Megara, and Olynthos. I start with Sparta because here the only monumental evidence is early. We are interested in these pre-dramatic performances in so far as they contain elements which survive in tragedy, satyr-play, and comedy. Athenaeus (651*d*) quotes Sosibios, an Alexandrian scholar of the early third century B.C., for 'an ancient form of comic entertainment in Sparta' performed by the *deikeliktai*, with whom he equates various other performers in other cities; of these we have already discussed the South Italian *phlyakes* and shall later consider the Boeotian *ethelontai*. He explains the name as meaning 'property-men and actors', probably because he knew two senses of *deikela* (from which the word comes), 'masks' and 'shows'. This suggests that the *deikeliktai* may have worn masks. He also quotes two examples of their performances 'men stealing fruit, or a foreign doctor talking like the one in Alexis' *Mandragorizomene*'. Sosibios evidently saw a parallel between their language and the language of the Middle Comedy poet, Alexis, and the *deikeliktai* may indeed have been still performing in the fourth century since according to Plutarch (*Vit. Ag.* 1) the Spartan king Agesilaos insulted the Athenian actor Kallippides by calling him a *deikeliktas*. 'Men stealing fruit' (and the word for fruit could be translated equally well 'grapes' or 'wine') belong to the general class of food stealers, which we know from the Sicilian comic poet Epicharmos (grape-stealers, fr. 23), from a Corinthian vase (F 11) where 'wine-stealers' are closely associated with padded dancers, and from a list of Laconian dances in Pollux (4, 104–5), among which are 'men imitating men being caught when stealing stale meat'. Thus the performances of the *deikeliktai* seem to belong to a general class which is known at many places and times in the Greek world. In Corinth the theme is closely associated with padded dancers, and we have supposed that Epicharmos' chorus in the west was also composed of padded dancers, but the quotation from Alexis shows that the themes of these early performances could also survive in the words of the actors of Attic comedy.

Sparta as well as Corinth and Athens had its padded dancers, and they appear on Laconian vases of the second and third quarter of the sixth century. These Laconian vases are less interesting than the Corinthian vases with padded dancers, but they have their importance because they show that padded dancers existed in Sparta and probably therefore illustrate the *deikeliktai*. They frequently dance on either side of a krater (mixing-bowl) with a flautist. They may be beardless or bearded; the padded short chiton is often represented, but sometimes it is left out so that the dancer only appears as abnormally fat, sometimes with a red belly. They are not phallic. There is one seeming exception (F 22); two nymphs are attacked by a hairy phallic Silen and a smooth phallic fat man, but this I think is the subject of the song, and only the two padded female figures with caps on their buttocks and purple anklets are actual performers. They are probably men dressed as women like their Attic counterparts. Pollux (4, 104), as we have said, speaks of Laconian dances in which they mimed men caught stealing stale meat. If this may be regarded as parallel with the fruit-stealers and also ascribed to the *deikeliktai*, the *deikeliktai* were dancers. Pollux says that the dances which he lists took place on Malea, the promontory in the South of Laconia, and the first one he mentions is 'Silens and with them Satyrs dancing in panic'. This must be the Silen of whom Pindar speaks (fr. 142): 'fierce is the dancer whom Malea reared, the bed-fellow of Nais'. Some such event as Pindar had in mind is depicted on the cup in Sparta with the attack on two Nymphs by a hairy Silen and a fat man.

Among the dances mentioned by Pollux are the *baryllicha*, which Pollux says were danced by women in honour of Apollo and Artemis; Hesychius mentions *bryllicha*, which were danced by men wearing ugly masks and female cloth-ing. These are probably the same, and may have been danced both by men in women's clothing and by women in men's clothing. Men wearing ugly female masks would be an apt description of the padded women on the cup in Sparta. Secondly, the words provide a predecessor for the naked hag who dances with a comic actor in the Bacchic thiasos on an Apulian vase of the fourth century (B 38) and for the other ugly female masks of comedy. Thirdly, a connection has been seen between them and the female masks of the early sixth century found in the sanctuary of Ortheia (F 21). These wrinkled masks, which are large enough to have been worn and therefore may well have been the moulds on which linen masks were made, have been regarded as the ancestors of the wrinkled fat old woman of comedy; there is a long history in between, but we may perhaps safely say that all the ugly old female masks of comedy and some of the dances have archaic predecessors of which the Ortheia masks and the *bryllicha* provide Spartan examples. But the Ortheia masks themselves also point Eastwards: R. D. Barnett is completely justified in stating that the earliest clay masks at the Ortheia site are of purely Phoenician appearance; more-over a very similar mask was found in a sixth-century grave at Samos (F 25). Another Eastern reference for Ortheia is given by the 'Procession of Lydians' mentioned by Plutarch with an untenable historical explanation.[1] Many of the Ortheia masks are ugly old women, but some at least are gorgons, although the boundary between them is difficult to draw; and Ortheia seems therefore to have been a Gorgon-

[1] *Aristides*, 17; D. L. Page, *Alcman*, 72.

headed queen of beasts such as appears on a Rhodian plate of the early sixth century (F 24). Again we are led Eastwards, and we can, I think, take one step further. In the ninth book of the *Iliad* (502) Phoinix tries to persuade Achilles by his picture of Infatuation as a strong runner and the Prayers as wrinkled, squinting, lame old women. The pattern, beautiful leader and not quite so beautiful chorus, is well-known, e.g. Artemis and her nymphs in the sixth book of the *Odyssey* (102–9); there may have been a similar pattern, ugly leader and not quite so ugly chorus. I suggest that Homer modelled his Infatuation and Prayers on a chorus of men dressed as wrinkled old women dancing in honour of a gorgon-headed Artemis, and that similar dances were performed in honour of Ortheia at Sparta. Another dance of a similar kind which passed over into comedy was the *kordax* which was danced in honour of Artemis Kordaka in Elis; this Pausanias derived from Asia Minor and it seems to have been very like a dance performed by Lydian maidens in honour of Artemis at Ephesos.[1]

The Eastern connections will have to be considered later. We can note for the moment the following points. Padded dancers wearing the costume later worn by comic choruses and actors were performing in Sparta in the sixth century and may have continued until the fourth century. They sang of and perhaps represented Silens and satyrs. As later in comedy, men represented women, both padded and ugly, in their dances in honour of Ortheia and probably of other deities.

2. CORINTH

The evidence for Corinth is much fuller.[2] Besides the main body of vases with padded dancers, which date roughly from the middle of the seventh to the middle of the sixth century,

[1] Pausanias 6, 22, 1; Autokrates fr. 1 K.
[2] I owe much to discussions with a young Norwegian scholar, A. Seeberg, who is publishing a full account of the Corinthian vases with padded dancers.

we have two from the fourth century, which Professor A. D. Trendall assures me are Corinthian (B 72, 73). Again therefore we have evidence for survival; these vases will be considered later with their contemporary terra-cottas. The early padded dancers generally appear dancing; they have certain definite steps and the dance takes certain definite forms; they often dance with naked women (but on the evidence of Laconian and Attic vases which we have discussed it seems likely that these are men dressed as women; the painter paints what he imagines rather than what he sees); they often have a flute-player with them and he sometimes wears long robes, sometimes the same clothes as the dancers; they often hold drinking horns and they sometimes dance round a mixing bowl. They normally wear belted chiton with short sleeves, which secures their padding in front and behind, and they are not phallic. But there are variations in costume, which tell us rather more about them; they are sometimes masked, they sometimes wear boots, and they sometimes wear a panther skin.

They also appear in scenes which tell us more about them. It was suggested long ago that they are satyrs, but they are of course men dressed up. We have to test the supposition that they are men dressed up as satyrs, remembering always that the vase painter will paint any stage that pleases him between what he sees and what he imagines. The following contexts are for one reason or another interesting: (*a*) stealing wine (F 11) (it will be remembered that stealing fruit (or wine) was attested by Athenaeus for the Spartan *deikeliktai*). On the front of the vase: two padded dancers, one with double flute and one dancing, who wears a mask—the one certain case of a mask; two naked men with a wine jar, named *Eunos* (well disposed) and *Ophelandros* (benefiter of men)—*Eunos* has marks on his arm which suggest a short chiton, *Ophelandros* is phallic; a naked man with two sticks, grossly phallic, named *Omrikos*. The names in spite of doubts seems to me to be fixed as names of *daimones* rather than men by the next vase which we shall consider (*Ombrikos* was a name of

Dionysos in Halikarnassos perhaps in his capacity as a rain god). On the back: two figures who seem to be padded, imprisoned in a cellar where a woman in a long dress feeds them. It is possible that as for the Laconian cup in Sparta (F 22) we should distinguish between the two padded dancers on the front and all the other figures, who may be the subject of their dance and song; the characters in the song are *daimones*, whether they are satyrs or not. (*b*) Herakles and hydra (F *12*). Six dancers on the other side have the names *Komios* (reveller), *Lordios* (backbender), *Loxios* (side-bender), *Paichnios* (sportive), *Vhadesios* (man of pleasure): *Lordios*, particularly, with its likeness to *Lordo*, named as a fertility spirit in a fragment of the comic poet Plato (fr. 174 K), must be a *daimon*; so therefore are the rest. They are the spirits of whom the dancers sing or whom they represent. The painter has carefully connected the two scenes by making Loxios dance up to the horses of Herakles, but this may be merely an archaic mannerism and it is perhaps too complicated to think that the padded dancers represent their *daimones* singing of Herakles and the hydra. (*c*) return of Hephaistos. We have spoken of this story before in connection with Attic pictures and with Epicharmos' play *Komastai* *or Hephaistos*. Hephaistos is brought back riding on a mule in the company of Dionysos and satyrs. Three Corinthian vases represent this subject. On the Musée Rodin mastos (F 16) the attendants of Hephaistos are normal padded dancers and some of them dance. On the krater in the British Museum (F 13) two are normal, two are naked, but there is a clear distinction between them; the naked men take part in the procession; the clothed men dance together at its head. On the amphoriskos in Athens (F 14) all wear short chitons, all are walking rather than dancing. Two are grossly phallic; of these one has a face like a satyr and a spotted chiton and stones in his hands; he is undoubtedly a stone-throwing satyr like the wild man of the woods, who may be a kind of proto-satyr, on an early Attic vase (F 1), and has ambushed the procession from a bush on the road. The explanation seems to me again that the painters are somewhere between two poles: the actual dance which the padded dancers perform, and the subject of their song and dance, which is the return of Hephaistos accompanied by Dionysos and satyrs. On the amphoriskos in Athens the dance is forgotten but the characters in the scene wear the short chitons of the dancers.

Therefore in Corinth too padded dancers are very closely connected with Dionysos and can be thought of as satyrs. Let us add the other evidence that they may represent satyrs. (1) On three vases a bearded draped man reclines on a couch (once with a woman) among the padded dancers, who are once joined by naked women and once by clothed women. This is the scene familiar in Attic of Dionysos or Dionysos and Ariadne with satyrs or satyrs and maenads. (2) The dancers (as we have said) often dance with naked women. A Corinthian krater in Dresden (F 17) gives one of the naked women the name of Poris. Poris recurs as the name of a maenad dancing with satyrs on a Chalkidian krater (F 18). (3) An aryballos in the British Museum (F 10) has five dancers. One at the back of the vase wears a panther skin, such as is often worn by satyrs on Attic vases. Next him is a dancer with something in both hands which has been interpreted as a piece of meat; he therefore may be a meat-stealer like the Laconian dancers listed by Pollux. Next him is a dancer with feet turned inwards, wearing boots and with a clearly indicated phallos, which seems to be artificial. The remaining pair are of no particular interest. Thus the first dancer suggests that these are men dressed as satyrs, and the second dancer gives a cross reference to Laconian dancers. The third dancer has two pieces of equipment which are of interest for the later history of drama, the phallos and boots. The comic actor representing a male always wore the phallos. If the comic actor was in origin the leader of the padded dancers, one would expect the leader of the padded dancers to wear the phallos. But on our vase it is unclear why the meat-stealer rather than the man with the panther skin should be the leader, and on another vase

two out of five dancers are phallic. Still we may note the fact
that on four vases one out of a company of dancers is phallic,
even while we remember that the vase painter may have
transferred this attribute from the satyr represented to the
dancer whom he saw. I owe, however, to Mr A. Seeberg the
knowledge of an aryballos in a private collection in Oslo with
a picture of a single dancer wearing a panther skin and a
large artificial phallos; here we seem clearly to have the phallic
leader of the dancers, possibly impersonating Dionysos
himself.

It is also interesting to find a dancer wearing boots,
because, as we have seen, boots are a distinctive part of the
equipment of the tragic actor. Boots are frequently worn by
another group of Corinthian fat men, who appear as moulded
vases. One of the best of these in the Louvre (F 15) wears
a panther skin as well as boots; many of them are spotted,
but, as with the dancers when they are spotted, the spots
appear to be on a chiton which leaves the arms and legs bare.
They are not hairy satyrs but men padded and provided with
hairy chitons to look like hairy satyrs.

The supposition that the dancers, whether painted on
vases or moulded to form plastic vases, are men dressed up
as satyrs seems to me to be justified. It is difficult not to
equate them with the satyrs speaking verses whom 'Suidas'
attributes to Arion, Arion who lived in the reign of Periander
(625–585 B.C.), who produced dithyrambs in Corinth and
went on a tour of South Italy. We seem here then to have a
form of entertainment which contained the seeds of later
tragedy, satyrplay, comedy, and dithyramb.

Our next Corinthian monuments belong to the fourth
century and consist of two vases and a number of terra-
cottas. One of the vases (B 72) is fragmentary and only
shows a bearded head of a kind known from Attic comic
terra-cottas and South Italian vases. The other (B 73) is a
bell-krater, on which two men similarly bearded, and dressed
in a short chiton with padding and apparently sleeves, drive
away geese from a large mortar in which they have been

pounding something with pestles. This is the kind of scene in which the early padded dancers might well have been shown, and it is likely that we have here a continuation of their performance into the fourth century, but the lines round ankles, shoulders, and wrists suggest that they are wearing tights like the Attic comic actors and we may here see a cross influence of Attic comedy. Such a performance could have taken place on the small stage in the fourth-century building in Corinth which seems to have been used as a tavern.[1] In it one of the terra-cotta comic actors was found (B 74). This and many of the other terra-cottas of this kind found in Corinth, both male and female, appear to be either direct copies or local variants of Attic types. Some however have no Athenian parallels: one (B 75), known both from Corinth and in a better preserved example in the British Museum, has a flared chiton which is unknown in Attic; he and the other male figures in terra-cotta, unlike the figures on the fourth century vase, are phallic; they are therefore actors rather than dancers.

So it seems likely that there was not only dancing by padded dancers but also comedy in Corinth in the fourth century, whether imported from Attica or home-made or both. In the early third century a bronze Corinthian mirror (C 53) was decorated with a Muse teasing Eros with a slave mask of New Comedy. The suggestion that comedy at least, if not also tragedy, was played in Corinth from the fourth century agrees with the evidence of excavation.[2] The earliest theatre of which there is any recognisable trace belongs to the late fifth century. It had a circular orchestra and a removable wooden stage-building like the contemporary Athenian theatre. From the late fifth century then plays were produced in Corinth on the same sort of scale as in Athens.

---

[1] C. Morgan, *Hesperia*, 22 (1953), 130.

[2] R. Stilwell, *Corinth*, vol. II, *The Theatre*. Cf. also the terra-cotta statuette, dated about 250 B.C., of a comic actor holding a *kore* mask, *Corinth*, vol. xii, no. 336 (*not* tragic as there stated, because no *onkos*).

Other theatres [1] also were built in the Peloponnese. A local copy of an Attic actor (B 29) may be too slight evidence for drama at Sikyon in the early fourth century, but in the early third century Sikyon had a stone theatre, and later at any rate this had a high stage, which was approached by ramps leading both to the stage itself and to the rooms behind the background. Epidauros had a theatre designed by the architect Polykleitos about 340 B.C., and this again seems to have been rebuilt in the Hellenistic age with a high stage. The large theatre at Argos was probably built in the late fifth or the early fourth century. Mantinea and Megalopolis had theatres from the third quarter of the fourth century, which were remodelled in the Hellenistic age.

Some idea of the repertory of a Peloponnesian actor in the third century may be formed from an inscription [2] set up by an actor at Tegea recording his victories: Euripides' *Orestes* at Athens, Euripides' *Herakles* and a play by the fifth-century tragic poet Archestratos at Delphi, Euripides' *Herakles* and *Archelaos* at Argos, and the *Archelaos* of Euripides and the *Achilles* of Chairemon (the fourth-century poet) at Dodona. From the third century at least actors in the Peloponnese could belong to the Isthmian and Nemean guild of the Artists of Dionysos.[3] This was formed, like the already existing Athenian guild, to look after the festivals at home, to ensure privileges for its members at home and abroad, to arrange for teams or representatives to appear at foreign festivals, and to honour benefactors. Their history can be followed into the Roman period. They must have contributed to the standardisation of production in the Hellenistic theatres all over the Greek world.

3. BOEOTIA

The list in Athenaeus which names the *deikeliktai* in Sparta and the *phlyakes* in South Italy also includes the

---

[1] See Pickard-Cambridge, *Theatre*, 198 f.; Dilke, *BSA*, 45 (1950), 21 ff.
[2] *IG*. v, ii, 118.
[3] See Pickard-Cambridge, *Festivals*, 292 f.

ethelontai in Boeotia. *Ethelontai* means 'volunteers', and it is tempting to think that Aristotle had this Boeotian title in mind when he wrote in the *Poetics* (1449 *b* 2) that comedy was late in becoming official; before that they were 'volunteers'. We have three groups of archaeological evidence; vases of the early sixth century, vases of the second half of the fifth century, and terra-cottas of the fourth century. The vases of the early sixth century have Komasts very like those of the Corinthian and Attic vases already described and may be taken as evidence for similar performances in Boeotia; these Komasts were presumably the 'volunteers'.[1] Some of the figures are grossly phallic, but here again the painter seems to have mixed the character and the actor. Two examples will make this clear. On a vase in Berlin (F 19) the painter has painted two pairs of dancers and a pair of satyrs, all dancing in the same way with cups and drinking-horns; the fourth pair consists of a flute-player in an elaborate flared chiton (like that worn twice by Corinthian dancers in the fourth century) and a little satyr running up to him. Here we have juxtaposition rather than conflation; on a vase in Göttingen (F 20) a pair of padded dancers wear the normal short chiton and one of them is ithyphallic and the other has a tail; they are given the attributes of satyrs because they represent satyrs. Here again we have evidence that padded dancers were men pretending to be satyrs.

The second group of vases are called Kabeiran vases because many of them were found in the sanctuary of the Kabeiroi at Thebes.[2] The men and women on these late black-figure vases of the second half of the fifth century look remarkably like their contemporaries on the Attic red-figure vases which we have associated with Old Comedy. The men are fat and phallic, the women decently dressed but ugly and snub-nosed. The artist does not show that the men are wearing tights, but it is difficult to suppose that he has any-

---

[1] For references see *Rylands Bulletin* 36 (1954), 575.
[2] Very fully published by Bruns-Wolters, *Das Kabiren-Heiligtum*.

thing but padded men in mind. But he thinks of them in their stories, and we can seldom say that the Kabeiran vases show us a stage scene. Odysseus watching Kirke mix him a potion (B 71) may very well have been a stage scene, but Odysseus blown across the waves by Boreas quite obviously was not. The range of mythological scenes is considerable and includes Kephalos, Bellerophon, Kadmos, and Perseus. But are these mythological scenes the songs which the dancers sang or are they the subjects of comedy? We have supposed that when the early dancers are phallic, except perhaps in the case of the leader, they are phallic because the painters are thinking of the satyrs whom they represent. Here the painter had no reason to make Odysseus or Kadmos phallic unless he so saw them. These therefore would seem to be actors in a mythological comedy of the same kind as contemporary Attic mythological comedy, and the miraculous events were presumably travestied in narrative speeches as well as songs. It is tempting to go one stage further and suppose that these were performances of Attic comedy in Boeotia, but for that we have not the evidence.

We can however say that terra-cotta statuettes of Attic comic actors were found in graves in the Kabeiran sanctuary, and this is some evidence of the popularity of Attic comedy there in the fourth century. It is not easy to decide (particularly on the evidence of photographs) whether a given terra-cotta is an Attic import, a Boeotian variant of an Attic type, or a Boeotian original. One example of the crosslegged standing Herakles (B *13*), which is known from the Pnyx in Athens, was found in the Kabeiran sanctuary and is certainly an Attic import. On the other hand a slave carrying a waterpot (B 76), which is said to come from Tanagra, is a variant of the hydrophoros of the New York set (B 11*f*) and has a different arrangement of the cloak and a different stance and pedestal. An instance of an original Boeotian terra-cotta (B 77) is a bald old man with pointed shoes and his cloak wrapped round his left arm, which was found in a tomb of the early fourth century at Halai: Halai is across the border in Locris, but the excavators are convinced that its terra-cottas were imported from Boeotia or else made in imported Boeotian moulds. We can be certain that some form of comic performance persisted in Boeotia in the fourth century. Whether the dances also continued and whether the comedy was Attic or native Boeotian we have not enough evidence to say. For New Comedy we can quote a wreathed, bald slave mask, also from Halai (C 52), and a flatterer's mask from Elateia (C 55); both are standard New Comedy masks and appear to date from the third century.

We have evidence from excavations and inscriptions for both theatres and performances in Boeotia. The theatre at Chaironeia has been dated to the late fifth century. The theatres at Thespiai and Tanagra cannot themselves be dated, but tragedies and comedies were acted at both in the first century, and the Isthmian and Nemean guild sent a deputation to the festival of the Muses at Thespiai about the middle of the third century.[1] The festival of Amphiaraos at Oropos was another occasion for dramatic performances, which are recorded in inscriptions of the Hellenistic age. A theatre seems to have been already in existence in the early fourth century; the present theatre was probably built in the third century, and rebuilt in the middle of the second century with a high stage approached by ramps as at Sikyon. Inscriptions [2] record the dedication of the *proskenion* and the *pinakes* and of the *skene* and the *thyromata*. The *proskenion* is the wall below the high stage; it had a row of columns on either side of its central door specially designed to hold painted panels (*pinakes*). The *skene* here is the back wall of the stage, and it supported much larger wooden panels about 12 ft. wide, known as *thyromata*. These, as Rumpf has seen, must have been considerable pictures, and he suggests that they were like the frescoes of the bedroom at Boscoreale (A 53, C 23). This is the clearest evidence from mainland Greece for the scenery of the late Hellenistic theatre.

[1] Pickard-Cambridge, *Festivals*, 293; *Theatre* 243; Dilke, *BSA, loc. cit.*
[2] *IG.* vii, 423 and 423a, cf. Rumpf, *JHS*, 67 (1947), 18.

4. MEGARA

The town of Megara is situated on the Isthmus between Corinth on the one side and Athens and Thebes on the other. We have some literary evidence but no reliable archaeological evidence for its comedy; I think it is safer to disregard two terra-cotta statuettes, one of the mid-fourth century and one of the New Comedy period, which are alleged to come from there. The literary evidence has been admirably discussed by Pickard-Cambridge[1] and may be summarised briefly. In Aristotle's time the Megarians claimed that comedy had originated with them in the time of their democracy, which lasted from about 581 B.C. to 424 B.C. It seems very likely that the Megarians like their neighbours had padded dancers in the sixth century, and the Megarian cult of Orthosia may have included dances of ugly women like the Spartan cult of Ortheia. In the fifth century Attic comic poets, wanting to point out how intellectual their comedy was, stressed its difference from the vulgar comedy of Megara, although we must in honesty admit that the instances which Aristophanes gives in the *Wasps* (54 ff.)— 'slaves throwing nuts to the audience' and 'Herakles cheated of his dinner'—are in no way alien to the spirit of Old Comedy. However that may be, they prove the existence of comedy as distinct from dances in Megara in the fifth century. We have already noticed two technical points about this comedy—the use of purple curtains, and the bald, red-haired Maison mask (P in Old and Middle Comedy, 25 in Pollux' New Comedy list), which according to Aristophanes of Byzantium was the invention of a Megarian actor called Maison. This evidence from Megara is valuable because it shows that local comedy survived in spite of the overpowering influence of Attica.

5. OLYNTHOS

Olynthos on the Chalkidike was sacked by Philip of Macedon in 348. A possible site for a theatre has been found

[1] *Dithyramb*, etc. 274 ff.

in the elaborate excavations, and a citizen of Olynthos, Satyros, was a famous comic actor at the time that the city fell. The excavations have revealed a number of terra-cotta statuettes and plastic vases of comic actors both from private houses and from graves; there was therefore considerable enthusiasm for comedy and it is difficult to believe that comedy was not performed there. The statuettes are all more or less nearly related to Attic. We can distinguish Attic imports, Boeotian imports, local copies of both, and free copies on an enlarged scale. Five of the fourteen terra-cottas from the New York sets (B 11, 12) have been found in Olynthos. These seem to be Attic imports, but the first of them, the standing weeping man with a felt hat (*11d*), exists in two further copies, which from their clay appear to have been made in Olynthos from a mould taken from the Attic import. I suspect that the same is true of the mould for a figure of a slave in short chiton with a basket on his head (B 79), although I do not know an exact Attic parallel. Similarly Boeotian terra-cottas seem to have been imported and copied. The Boeotian variant (76) of the Attic hydrophoros (*11f*) is also found in Olynthos. The group of Hephaistos on his mule is probably Boeotian (B 78) although it also is likely to have been derived ultimately from an Attic original; five copies are known in Olynthos, of which four are said to come from the same mould and are likely to be of local manufacture. On the other hand some of the larger masks and plastic vases are local in the sense that they have no near parallel elsewhere; but they seem to be free adaptations of Attic masks and figures. One of the most interesting is the mask of a young man with wavy hair (B 80). This is, as we have said, one of the earliest surviving clean shaven comic masks; the destruction of Olynthos dates it before 348. It is not unlike the mask of the worried lover on the Attic relief from Aixone (B *31*), which is dated 340; the same mask recurs on a South Italian vase (B *52*) which can be dated 350–25 and thus shows the uniformity of practice over the Greek world. Another interesting cross connection between North-East and West is given by a terra-cotta statuette in Olynthos (B 81); it is a young man, wearing a wreath, with raised eyebrows and clean shaven, draped in a long himation which descends to the region of his knees. He is very like in face and dress a youth on an Apulian vase (B 43) of the middle of the century, who is receiving a bundle from an elaborately dressed lady while an old man looks on. All these terra-cottas may have been made in the last years of the city's existence when it was allied to Athens.

6. DELPHI

We have already noted that an actor from Tegea won a victory at the Soteria at Delphi with the *Herakles* of Euripides in the third century.[1] The theatre at Delphi is Hellenistic, and the festival of the Soteria was instituted to commemorate the defeat of the Gauls in 279–278. We have inscriptional records of these festivals from the third century and later. The performers were sent by the different Guilds and each troupe seems to have consisted of three tragic or three comic actors with a flute-player and a trainer. Some of the actors are known elsewhere, as victors in Athens or at Delos; they include not only the actor from Tegea, who was also victorious at Athens, Argos, and Dodona, but also Drakon of Tarentum who is interesting as giving one of the few clear non-archaeological indications that the West in fact belonged to this international dramatic tradition, as the monuments have led us to believe.

Early in the third century the Amphiktyonic council recognised the priority of the Athenian guild of Artists of Dionysos and granted it special privileges, but it is at least probable that long before this Delphi had extended its protection to actors and accorded them the freedom of travel and immunity from hostile action which made it possible for them to act in different parts of the Greek world

[1] See above p. 137. On Delphi see Pickard-Cambridge, *Theatre*, 240, 243; *Festivals*, 153, 286 f.; Tod, *Greek Historical Inscriptions*, II, 120.

and also to serve as ambassadors in political negotiation. When the temple of Apollo was burnt down or otherwise destroyed in 373/2, the highest gifts from individuals towards its rebuilding were the two sums of 70 drachmai (not less than £50) contributed by an unknown man of Apollonia and the Athenian tragic actor Theodoros. It may be therefore that Delphi was already giving some sort of special privileges to actors in the early part of the fourth century. Terra-cottas of Attic comic actors of the same period (B 11a, 13) have been found in Delphi, but nothing can be built on this.

This survey of mainland Greece has been useful in showing the wide spread of local pre-dramatic performances in the Peloponnese and Boeotia as well as in Attica and their survival into classical times. Where they became local comedy it seems extremely likely that this local comedy was strongly influenced by Attic comedy and probable that Attic comedy was imported, since terra-cottas of Attic comic actors were so universally popular even in the distant northern town of Olynthos. Early in the third century at latest the local guilds were formed and ensured protection for their members, but probably Athenian actors at any rate had enjoyed some kind of immunity from Delphi long before. Where we know anything about the plays performed in the Hellenistic period they seem to be the old Athenian classics, and their revival as well as the existence of the guilds must have helped to standardise production. It is likely therefore that if in one theatre, such as Oropos, the action was removed from the orchestra to the raised stage and played before large pictures inserted in the back wall, this practice would soon become general.

IV. THE ISLANDS

THE islands may conveniently be treated together in a brief chapter. Chance finds of Middle Comedy terra-cottas in Melos or of New Comedy terra-cottas in Thera need not delay us. It is however interesting, in view of the cross connections between Athens and Cyprus in the fourth century (Isocrates and Euagoras, Aristotle and Themison) and the occasional mentions of Cyprus in the fragments of Middle and New Comedy as a place where braggart soldiers feast in luxury, to note that about a dozen statuettes and masks of comic actors have been found in Cyprus. Some of these are probably imports; for instance the Middle Comedy man with a pitcher (B 28), of which examples were also found at Larisa on the Hermos and in Cyrenaica, is almost certainly Attic; but others are local products, particularly the fine series in the Nicosia Museum, knowledge of which I owe to V. Karageorghis: these include a Middle Comedy terra-cotta (B 82) of a standing man with a long beard and a himation over the left shoulder, and a bronze (B 83) of a man similarly dressed with a short beard; his left arm was raised, and his right arm extended; he is parodying a mythological hero standing with a spear in one hand and a phiale in the other. The New Comedy terra-cottas in Nicosia include a grinning, wreathed procurer, draped in an elaborate cloak (C 58), a youth with smooth brows and wavy hair (C 59), and a large slave mask with trumpet mouth (C 60) which may very well have been a mould on which an actor's mask was made. It may also be noted that in Euboea the theatre at Eretria dates from the late fifth century, and from the early third century we have an inscription [1] which makes arrangements, including payments and rations for actors

---

[1] *IG*. xii, pt. 9, No. 207. Pickard-Cambridge, *Festivals*, 289.

and choruses for dramatic festivals at Karystos, Eretria, Chalkis, and Oreos.

The island about which we know most is Delos. For Delos we have first a series of inscriptions relating to the festivals in the third century, secondly a series of inscriptions relating to the rebuilding of the theatre in the third and second century, and thirdly a very fine set of mosaics from a house of the second century. Various New Comedy statuettes have been found in Delos, but there is no clear evidence that they are of local fabric (e.g. C 62). The festival inscriptions [1] give the names of poets and actors of tragedy and comedy, and their chief interest is that they show the international quality of this third century drama in that names known from Athens and Delphi recur here and the poets and actors come from a very wide spread of towns. Thus in 284 tragic victors came from Megara and Chalkis and comic victors from Athens and Sinope. These last are both called Diodoros and are probably both relations of the well known comic poet Diphilos; they both had successful comedies produced at the Lenaia in the early third century. Kephisios of Histiaia in Euboea, who was the chief actor in one of these comedies at the Lenaia, was successful at Delos in 282 and again in 279, when the other comic actors were Teleson of Megara, Simias of Athens, and Aristophanes of Soloi. On the second occasion in Delos the tragic actors were Nikokles of Epeiros, Drakon of Tarentum (whom we have already noted at Delphi), and Kleodoros, whose name also appears in the list of the tragic actors victorious at the Lenaia in Athens. In the year before, 280, Ameinias, Philemon, and Nikostratos are quoted as comic poets, all of whom are known from the Athenian lists, as are also the comic actors Polykles and Menekles. A glance down the lists shows further places from which the actors come; Paros, Arcadia, Kassandreia, Chalkis, Acarnania, Boeotia, Knidos. Thus drama was truly international in the third century.

During all this period the theatre was being rebuilt, and

[1] *IG.* xi, 2, 105–133. Pickard-Cambridge, *Theatre*, 241 f.

we have incomplete records of this in the inscriptions [1] of
the Hieropoioi, magistrates whose title might perhaps be
translated Inspectors of Holy Places. They begin in the
fourth century and continue into the second. The vocabulary
is difficult, and though the following account seems to me
the most probable, many points are still open to discussion.
We need not consider here the rebuilding of the auditorium
in stone, which is discussed in detail by Mr Dilke. In the
late fourth century 550 drachmai were paid for the wood for
the *skene*. We may suppose that *skene* here has its normal
meaning of stage-building. Then in 290 a payment of 450
drachmai was made to those who had contracted to make
the *skene* and the *proskenion*. The *proskenion* here would seem
to be a wall in front of the *skene*; this makes sense if it
supported a platform for roof scenes or for the appearance
of gods; this platform would have as its background the
upper portion of the *skene* itself. In 282 two payments each of
200 drachmai were made for painting four panels for the *proskenion*, one payment for making one panel for the *proskenion*,
and one payment for making one panel for the *proskenion* out
of existing fir wood; it is unclear whether the last was one of
the four painted panels or not. These are the painted panels
(*pinakes*) of the background which we have already noticed
at Oropos. Money was also spent on pitch for the doors,
lintels, and other needs of the *skene*, which again confirms
that the stage-building was of wood at this date. The panels
were set in place in 281 and money was also spent on an
unknown bronze object. In 279 much was spent on the
auditorium and the roof of the stage-building was washed
over (or whitewashed) and an eleven-cubit beam was bought
for the *logeion* of the *skene*; the word *logeion* simply means
speaking place, and we cannot say whether it refers here to a
low stage in front of the *proskenion* or to the high platform
above the *proskenion*. A *torniskos* for the theatre is mentioned

---

[1] *IG*. xi, 2, Nos. 142 ff. Pickard-Cambridge, *Theatre*, 169 f., 187, 208–9.
Dilke, *BSA*, 45 (1950), 59. Bulle, *Untersuchungen an griechischen Theatern*,
174 ff.

both this year and next, and Bulle interprets this as the crane or *mechane*. In 276 there was a second payment for seating and a first payment 'for the remaining work in the theatre'.

A great deal was done in 274: (1) the doors of the *skene* were colour-washed; (2) stone was brought to the theatre for the *paraskenia* and the *paraskenion* was constructed in ten days; (3) wood of various lengths from eleven to thirty cubits were brought for the *skenai* (and the *palaistra*), and planks for the doors and some other part (undecipherable) of the *skenai* and *paraskenia*, and moulds for rivets for the *skenai*; (4) arrangements were made for the wood to be sawn, and nails were provided for the *skenai* and the *paraskenia*; (5) Theodemos was paid for making the middle *skene* and the lower *paraskenia*; (6) Epiklytes was paid for scraping and restoring the old *skenai*, renewing the two upper *skenai* and two upper *paraskenia*, making an enclosure round the old panels of the *paraskenia*, and restoring the *exostra* and the ladder and the altars; (7) two men were paid for painting the *skenai* and the upper and lower *paraskenia* (or more probably, the *skenai* and the *paraskenia*, above and below); (8) a man was paid for making the *paraskenion* in the theatre; (9) a man was paid for colour-washing the wall of the *skene*.

The terminology of this inscription is confused. In (2) we have stone brought for the *paraskenia* and one *paraskenion* is constructed; the other *paraskenion* is probably the subject of the contract in (8), and the stone for it was paid for five years later. I am inclined to interpret these as stone wings at either end of the stage-building, but it may be, as Bulle suggests, that these are only stone foundations for wooden wings. But then we have *paraskenia* also mentioned in close connection with *skenai* in (3), (4), (5), (6), (7); these are wooden, have doors, are painted, and may be described as upper and lower. *Skenai* in these contexts is always plural except in the phrase 'middle *skene*' in (5); we should not therefore be justified in translating it here as stage-building. It must mean 'background', and the *paraskenia* in these passages are 'side backgrounds' on either side of the 'middle background' both for the lower storey (which in the earlier inscription was called *proskenion*, a word not occurring in this inscription at all) and for the upper storey (there they are supported by the *skene* in the old sense of stage-building, which sense recurs in (1) and (9), where its side and/or back walls and doors are colour-washed). These backgrounds are made of wood and have practicable doors, (3) (4); presumably the centre door belongs to the 'middle background' and the side-doors to the 'side backgrounds'. But the 'middle background' may be called simply 'backgrounds' (plural) when it is thought of as two backgrounds on either side of the central door. These 'backgrounds' and 'side backgrounds' on both storeys were painted (7), and this must mean that they had decoration or pictures, because a different verb is used for colour-washing.

We now come to the very interesting passage which I have numbered (6): Epiklytes was paid first for scraping and restoring the old 'backgrounds' and renewing the two upper backgrounds and two upper side backgrounds. Two points are clear, first that the total number of a set of backgrounds for the upper storey is four, one at each side and two in the middle, secondly that there is more than one set for the upper and the lower storey—a new lower set made in (5) and painted in (7), an upper set renewed in (6) and painted in (7) (if in fact 'renewed' rather than 'newly made' is the right translation), an old set scraped and restored in (6). Secondly, Epiklytes 'made an enclosure round the old panels of the *paraskenia*'. The translation is doubtful here. It would be rather simpler linguistically to render 'used the old panels, etc., as a border for the backgrounds (already mentioned)'. I should prefer to take it with Bulle as 'made a border round the old panels'. In either case the old panels (whether those made and painted in 282 or others) were evidently useless as 'backgrounds'; they were either converted into frames for the new backgrounds or were themselves enlarged by frames. It seems therefore very probable that the backgrounds were larger than the earlier panels, in fact that they were something like the later *thyromata*, for which we have quoted inscriptional evidence at Oropos. Finally, Epikrates restored the *exostra* (and there is no reason why this should not be the *ekkyklema*, in the normal sense of a platform rolled or pushed through the central door, as described in the first chapter), the 'ladders', which I take to be short staircases up to the low stage, as we see them on South Italian vases [1] and on one Attic vase, and the altars, which were movable stage properties and are often pre-supposed by the texts of surviving tragedies and comedies.

This makes a convincing picture of a theatre of the normal type, with wings, and a low stage in front of a *proskenion* carrying wooden painted backgrounds between and outside its three doors and supporting a high platform, which in its turn had wooden backgrounds set in the front of the stage-building. The chief changes in 274 were the reconstruction of the wings in stone and the substitution both on the stage level and on the upper level of large backgrounds for the smaller panels, and several sets of these large backgrounds existed. The later inscriptions do not yield much of interest for the stage arrangements. I have noted already that stone for 'the *paraskenion* in the theatre' was paid for in 269. In 250 Neogenes was paid for making an inscription on the *proskenion*. The other inscriptions for which he was paid in the same year are undoubtedly inscriptions on stone, and it is at least doubtful whether an inscription on the wood of the *proskenion* would either be made or payment for it recorded. This may therefore suggest that after the completion of the stone wings, the stage-building itself with its *proskenion* was gradually rebuilt in stone. Later still in 180 B.C. wood was used for panels for the *logeion*; the sense of *logeion* is no clearer here than in the earlier inscription, so that we cannot say whether these new panels are for the upper or the lower storey. The terminology is evidently not fixed, and what are here called *pinakes* are presumably the same as what was in 274 called *skene*.

[1] Cf. above p. 109.

The theatre of which the remains are visible today appears to be later and perhaps dates from the second century. A curious feature of this theatre is the absence of wings. The action evidently took place on a stage above the *proskenion*, and this stage was continued round the sides of the central stage-building. This arrangement must have involved considerable further rebuilding, but for this we have no records. The records however give us some idea of the third century theatre; not the least interesting point is that this reconstruction went on during a period of considerable dramatic activity.

A hundred yards from the theatre a house with large rooms was excavated, which dates from the first half of the second century B.C. M. Chamonard has suggested that it was put at the disposal of the theatre for storing properties, and perhaps entertaining actors, by a choregos or poet, who was the father of a victorious athlete; statues of an elderly man and a youth were found in the house, and the subjects of the mosaics are suitable to commemorate dramatic and athletic triumphs. Three of the mosaics have subjects connected with the theatre. The first (A 74) is a beardless figure with thyrsos and tympanon riding on a leopard. M. Chamonard discusses whether the rider is Dionysos or Ariadne. But although it is unexpected that Dionysos should have a tympanon, the face seems to me too strong and the complexion too dark for Ariadne. With its elaborate wreath and piled fair hair (not a tiara) it resembles the young mask known in marble and from wall paintings at Pompeii (which I have suggested above is Dionysos).[1] M. Chamonard's original suggestion of Dionysos is therefore the more probable. In either case the figure is wearing tragic costume, a long pale-grey robe with long sleeves, which are red between shoulder-piece and cuff. The robe has patterns of white and gold on the breast and round the bottom. It falls at the bottom in heavy formal folds, like those seen some two hundred years earlier on the Copenhagen relief (A 20). It has a narrow yellow girdle, set

[1] Cf. above p. 125.

very high like the wider girdle of the tragic actor in the painting from Herculaneum (A 57). A yellow himation is worn over this. The footwear is red with thin soles; these may be *kothornoi* but the uppers are concealed by the long robe; again they look remarkably like the footwear of the actor on the Copenhagen relief. The excellent coloured reproduction in the Delos publication gives a good impression of the splendour of a Hellenistic tragic actor.

In another room the floor has a kind of mosaic carpet of which the main pattern consists of cubes in perspective painted in black, white, dark red, and light red. These are bordered on two sides by a row of masks (C 61a) set in a pattern of ivy and helichryse of the kind commonly seen on vases from the fifth century onwards. The ancestors of this border can be seen on the Gnathia vases with single hanging masks or the Paestan vase (B 64) with three masks hanging from an ivy trail, but there the painter was recording the decoration of the room for a special occasion, the actors' victory party. This is the first use of masks set in a floral pattern to form a border that we have seen; but later borders of masks set in floral bands surround several Pompeian mosaics (e.g. C 21) and we have literary evidence for floral borders from the middle of the second century—the time of our mosaics; in an epigram [1] on a painting by Apelles the poet congratulates also the anonymous flower-painter, who evidently supplied a floral border to the picture of the master.

The masks may be described in order from the South end of the West border; the numbers are the same as those in the Delos publications. They come from Comedy. 1. The first mask has wavy hair, which is black with some red in it, black slave beard outlined on the left by a white line (which renders a highlight on the edge of the trumpet mouth), red complexion, raised brows. This is the wavy-haired leading slave (No. 27 of Pollux' list). 2. The second is a woman. Unfortunately it is badly damaged. She wears a kind of veil over

[1] C. H. Roberts, *Journal of Juristic Papyrology*, 4 (1950), 215; T. B. L. Webster, *ibid.*, 5 (1951).

her head with a red border; eyes and brows look too old for the wimpled hetaira, and traces can be seen of fat wrinkles round the mouth; she is therefore the fat old woman (No. 29), and mask and head-dress were not unlike that of the old woman on the Dioskourides mosaic (C *19*). 3. The third is a Pan, bearded with a long square-cut beard with fair streaks, red complexion, and highlights in the arch between the brows and the eyes (these we have noticed before on Paestan vases).[1] 4. The fourth is a young man with wavy hair; his hair is lightish brown; the brows are not so much raised as the brows of the slave; the complexion varies from red through pink to yellow; it is meant to be lighter than the complexion of the slave. He must therefore be the second young man with wavy hair (No. 16), who in contrast to the soldier with dark colouring and hair is more delicate and has fair hair. 5. The fifth is an old man with neat dark hair, medium length beard with white streaks, red to yellow complexion, one brow level and the other raised. This is a very fine example of the leading old man described by Pollux (No. 3). The hair sits on the forehead like a cap, whereas wavy hair sprouts from a point in the centre of the forehead.

The East border has five further masks which I describe from the Northern end. 6. The first is difficult to identify; the hair is long and dark, the beard is half length with white and yellow streaks (more I think to lighten the tone than to indicate the colour of the hair), the brows are level and the complexion red rather than yellow. The difficulty is increased by the fact that the mask looks rather different in the two illustrations. It is either a variant of the leading old man with both brows even (for this many parallels could be quoted) or, as I am rather inclined to think, a satyr. 7. The next mask belongs to a youth with neat dark hair and smooth brows; the complexion varies from red to pink. This is the dark youth (No. 11), who it will be remembered is 'cultured rather than addicted to exercise'. 8. The third mask is the mask of the old man with wavy hair (No. 4). He has a very

[1] Cf. above p. 115.

fine long beard with yellow streaks, which justifies Pollux' adjective 'well-bearded'. 9. The fourth mask is bald, has a very yellow complexion, and a square beard with a great deal of white in it. This is certainly a *pornoboskos* (No. 8). 10. The fifth mask is a very fine leading slave (No. 22) with neat black hair, one level and one raised brow, red to yellow complexion, black slave beard outlined on the right with a white line as in the first mask of the series.

If the excavator's conjecture that the house has some special connection with drama is right, it is not impossible that the mosaics were designed to celebrate some particular performance. In that case the masks and ivy trails may like those on the Paestan bell-krater have some relation to the celebration of a dramatic victory, but here they have been taken out of their context to become the border for a carpet of cubes. I am inclined to think that the masks may recall the chief characters of two comedies. In the comedy illustrated in the West border the prologue was spoken by Pan, and the wavy-haired slave intrigued to get a girl from the possession of the fat old woman for his wavy-haired young master; the old man is not his father but perhaps the father of his friend and helper. The East border illustrates a comedy in which the prologue was spoken by a satyr (if that interpretation of the mask (No. 6) is right), and the dark youth was in love with a girl owned by the brothelkeeper. His slave of course helped him. The girl possibly turned out to be the daughter of the wavy-haired old man.

The third mosaic (C 61*b*) is interpreted by the excavators as a Silen dancing to a flautist. The flautist is apparently male and naked, and he is sitting on a rock. He seems to be a creature of imagination rather than of the stage. The dancer is bald, wreathed, and bearded; he wears a short chiton which shades from green to grey and blue and reaches to near his knees, a yellow cloak wrapped round his middle (as worn by the revellers on the Dioskourides mosaic (C 20), and yellow shoes with white soles. He looks like a dancing slave of comedy, and I think this is the most probable interpretation; even if a tailless satyr is possible in the Hellenistic period, he has neither the tights covered with flocks of wool worn by Papposilenos nor the loincloth of the younger satyr. Here again then I think we have a moment of comedy partly imagined and partly seen.

I have described the monuments at Delos at some length because of their peculiar interest. Perhaps nowhere else are festivals, theatre details, and costumes of approximately the same date recorded and preserved so well. This is our most complete set of original records of Hellenistic production, and because Hellenistic drama was international, as the records of the artists show, the picture which we can draw from them is probably valid for other Greek cities in the third and second centuries.

V. ASIA AND AFRICA

WHEN discussing the early dances in Sparta [1] which form
part of the pre-history of drama I noted the various threads
which led across the Aegean to Asia Minor; the most
interesting of these is the evidence for dances of ugly women
(or men dressed as women) in honour of a Gorgon-headed
Artemis. There are three separate pieces of evidence which
suggest this. The Gorgon-headed Artemis is seen on a
Rhodian plate of the early sixth century (F 24). A mask of
a bald, wrinkled, ugly woman very like the Ortheia masks
was found with sixth-century pottery in Samos (F 25).
Thirdly we have Homer's picture (*Iliad* 9, 502) of Infatuation as a strong runner and the Prayers as wrinkled,
squinting, lame old women, which may well be modelled
on such a dance of ugly women round an uglier leader.
Thus it seems reasonable to suppose that dances of men
representing ugly women occurred in the Greek cities of
Asia Minor as well as in the Peloponnese.

Padded dancers like those of Athens, Corinth, and Sparta
are not found in East Greek art, but we have several indications of performances which belong to the same general
class. Dancers whose postures and gestures are like those of
the padded dancers are illustrated on vases of various fabrics
produced in the late seventh or sixth century.[2] On Chiot
pottery of the early sixth century the dancers habitually wear
a cap made of stuff rolled round like a turban and a peculiar
loin-cloth, which looks very like the buttock-caps worn by
the ugly women on the Laconian kylix (F 22); these Komasts
seem to me to be in all probability men representing women.
East Greek Komasts are not fat, but Rhodes at any rate
produced in the sixth century a peculiar type of fat men of

[1] See above p. 129.
[2] References are given in *Rylands Bulletin*, 36 (1954), 578. For Chiot
dancers see E. R. Price, *JHS*, 44 (1924), pl. 11.

its own: a number of terra-cotta statuettes [1] of grossly fat little men have been found in Lindos and elsewhere; they are generally explained as deriving from Egyptian proto-types, but Boehlau long ago suggested a connection with Corinthian padded dancers, and it seems to me possible that they may be a local variant produced under Eastern influences. A much earlier fat man was found in Samos (F 23), a jug with bearded head and spout modelled as a phallos; Buschor compared this with the very early satyrs on the roughly contemporary early Attic amphora (F 1) and with the later Corinthian plastic vases of squatting fat men (e.g. F 15). The example in Samos is phallic and may recall therefore the leader rather than the chorus.

It seems therefore not unreasonable to assume that there were padded dancers in the Eastern Greek world as well as elsewhere in the seventh century. In Attica we believe that the normal satyr costume—snub-nosed mask with equine ears and shaggy or smooth loin-cloth supporting tail and phallos—was introduced at the beginning of the fifth century. Mr Higgins has lately suggested that a very fine terra-cotta mask from Samos in the British Museum (F 26) 'is probably a faithful copy of a mask as worn in a satyr-play'. He dates it in the sixth century, which seems to exclude the satyr-play in the accepted sense. Moreover the mouth is closed, so that the original was not worn by a singer in a chorus. But the nostrils are pierced, and it is therefore possible that this large mask was a mould from which the masks of silent satyrs were taken. Very tentatively I should like to combine this with two other pieces of evidence: Herakleitos of Ephesos [2] says that in his time, the late sixth century, they made a procession in honour of Dionysos and sang a song to genital organs. A much later relief [3] shows a large phallos carried by a walking man and preceded by a

---

[1] See *British Museum Catalogue of Terra-cottas* I, No. 88 f. for examples and references.

[2] B 15, Diels-Kranz.

[3] Keil, *Ö. Jh.*, 29 (1934), 91.

man with a tail, evidently a man dressed as a satyr, and this procession in Ephesos was still held in the first century A.D. This procession in honour of Dionysos worshipped in the form of a phallos is dated back to the sixth century by Herakleitos (and is probably very much older); the mask from Samos suggests that men masked (if not dressed) as satyrs may here already have taken part in it at that date. We should not lay too much stress on this combination; it might for instance be possible to bring down the date of the mask to the early fifth century and to suggest cross influence from Athens and in any case there is plenty of time for such cross influence before the Ephesos relief. In Delos also a similar procession is known from monuments and inscriptions [1] dating from the late fourth to the second century B.C. However these various pieces of evidence from different sites show that several of the pre-dramatic performances which we have identified in mainland Greece and the West were also known in the Greek cities of Asia Minor and the islands.

Between the late sixth century and the Hellenistic age there is little to record, although it should be noted that terra-cottas of comic actors from the early fourth century have been found in some quantity in the Greek cities of South Russia and sporadically in Asia Minor. In the Aeolian town of Larisa on the Hermos about a dozen terra-cotta figures of actors were found, and ten of these are said in the publication to be of Attic clay whereas the other two are local imitations. Thus on a small scale we have the same kind of picture as we have seen elsewhere. The town was destroyed in 300 B.C. and some of the non-dramatic terra-cottas are certainly not long before that date. But the dramatic terra-cottas include a replica of the cross-legged Herakles (B *13*) and another which is extremely like, if not actually a replica of, the seated man with a purse in the New York series (B 12*e*); these two must be at least as early as 350. Of the others the man with a pitcher (B 28), of which there is a replica in the Louvre

---

[1] *BCH*, 31 (1907) 430, 499 f.; Vallois, *BCH*, 46 (1922), 96 f. Cf. Buschor, *Ath. Mitt.*, 53 (1928), 96 f. (Athens).

from Cyprus and another extremely close relative from Cyrene in the British Museum, also belongs to Middle Comedy rather than New, but a mask of a slave with trumpet mouth and the beard shown by incisions inside the trumpet seems to me to belong to New Comedy (C 63) and is one of the few New Comedy monuments which can be confidently dated in the fourth century.

Another is provided by a terra-cotta mask of the leading old man, No. 3 in Pollux' list, which was found in the Chatby Necropolis at Alexandria (C 64); the finds here all seem to date from the last third of the fourth century, and the leading old man is one of the masks introduced for New Comedy, so that here again we have some evidence that these masks were introduced before the end of the fourth century. This brings us to the Hellenistic period. Alexandria had its own group of tragic poets, known as the Pleiad, in the early third century, and its own Guild of Artists of Dionysos.[1] In the great procession organised by Ptolemy Philadelphos,[2] which included Silens and Satyrs in quantity and such figures as a man in tragic robes and mask with a golden horn of plenty, called Eniautos (year), the Artists of Dionysos were led by Philikos the poet, priest of Dionysos. This Philikos was one of the Pleiad, and had his picture painted by the famous painter Protogenes; it is possible that it is the original of the picture from Pompeii (A 58) with a poet contemplating a tragic female mask which is held by a servant; this is a variant of the old theme of the poet seeking inspiration from the mask as he writes.

The performances in the Greek cities of Asia Minor came under another Guild of Artists, the Guild of Ionia and the Hellespont. This was in existence by the third quarter of the third century.[3] The geographical range implied in the title is very wide, and perhaps included Amisos on the South shore of the Black Sea and Selymbria on the North coast of

[1] Cf. Pickard-Cambridge, *Festivals*, 289 f.
[2] Athenaeus, 198*c*.
[3] Cf. Pickard-Cambridge, *Festivals*, 298 f.

the Sea of Marmara. At any rate it is convenient to mention
these two places here. Amisos (not far from Sinope, the
home of Diphilos) has yielded a number of terra-cotta
statuettes and masks; those of New Comedy are of well-
known types—youth, slaves, and hetairai—and there is no
need to describe them in detail; they are pleasing and careful
examples, probably of the second century B.C. More interesting is the statuette of the tragic Herakles (A 75), wearing
the long high-girded robe, and boots with thick soles, and
carrying a mask with a high *onkos*. This was probably not
made later than the first century B.C. and is evidence for the
high-soled boots at that time. Selymbria has produced a
pair of very pretty comic masks mounted on disks (C 67),
the curly-headed youth and the wimpled hetaira.

The headquarters of the Ionian and Hellespontine Guild
was originally at Teos but was subsequently at Ephesos and
at various other places. Teos is not very far from Myrina,
and it has been suggested that the large numbers of dramatic
terra-cottas manufactured at Myrina reflect the dramatic
practice of this guild. This seems likely, but by the time of
the Myrina terra-cottas (most of the dramatic terra-cottas
can be dated in the second century although some of them
are later) [1] practice would seem to have been standardised
over the Greek world. A few tragic terra-cottas and many
comic terra-cottas were found at Myrina; some have been
published in the official account [2] of the excavations and
many more are credibly asserted to come from there. There
is a wide range of comic types and most of the masks which
Pollux mentions are found; moreover in most cases not only
the mask but the whole actor was represented and the figure
is seen in action: thus the procurer (C 65) walks forward in
an elaborate cloak with a huge wreath round his head; the
foreigner in the *eikonikos* mask (C 66) stands rather super-
ciliously with his hands in the folds of the long cloak which
falls to his ankles; the parasite (C 69) is shivering hungrily

[1] Cf. D. Burr, *Terra-cottas from Myrina.*
[2] Pottier and Reinach, *Nécropole de Myrina.*

huddled up in his small cloak and short chiton, carrying his own oil bottle and scraper because he is too poor to have a slave; the soldier (C 68) wears a civilian cloak and is evidently lovelorn like Polemon in Menander's *Perikeiromene*; the hetaira's maid (C 75), wearing only a chiton but a smartly arranged chiton, is making a pert reply to one of her mistress's lovers; and the straight-haired slave (C 70) is finishing a lengthy oration.

To the second century also belong the tragic and comic masks of a marble frieze from the gymnasium at Pergamon (A 77c, C 72)—an old woman and a young woman and a fair-haired man of tragedy, and a cook (tettix) of comedy—and the terra-cotta statuette of the tragic messenger (A 76). The masks on the marble frieze are set in an ivy spray like the masks on the Delos mosaic (C 61), but the leaves and fruit are much thicker than on the mosaic and more like the rich garlands in which masks are set on some of the Pompeian mosaics. Pergamon under her kings took an interest in drama and in the Ionian and Hellespontine Guild. A theatre was built at the beginning of the second century with a wooden stage-building, but this was rebuilt in stone at the end of the century.

At one moment in the later second century the guild moved its headquarters to Ephesos. Here a theatre had been built in the third century and was rebuilt in the second century.[1] This rebuilding gave the typical late Hellenistic form with a high stage over the *proskenion* and wide openings in the background. The theatre of Ephesos was peculiar in having an unusually long stage-building so that the ends stretched a considerable distance beyond the orchestra. This meant in practice that actors entering from the wings came out of the outside sections of the stage-building instead of coming from beyond it. A more usual form can be seen in the reconstructions of the theatre at Priene.[2] The theatre here was built in the fourth century

---

[1] Bulle, *Untersuchungen*, 253.
[2] Cf. Pickard-Cambridge, *Theatre*, 202.

and rebuilt about the middle of the second century. The rebuilt theatre had a high stage above a *proskenion* wall, the columns of which were arranged to hold wooden panels; the stage was longer than the stage-building which formed its background so that entrance from the wings would appear to be round the ends of the stage-building, and the background was formed of three wide openings set between narrow walls. These openings would take wooden panels of the kind called *thyromata* in the inscription from the theatre at Oropos.[1] This then is a standard type of late Hellenistic theatre with variations in different theatres. Bulle [2] assumes that the wide openings really were used as openings, and has very ingeniously reconstructed many of the pictures of comedy so that the figures are placed inside them. Thus for him the Dioskourides mosaic of the women at breakfast (C *19*) is a picture of such an opening; the steps lead down from the opening on to the stage and the women are arranged inside the opening. He believes that in theatres of this kind the action took place not on the stage but in the openings. This would increase quite unnecessarily the acoustic difficulties of an enormous open-air theatre; and if the Boscoreale picture of houses (C *23*) is in fact a copy of a comedy scene in a late Hellenistic theatre, the scenery included a practicable door in the front wall of the painted architecture. This suggests that the *thyroma* was a wooden panel filling the opening and including when necessary a practicable door; the action took place in front of the *thyroma* whether it was nominally taking place inside the house or not.

We are not only dependent on Boscoreale for an idea of the *thyromata*. Vitruvius (vii, 5, 5) describes a scene painted in a small theatre at Tralles in Asia Minor sometime before his day and probably in the second century. It had painted 'columns, statues, centaurs supporting architraves, domes, projecting gables, cornices with lion heads, and over that an

---

[1] See above p. 140.
[2] *Untersuchungen*, 277 f.

upper scene with round buildings, temple fronts, and half gables'. This is exactly the kind of illusionistic architecture which we find in Boscoreale and is here attested for a small theatre in Asia Minor.

It is probably not chance that the earliest monuments which show tragic actors with thick soles to their boots are dated at about the same time as the introduction of the *thyromata*. Priene itself, besides a number of dramatic terra-cottas which do not need specific mention, gives us a fine example of the *kothornos* with thick soles—they are worn by the personification of Tragedy on the relief showing the Apotheosis of Homer (A 78). The connecting link is the raised stage which seems to have been introduced in many theatres when the stage-building was rebuilt to accommodate *thyromata*, and indeed although a raised stage could have been and may have been introduced without *thyromata*, *thyromata* only have meaning if used as the background of the raised stage. Two objects were achieved by the heightened soles: the heroes and heroines looked more stately and it was possible for those occupying the lower rows of the theatre to see their feet.

VI. CONCLUSION

DRAMATIC monuments have so far been grouped under the areas which produced them. It is time now to attempt to sketch a general history. The origins lie in the Mycenaean age,[1] when we have evidence both for masks and for the worship of Dionysos and Artemis but not yet, I think, for Ortheia—the third deity whose cult we know admitted pre-dramatic dances. For the history of theatre production we can be content with the statement that pre-dramatic dances were very old and very widespread: in archaic, as distinct from Mycenaean, times they existed in the Greek cities of Asia Minor, in the Peloponnese, Attica, and Boeotia, and as they can be traced back to the early seventh century and even before, they were presumably taken by Greek colonists to the West. They survived long after the institution of the Athenian dramatic festivals. For this we have the testimony of Aristotle, of the various writers quoted by Athenaeus, and the monuments, particularly the various original local types of comic performer, whom we have seen in Corinth and the West, and the phallic procession on the late relief from Ephesos described in the last chapter. But when the Athenian dramatic festivals were instituted they exercised a powerful influence on the surviving pre-dramatic performances, which then became sub-dramatic: we have noted for instance that the Corinthian padded dancers had adopted the sleeves of the Athenian comic actors by the early fourth century, and Rhinthon of Tarentum, who made the South Italian *phlyakes* literary in the very late fourth and early third century, wrote parodies of Euripides in broad Doric, which revived on a small scale the mythological parodies of Old and Middle Comedy in the New Comedy

[1] See most recently Sir John Forsdyke on the Harvester Vase from Hagia Triada, *Journal of the Warburg and Courtauld Institutes*, 1954, 1, and Möbius, *Arch. Anz.*, 1954, 209 f.

period. Similarly we may suppose in the fifth century inter-change of ideas between Athens and the local comedies of Syracuse, Megara, and Boeotia.

The essential elements of Athenian dramatic costume can be found in these pre-dramatic performances: masks, the sleeved chiton and the boots of tragedy, the tights and padding of comedy. Choruses of fat Komasts singing songs on themes which recurred frequently in comedy, of men representing nymphs or ugly old women, of men disguised as animals, perhaps also in the late sixth century dances without song of men disguised as satyrs, all preceded the institution of the Athenian festivals. The choruses could perform anywhere, but it would at least be convenient if the spectators could watch them from some kind of grand-stand such as was adopted in Athens at least in the early sixth century for other kinds of contest. When there was a leader and he sang and danced a solo, it would be con-venient if he were raised above the level of the chorus; at the wedding of Agariste Hippokleides called for a table to dance on, and Thespis, the founder of Attic tragedy, is credited with a wagon. We may therefore suppose that the earliest performances of drama in the Athenian agora had at least a primitive low stage and raised seats round the dancing floor —the name of this *orchestra* survived in the Agora after the theatre of Dionysos was built, and these minimum require-ments were necessary for local comedy elsewhere.

The architectural evidence suggests that the Athenian theatre was rebuilt four times and we can therefore speak of the pre-Periclean theatre, the Periclean theatre, the theatre of Lykourgos, the late Hellenistic theatre, and the Roman theatre. The pre-Periclean theatre was constructed in the early fifth century, certainly before the earliest surviving play of Aeschylus, the *Persae*, which was produced in 472. This already needs (as does Phrynichos' *Phoinissai* which was produced four years earlier) a solid background to form Dareios' tomb; whether the ghost appeared on the roof or through a practicable door half-masked by a screen, the

actor had appeared in the previous scene as the messenger
and must have been able to get off, change mask and clothes,
and come on again without being seen by the audience until
he appeared above his tomb. As Aeschylus took this play
to Syracuse, similar arrangements must have been possible
there, and the curious passage about the comic poet Phormis,
the contemporary of Epicharmos, using purple hangings
instead of skins also implies a background for comedy in
Syracuse.

Aeschylus in his plays is so keenly aware of the possibilities of spectacle of every kind that we must believe that
the main equipment of the Periclean theatre was already in
use in his day. The pre-Periclean theatre must have already
had a low stage, up the steps of which Klytemnaistra could
entice Agamemnon, a wide central doorway through which
a platform could be rolled to display Orestes seated among
the Furies, a high platform from which the watchman could
open the *Agamemnon*, a crane by which Eos removed the
body of Memnon, and movable screens to represent the
rocks of the Caucasus in the *Prometheus*. The chief additions
of the Periclean theatre were wide wings, which gave the
stage an architectural framework but were not in any other
sense part of the scenery, and two small doors on either side
of the wider central door which could be used for separate
houses in comedy; these houses could be isolated from each
other by curtains. The new technique of perspective and
shading made more realistic backgrounds possible, but the
intervals for scene-changing did not allow for much more
than the carrying on or off of the minimum of screens,
statues, and altars necessary to show that for the next play
the scene had changed to a deserted island, the forecourt of
a Homeric palace, or a street of private houses in contemporary Athens. We may imagine the essential background as having a central door with pediment and columns
and two side doors with flat porches above them (or at any
rate flat roofs), which could serve both for the high platform
on which gods appeared in tragedy and for the roof scenes

of comedy. Perhaps the row of wooden columns along the backwall which is amply attested on South Italian vases between 360 and 320 is a fourth-century development, heralding the later stone backgrounds. The low stage itself was probably mounted by portable flights of steps which could be placed opposite whatever doors were is use for the particular play. We have always to remind ourselves that realism is a relative term and that an ancient Greek audience would have been as troubled by our footlights as we are by a palace door on a deserted island.

The clue to understanding costume lies in Aristotle's remark that the heroes of tragedy are better and the heroes of comedy worse than ourselves. Aristophanes had already said that the heroes of tragedy wear much more dignified robes than we do (*Frogs* 1061). There is no suggestion that the costume of Agamemnon should be historically accurate, only that it should be magnificent. The Athenian monumental evidence for the fifth and early fourth century agrees with this; costume appears to change slightly with the slight changes of contemporary fashion, and the hairdressing of the masks is in line with contemporary hairdressing. So we should imagine the heroes and heroines with their long elaborately patterned robes as not essentially unlike the richest and most elegant Athenians (though more magnificent and equipped with long sleeves and special footwear). Only the long supple boot, elaborately patterned for men but simpler for women and for the chorus, and perhaps the use of sleeves marked the performers in tragedy as servants of Dionysos, but the satyr play followed each group of tragedies and there members of Dionysos' train appeared as artists had represented them from the early sixth century: Papposilenos white and hairy, the satyrs red with tail and phallos, snub-nose, and horse-ears.

Aristotle's judgment on the characters of comedy is immediately intelligible when we consider the illustrations of comedy, which are known in quantity from the time of Aristophanes to the third quarter of the fourth century, by

when Aristotle had formulated the main doctrines of the
Poetics. Comedy took over and modified the costume of pre-
dramatic dancers: ugly masks, tights covering padding and
supporting the phallos as the dramatic skin of male
characters, white tights covering the padding as the dramatic
skin of female characters, and over the tights other garments
as worn by the kind of Athenians whom the aristocrat could
easily confuse with slaves. In mythological comedy the
contrast between earthy appearance and sentiments on the
one hand and divine and heroic names on the other was
continually exploited. When Aristophanes was serious, the
improbability of such figures having serious views made
their serious views more memorable.

Plato tells us that a foreigner who wanted to be a tragic
poet had to win his spurs in Athens, and we know how
ardently Dionysios I of Syracuse desired Athenian recognition for his tragedy. We have records of Athenian poets and
actors who went abroad and of foreign playwrights and
actors who came to Athens in the early fourth century.
When therefore we find on vases from Tarentum, Paestum,
and Campania the same tragic costume worn by the
characters of Athenian tragic stories and the same comic
costume with minor local variations worn by the characters
of comedy, we can assume that Athenian theatre practice
was the norm and that Athenian comedy as well as tragedy
was exported to the West. Then we may reasonably go
further and suppose that the discovery of terra-cotta statuettes (originals, local replicas, or local variants) of Athenian
comic actors all over the Greek world from Cyrene and
Paestum in the West to Priene and South Russia in the East
indicates a widespread knowledge of Athenian comedy,
whether based on the circulation of texts or on local performances. Drama in this period is an Athenian export and
not yet an international possession.

The rebuilding of the Athenian theatre by Lykourgos
about 330 marks more than an architectural change. The
spatial relations between actors, chorus, and audience

remained the same, but the stage buildings, wings and back-ground, were now reconstructed in stone, and this must have been more obtrusive than the preceding wooden structures and more difficult to mask with screens. At the same time the *onkos* masks were introduced, so that for the first time the heroes and heroines of tragedy looked not indeed like their Mycenaean originals but more like Athenians of the time of Thespis than their fourth-century contemporaries. Aristotle had introduced historical scholar-ship into the *Poetics*; now it invaded the theatre, if we may assume that the new masks looked archaic. The great fifth-century classics were acted from an established text, and the mythological heroes and heroines of both old and new tragedies were relegated to a distant past by their masks and their costumes.

Tragedy became hieratic and comedy became respectable. We have enough evidence from literary fragments and from vases and terra-cottas to tell that the character of comedy changed in the fourth century from brilliant, intellectual, political, obscene phantasy to the comedy of intrigue and the comedy of manners, and we can see that new masks were introduced for the worried lover and the distressed maiden by the middle of the century. But in the last quarter of the century not only new masks but also new costumes without padding and with long chitons were introduced, and the fathers and sons of Menander's comedy looked like well-to-do Athenians of their own day. This meant that New Comedy showed almost no trace of its origin in pre-dramatic dances; it is true that the ancestry of some of the masks, particularly the slaves and the ugly old women, can be traced right back, but the ugly old women were only minor characters and the slave now wore a respectable chiton which reached nearly to his knees. This is a complete revolution, and New Comedy is a new form of drama with a long history before it, which shows no signs of ending with the twentieth century.

Hieratic tragedy and respectable comedy were the international drama of the Hellenistic world, and besides being performed in Greek cities made their way to Rome in Latin translation soon after the middle of the third century B.C. We know a good deal about the guilds of the Artists of Dionysos formed in various parts of the Greek world on the model of the Athenian guild, which had probably been started by the middle of the fourth century. We also know something of the dramatic festivals, particularly at Athens, Delos, and Delphi. From Tarentum Drakon went to Delphi and Delos and Livius Andronicus to Rome. The fact that actors from all over the Greek world performed in competition with each other at many different festivals suggests that production must have become largely standardised. The wooden stage-building in the theatre of Delos was rebuilt in stone during the course of the third century and probably became very like that in the theatre of Lykourgos. The comic masks on the mosaic floor of a second-century house in Delos can be paralleled from all over the Greek world by masks in many different materials dating from the fourth century B.C. to the fourth century A.D. and later. Hellenistic theatre production was international.

One great change was made in the second century, the removal of the action from the low stage connected with the orchestra to a high stage some thirteen feet above the orchestra. This in fact destroyed the link between the audience and the actors, and confined the actors to a distinct world of their own, which the audience observed from afar. In this way it is the beginning of the modern theatre with its dark auditorium and illuminated stage, but before this change could be perfected many centuries elapsed. The high stage became possible when the large chorus disappeared, and we have evidence that in the Hellenistic age even classical tragedies were acted with a reduced chorus. The reduction of the number of the chorus is of course itself only a sign of a much more important change: Thespis' actor had been the leader of the chorus, and all through the fifth century the chorus had been intermediaries in more than one sense between the audience and the characters. In tragedy and comedy the orchestra, where they sang and danced or stood and waited, was between the auditorium and the stage; in tragedy they represented ordinary men and women of the heroic past intermediate in status between the audience and the kings and queens on the stage, intermediate also as ideal commentators on the action; in comedy although they might take a great part in the action, in the *parabasis* at least they spoke as ordinary Athenian citizens. From the time of Agathon in tragedy (late fifth to early fourth century) and from the time of Aristophanes' *Ekklesiazousai* (391) the chorus began to sing transferable interludes instead of special songs composed for the particular play. The fragments of Menander show no signs of choral lyrics or of commentary in the dialogue by the leader of the chorus. When the chorus only appeared to sing interludes, they were no longer intermediaries in any sense. Drama now consisted only of characters and spectators, and it was logical to emphasise their separation by the introduction of the high stage which gave the characters a world apart. Archaeological evidence suggests that theatres in Greece, Asia Minor, and the West were rebuilt in the second century to accommodate the high stage.

The background of the high stage was formed by large panels set in wide openings and surrounding the three practicable doors (or masking doors which were not needed). They probably gave a better field for illusionistic scene painting than anything that had been known in the theatre before, and in some theatres, which had a specially long stage-building, additional openings incorporated further panels which could be revolved; sometimes only the panels turned, sometimes they took a section of the stage with them. This was the furthest that the Greek theatre got towards creating a separate and complete world for the characters of a particular play, and, where the revolving panels were used, a world that could be partly changed within the compass of a single play. This world was as three dimensional as perspective and shading could make it, but it was not, if we may judge from Boscoreale, the world of everyday reality; comedy played before a rich man's dream of town houses, tragedy before fantastic palaces and temples, and the satyr play in some imagined Arcady. It was therefore not out of keeping with the fantastic nature of the background that the tragic hero and heroine should now at last be mounted on high soles so as both to look more stately and be better seen by the audience.

It only remained for this imaginary architecture to be solidified to form the typical *scaenae frons* of the Graeco-Roman theatre, but that belongs to the history of the Roman Stage rather than to Greek theatre production.

LIST OF MONUMENTS

This list of monuments mentioned in the foregoing pages is extracted from my fuller list, which is deposited in the Classical Institute of London University. The numbers in brackets refer to the fuller list. The primary division was into A. Tragedy, B. Old and Middle Comedy, C. New Comedy, D. Satyr play, E. Theatres and Scenery, F. Origins. For the present list D and E have been included under A, and I have therefore, where necessary, added D and E to the numbers in brackets to distinguish these objects. Within these categories the monuments are divided by localities corresponding to my chapter headings: (i) Athens, (ii) Sicily and Italy, (iii) Mainland Greece, (iv) Islands, (v) Asia Minor and Africa. Within the geographical sections the monuments are grouped in broad chronological divisions; I have been content for the most part to date by twenty-five year periods; this span seems to me the smallest that is safe for the production date of the objects in question. Within these periods the objects are as far as possible arranged in the order in which they appear in the book. My bibliography is not intended to be complete but only to refer to handy illustrations or discussions relevant to my present purpose.

I have used the following abbreviations:

A.A.	Archäologischer Anzeiger (of J.D.A.I.).
A.J.A.	American Journal of Archaeology.
A.M.	Athenische Mitteilungen.
A.R.V.	J. D. Beazley, *Attic Red-figure Vase-painters*.
A.Z.	Archäologische Zeitung.
B.C.H.	Bulletin de Correspondance Hellénique.
B.D.	M. Bieber, *Denkmäler zum Theaterwesen*.
B.H.T.	M. Bieber, *History of the Greek and Roman Theatre*.
B.S.A.	Annual of the British School at Athens.
C.V.	Corpus Vasorum Antiquorum.
J.D.A.I.	Jahrbuch des deutschen archäologischen Instituts.
J.H.S.	Journal of Hellenic Studies.
J.OE.A.I.	Jahreshefte des oesterreichischen archäologischen Instituts.
Mon. Piot.	Monuments et Mémoires de la Fondation Eugène Piot.
M.U.Z.	Malerei und Zeichnung.
N.Sc.	Notizie degli Scavi.
P.C.D.	A. W. Pickard-Cambridge, *Dithyramb, Tragedy, and Comedy*.
P.C.T.	A. W. Pickard-Cambridge, *Theatre of Dionysus at Athens*.
P.C.F.	A. W. Pickard-Cambridge, *Dramatic Festivals of Athens*.
R.M.	Römische Mitteilungen.
S.C.T.	A. K. H. Simon, *Comicae Tabellae*.
T.F.I.	A. D. Trendall, *Frühitaliotische Vasen*.
T.P.P.	A. D. Trendall, *Paestan Pottery*.
T.P.P.S.	A. D. Trendall, Paestan Pottery: a revision and a Supplement, in *Papers of the British School at Rome*, 20 (1952).
W.A.L.A.	T. B. L. Webster, *Art and Literature in Fourth-Century Athens*.
W.E.A.	T. B. L. Webster, in *Arkhaiologike Ephemeris* (forthcoming).
W.G.C.C.	T. B. L. Webster, Greek Comic Costume, in *Bulletin of the John Rylands Library*, 36 (1954).
W.G.M.	T. B. L. Webster, Masks on Gnathia vases, in *J.H.S.*, 71 (1951), 222.
W.L.G.C.	T. B. L. Webster, *Studies in Later Greek Comedy*.
W.W.S.	T. B. L. Webster, Scenic notes, in *Wiener Studien*, 69 (forthcoming).

A. TRAGEDY AND SATYR PLAY

I. ATHENS

1 (E 28) ODYSSEUS AND THE SIRENS.   Black-figure lekythos, 500/475.
Athens, N.M. 1130.   Haspels, *Attic Black-figured Lekythoi*, 217, no. 27, pl. 29, 3; Kenner,
J.OE.A.I., 39 (1952), 51.
See above p. 16.

2 (D 27) SATYR CHORUSMAN.   Red-figure cup, 500/475.
Munich 2657.   *A.R.V.* 312, no. 191; Brommer, *Satyrspiele*, fig. 5.
See above p. 31.

3 (D 19) MASKED SATYR CHORUSMEN BUILDING A COUCH.
Red-figure hydria, 475/450.
Boston 03.788.   *A.R.V.* 377, no. 5; Brommer, *Satyrspiele*, fig. 6.
See above p. 31.

4 (1)   BOY HOLDING WHITE MASK OF GIRL.
Red-figure oenochoe fragment, 475/50.
Athens, Agora Museum, P 11810.   Talcott, *Hesperia*, 8 (1939), 269, fig. 1; P.C.F., fig.
25; *Greece and Rome*, 1954, pl. 141; W.W.S., I.
See above pp. 37, 38, 39, 52.

5 (D 12) CHORUS OF GOAT MEN AND FLUTE-PLAYER.
Red-figure kalyx-krater, 475/50.
British Museum, E 467.   *A.R.V.* 420, no. 21; B.D., no. 39; P.C.D., fig. 14; Rumpf,
J.D.A.I., 65/6 (1950/1), 171.
See above p. 32.

6 (104) MAENAD AND FLUTE-PLAYER.   Red-figure pelike, 475/50.
Berlin, inv. 3223.   *A.R.V.* 397, no. 39; Weinreich, *Epigrammstudien*, pl. 1.
See above p. 37 f.

7 (2)   MEN PREPARING FOR FEMALE CHORUS.   Red-figure pelike, 450/30.
Boston 98.883.   *A.R.V.* 655, no. 38; B.H.T., fig. 108; P.C.F., fig. 39; *Greece and Rome*,
1954, pl. 141.
See above pp. 37, 39, 41.

8 (E 27) EURIPIDES, *IPHIGENEIA IN TAURIS.*
Red-figure kalyx-krater, 400/375.
Ferrara T 1145.   *A.R.V.* 875; Metzger, *Réppresentations*, 287, no. 39.
See above pp. 15, 102; pl. 7.

9 (93)   ACTORS AND CHORUS OF SATYR PLAY.
Red-figure volute-krater, 400/375.
Naples 3240   *A.R.V.* 849, no. 1; *B.D.*, no. 34; B.H.T., fig. 20; P.C.D., fig. 28; W.A.L.A.,
pl. 3*b*.
See above pp. 31, 37, 40, 43, 46, 52, 111; pl. 8.

10 (73) EURIPIDES, *ANDROMEDA.*   Red-figure kalyx-krater.
Berlin, inv. 3237.   B.D., no. 40; B.H.T., fig. 61–4; P.C.F., fig. 164.
See above p. 40.

11 (11) DIONYSOS AND ACTORS.   Marble relief, 400/375.
Athens, N.M. 1500.   B.D., no. 41; B.H.T., fig. 66; P.C.F., fig. 26; Buschor, *Studies
presented to D. M. Robinson*, 2, 91.
See above pp. 41, 43, 46.

12 (41)   ACTORS AND CHORUS.   Red-figure fragments, 400/375.
Würzburg.   *A.R.V.* 965; P.C.F., fig. 40; *Greece and Rome*, 1954, pl. 142; Buschor, *loc. cit.*; Bulle, *Corolla Curtios*, pl. 54–6.
See above pp. 40, 48, 52.

13 (64)   PAPPOSILENOS WITH INFANT DIONYSOS HOLDING MASK.
Marble copy, original early 4th cent.
Athens, N.M. 257.   B.D., no. 37; P.C.F., fig. 29.
See above p. 42.

14 (63)   MUSE HOLDING BEARDED MASK.
Marble copy, original early 4th cent.
Mantua.   Bieber, *J.D.A.I.*, 32 (1917), 79; P.C.F., fig. 27.
See above p. 42 n. 1

15 (47)   MASK OF YOUTH.   Marble, 350/25.
Athens, Kerameikos Museum.   *A.A.*, 1942, fig. 26/7.
See above pp. 42, 48.

16 (77)   MASK OF OLD WOMAN.   Marble, 350/25.
Athens, Small Acropolis Museum, inv. 2294.   Walter, *Beschreibung*, no. 415.
See above pp. 42, 53.

17 (78)   MASK OF SHORN MAIDEN.   Marble, 350/25.
Athens, Small Acropolis Museum, inv. 2367+2353.   Walter, *Beschreibung*, no. 417.
See above pp. 42, 54.

18 (76)   MASK OF WOMAN WITH LONG HAIR.   Marble, 350/25.
Athens, Small Acropolis Museum, inv. 2292.   Walter, *Beschreibung*, no. 413; P.C.F., fig. 37; *Greece and Rome*, 1954, pl. 143.
See above p. 42.

19 (79)   MASK OF WOMAN WITH LONG HAIR.   Marble, 350/25.
Athens, Small Acropolis Museum, inv. 2295.   Walter, *Beschreibung*, no. 420.
See above p. 42.

20 (151)   ACTOR DRESSED AS WOMAN, HOLDING MASK.
Marble relief, 350/25.
Copenhagen, Ny Carlsberg Glyptotek, 233.   *Billedtavler*, pl. 17.
See above pp. 43, 151; pl. 9.

21 (19)   AESCHYLUS(?) HOLDING BEARDED MASK
Marble copy, original about 330.
Rome, Vatican, Braccio Nuovo 53.   B.D. no. 27; B.H.T., fig. 35; P.C.F., fig. 45; *Greece and Rome*, 1954, pl. 144; Webster, *J.H.S.*, 71 (1951), 229; *Hermes*, 82 (1954), 307.
See above pp. 43, 46.

22 (7)   EURIPIDES HOLDING BEARDED MASK.
Marble relief, original about 330.
Constantinople.   Mendel, *Catalogue*, ii, no. 574; B.D., no. 29; B.H.T., fig. 60; P.C.F., fig. 48; Webster, *J.H.S.*, 71 (1951), 229.
See above p. 48.

23 (110)   ACTOR IN BEARDED MASK, BOOTS, AND CLOAK.
Bronze statuette, 1st to 3rd cent. A.D.
Athens, Agora Museum.   *Hesperia* 6 (1937), 351; P.C.F., fig. 161.
See above p. 55.

24 (109)   MASK OF WOMAN.   Marble mask, 4th cent. A.D.
Athens, Agora Museum, S 1144.   *Hesperia* 10 (1950), 292; P.C.F., fig. 67.
See above p. 55.

II. SICILY AND ITALY

25 (D 5)   EURIPIDES, *CYCLOPS*.   South Italian kalyx-krater, 425/400.
British Museum.   T.F.I., no. A 139, pl. 12*b*; Brommer, *Satyrspiele*, fig. 8.
See above p. 101.

26 (E 26)   EUROPA AND SARPEDON.   South Italian bell-krater, 400/380.
New York 16.140.   T.F.I., no. B 88; B.H.T., figs. 200–1; P.C.T., fig. 30.
See above pp. 12, 103, 105.

27 (53)   SATYR CHORUSMEN.   South Italian bell-krater, 400/375.
Sydney 47.05.   Tillyard, *Hope Vases*, no. 210, pl. 30; Trendall, *Handbook to Nicholson Museum*, pl. 10.
See above, p. 111.

28 (150)   TRIUMPH OF AN ACTOR.   South Italian bell-krater, 400/375.
Rome, Vatican T 7.   Trendall, *Vasi Dipinti*, 1, pl. 23*b*.
See above p. 118.

29 (48)   DIONYSOS HOLDING MASK.   South Italian bell-krater, 375/350.
Bari 1364.   T.F.I., 26 n. 41; B.H.T., fig. 40; P.C.F., fig. 41.
See above p. 42.

30 (E 29)   IPHIGENEIA IN TAURIS.   Apulian volute-krater, 375/350.
Naples 3233.   F.R., pl. 148; B.H.T., fig. 69; P.C.T., fig. 19.
See above p. 102.

31 (E 34)   PELOPS AND OINOMAOS.   Apulian situla, 375/350.
Rome, Villa Giulia.   P.C.T., fig. 23.
See above p. 106.

32 (E 33)   DEATH OF MELEAGER.   Apulian volute-krater, 350/25.
Naples, Santangelo 11.   P.C.T., fig. 22.
See above p. 106.

33 (49)   MESSENGER.   Apulian kantharos, 350/25.
Ruvo, Jatta 1394.   W.G.M., no. 44; P.C.F., fig. 47.
See above pp. 51, 111.

34 (3)   ACTOR HOLDING FAIR MASK.   Gnathia fragment, 350/40.
Würzburg 832.   B.H.T., fig. 216; P.C.F., fig. 34/5; W.G.M., no. 37; *Greece and Rome* 1954, pl. 144; W.A.L.A., pl. 3*a*.
See above pp. 44, 46, 111, 118.

35 (4)   CHARACTERS AND STAGE-BUILDING.   Gnathia fragment, 350/40.
Würzburg.   P.C.T., fig. 55–6; Rumpf, *M.U.Z.*, 136, pl. 44/1.
See above p. 105; pl. 10.

36 (6)   PROLOGUE OF AESCHYLUS, *EUMENIDES*.
                                          Gnathia kalyx-krater, 350/40.
Leningrad, St. 349.   P.C.T., fig. 11; P.C.F., fig. 177.
See above pp. 103, 107.

37 (153)   MASK OF YOUTH.   Gnathia oenochoe, 350/25.
Copenhagen, N.M., Chr. viii, 70.
See above pp. 49, 111.

38 (5)   PROLOGUE OF EURIPIDES, *IPHIGENEIA IN TAURIS*.
                                          Campanian bell-krater, 350/25.
Louvre K 404.   Beazley, *J.H.S.*, 63 (1943), 82; B.H.T., fig. 175; P.C.T., fig. 58.
See above p. 104.

39 (13)   MADNESS OF HERAKLES.   Paestan kalyx-krater, 360/40.
Madrid 11094.   T.P.P.S., no. 39; P.P., pl. 6/7; B.D., no. 43; B.H.T., fig. 351/2; P.C.T.,
fig. 83-4.
See above p. 107.

40 (D 8)   SILENOS AND SPHINX.   Paestan bell-krater, 350/25.
Naples 2846.   T.P.P.S., no. 155; P.P., pl. 21a; B.D., no. 36; Brommer, *Satyrspiele*,
fig. 44.
See above p. 111.

41 (E 30)   EURIPIDES, *IPHIGENEIA IN TAURIS*   Apulian volute-krater, 330/20.
Leningrad, St. 420.   P.C.T., fig. 15.
See apove p. 103.

42 (12)   MEDEA.   Apulian volute-krater, 330/20.
Munich 810 (Jahn).   B.D., no. 42; H.T., figs. 72-5; P.C.T., fig. 21.
See above pp. 103, 106, 111.

43 (E 31)   EURIPIDES, *HYPSIPYLE*.   Apulian volute-krater, 330/20.
Naples 3255.   P.C.T., fig. 20.
See above pp. 104, 106, 110.

44 (E 32)   AESCHYLUS, *NIOBE*.   Apulian volute-krater, 330/20.
Naples 3246.   P.C.T., fig. 10.
See above p. 104.

45 (17)   MASK OF FIRST SHORN MAIDEN.   Gnathia oenochoe, 325/300.
Reading City Museum.   W.G.M., no. 5a, pl. 45c.
See above pp. 54, 111; pl. 11a.

46 (44)   MASK OF FAIRER MAN.   Gnathia oenochoe, 300/275.
Würzburg 841.   W.G.M., no. 3.
See above pp. 46, 111.

47 (10)   MASK OF FRESHLY HALF-SHORN WOMAN.
                                               Gnathia oenochoe, 300/275.
Louvre K 596.   W.G.M., no. 4; P.C.F., fig. 46.
See above pp. 54, 111, 117.

48 (16)   MASK OF SECOND SHORN MAIDEN.   Gnathia oenochoe, 300/275.
Louvre K 597.   W.G.M., no. 5, pl. 45b.
See above pp. 54, 111; pl. 11b.

49 (E 35)   STAGE-BUILDING.   South Italian terra-cotta, 300/275.
Naples, C.S. 362.   B.D., no. 23; B.H.T., fig. 353; P.C.T., fig. 82; T.P.P., 32.
See above p. 110.

50 (135)   MASK OF DARK MAN.   Paestan terra-cotta mask, 3rd/2nd cent.
Paestum, M.N., Case 50.
See above p. 122.

51 (136)   MASK OF FAIRER MAN.   Paestan terra-cotta mask, 3rd/2nd cent.
Paestum, M.N., Case 50.
See above p. 122.

52 (9)   ACTORS IN SCENERY.   Roman terra-cotta relief, 1st cent. B.C.
Rome, Terme 602.   B.D., no. 46; B.H.T., fig. 421; P.C.F., fig. 57; Webster, *Hermes*,
82 (1954), 299.
See above p. 28.

53 (70)   SCENE FOR TRAGEDY AND SATYR PLAY.
                       Paintings from cubiculum, Boscoreale, 1st cent. B.C.
New York.   B.H.T., figs. 344, 347; P.C.T., fig. 69; Rumpf, *J.H.S.*, 67 (1947), 18;
M.U.Z., pl. 54/3, 5.
See above pp. 26, 140.

GTP—M

54 (72)   MASK OF LONG-HAIRED PALE WOMAN.
                                    Silver cup from Boscoreale, 1st cent. B.C.
Louvre.   Héron de Villefosse, *Mon. Piot*, 5 (1899), 58; Schefold, *Bildnisse*, 167, fig. 4.
See above p. 53.

55 (71)   LYKOPHRON WITH MASK OF KASSANDRA.
                            Silver cup from Bernay-Berthouville, 1st cent. B.C.
Paris, Bibliothèque Nationale.   Schefold, *Bildnisse*, 226; Picard, *Mon. Piot*, 44, 53.
See above pp. 53, 54.

56 (22)   HEROINE, NURSE, AND WOMAN.
                    Painting on marble (from original of 340/30), 1st cent. B.C.
Naples 9563.   B.D., no. 47; B.H.T., fig. 423; P.C.F., fig. 70; Rumpf, *M.U.Z.*, 136;
Greece and Rome, 1954, pl. 143.
See above pp. 42, 53.

57 (20)   ACTOR AS YOUNG KING.
                            Painting (from original 310/280), 1st cent. B.C.
Naples 9019.   B.D., no. 44; B.H.T., fig. 217; P.C.F., fig. 43.
See above pp. 44, 45, 48, 152; pl. 13.

58 (45)   POET CONTEMPLATING MASK.
                            Painting (from original 300/275), 1st cent. B.C.
Naples 9036.   B.H.T., fig. 218; P.C.F., fig. 44.
See above p. 159.

59 (134)   MASKS ON TABLE.   Painting, 1st cent. B.C.
Pompeii, House of the Menander.   Maiuri, *Casa del Menandro*, fig. 51, pl. 13.
See above p. 49.

60 (25)   MASTER AND SERVANT.   Painting, 1st cent. A.D.
Palermo.   B.D., no. 50; B.H.T., fig. 512; P.C.F., fig. 76; Bieber, *R.M.*, 60/61
(1953/4) 103.
See above pp. 46, 51.

61 (18)   MASK OF YOUTH IN ARCHITECTURE.   Painting, 1st cent. A.D.
Naples (from House of the Gladiators).   B.D., no. 24.
See above p. 48.

62 (62)   MASK OF YOUNG MAN AND OLD MAN.   Painting, 1st cent. A.D.
Naples 8594.   P.C.T., fig. 93.
See above p. 49.

63 (26)   MAN WITH JUG AND WOMAN WITH CHILD.
                                            Painting, 1st cent. A.D.
Naples 9039.   B.D., no. 51; B.H.T., fig. 513; P.C.F., fig. 77.
See above p. 54.

64 (23)   HERAKLES, OLD MAN, YOUNG WOMAN, SEATED MAN.
                                            Painting, 1st cent. A.D.
Pompeii, House of the Centenary, atrium.   B.D., no. 48; B.H.T., fig. 522; P.C.F.,
fig. 72.
See above pp. 46, 51, 122.

65 (15)   MEDEA, OLD MAN, AND CHILDREN.   Painting, 1st cent. A.D.
Pompeii, House of the Centenary, triclinium.   B.D., no. 49; B.H.T., fig. 521; P.C.F.,
fig. 75.
See above pp. 51, 53, 54, 122.

66 (24*b*)   ACHILLES AND PRIAM.   Painting, 1st cent. A.D.
Pompeii, House of the Centenary, triclinium.   B.D., no. 49; B.H.T., fig. 520; P.C.F.,
fig. 74.
See above pp. 44, 46, 48, 122.

67 (24*a*) PRIAM AND HEKABE. Painting, 1st cent. A.D.
Pompeii, House of the Centenary, triclinium. B.D., no. 49; B.H.T., fig. 519; P.C.F., fig. 73.
See above pp. 46, 53, 122.

68 (23*a*) OLD MAN, YOUNG WOMAN, SEATED MAN. Painting, 1st cent. A.D.
Pompeii, I, vi, 11. Maiuri, *N.Sc.*, 1929, 408; B.H.T., fig. 523.
See above p. 123.

69 (140) YOUTH AND HEROINE. Painting, 1st cent. A.D.
Pompeii, I, vi, 11. Maiuri, *N.Sc.*, 1929, 411, fig. 32.
See above p. 124.

70 (36) GROUPS OF TRAGIC MASKS. Painting, 1st cent. A.D.
Pompeii, I, ii, 6. Robert, *A.Z.*, 1878, 13 f. (*a*) Robert, pl. 3/1; B.D., no. 63; P.C.F., fig. 71, (*b*) Robert, 20, (*c*) Robert, pl. 4/2, (*d*) Robert, pl. 5/1.
See above p. 124.

71 (118) MASKS OF TWO WOMEN AND BEARDED MAN.
Marble relief, 1st cent. A.D.
Pompeii, House of the Golden Cupids. *N.Sc.*, 1907, 561, fig. 11.
See above p. 127.

72 (119) MASK OF YOUTH. Marble relief, 1st cent. A.D.
Pompeii, House of the Golden Cupids. *N.Sc.*, 1907, 561, fig. 12.
See above p. 127.

73 (8) HEROINE, Ivory statuette, 2nd cent. A.D.
Paris, Petit Palais. B.D., no. 59; B.H.T., fig. 533; P.C.F., fig. 66.
See above pp. 44, 53.

III. MAINLAND GREECE

73*a* (37) MASK OF ORIENTAL. Terracotta (Thebes), 2nd cent. B.C.
Berlin 8328. B.D., no. 64; P.C.F. fig. 54.
See above p. 51.

IV. THE ISLANDS

74 (154) DIONYSOS RIDING LEOPARD. Mosaic, 200/150 B.C.
Delos, House of the Masks. Chamonard, *Délos*, XIV, pl. 3; Rumpf, *M.U.Z.*, pl. 56/5.
See above p. 151.

V. ASIA MINOR AND AFRICA

75 (51) HERAKLES. Terra-cotta statuette (Amisos), 2nd cent. B.C.
Louvre CA 1784. B.H.T., fig. 203; P.C.F., fig. 52.
See above pp. 44, 46, 160.

76 (32) MESSENGER. Terra-cotta statuette (Pergamon), 2nd cent. B.C.
Berlin 7365. B.D. no. 58; B.H.T., fig. 208; P.C.F., fig. 51.
See above pp. 51, 161.

77 (40, 107) MASKS OF WOMEN AND BEARDED MAN.
Marble frieze (Pergamon), 2nd cent. B.C.
Berlin. B.D., no. 69; P.C.F., fig. 53*a, b*.
See above p. 161.

78 (97) TRAGEDY WEARING MASK AND KOTHORNOI.
Apotheosis of Homer (Priene), 150/50.
British Museum 2191. P.C.F., fig. 194.
See above, pp. 44, 163; pl. 12.

79 (108) TRAGEDY WITH BEARDED MASK. Muse base (Halikarnassos), 150/50.
British Museum 1106. Winter, *Kunstgeschichte in Bildern*, 363/2.
See above pp. 44, 46.

B. OLD AND MIDDLE COMEDY

I. ATHENS

1 (2)   PERSEUS ON THE STAGE: MASK H (?).
                                                Red-figure oenochoe, 425/400.
Athens, Vlastos.   Brommer, *Satyrspiele*, fig. 17–19; Karouzou, *J.H.S.*, 65 (1945),
pl. 5; Van Hoorn, *Choes*, no. 276; W.E.A.
See above pp. 7, 20, 109; pl. 14.

2 (3)   HERAKLES IN A CENTAUR CHARIOT: MASKS, T, HERAKLES, N.
                                                Red-figure oenochoe, 425/400.
Louvre L 9.   *A.R.V.*, 848/22; Van Hoorn, *Choes*, no. 826; Rumpf, *A.J.A.*, 55 (1951),
8, figs. 5–7; W.E.A.; W.A.L.A., pl. 5a.
See above pp. 58, 61, 64, 65, 67.

3 (64)   YOUTH, ACTOR, AND DOG: MASK F.   Red-figure oenochoe, 425/400.
Louvre CA 2938.   Van Hoorn, *Choes*, no. 854; W.L.G.C., pl. 2a.
See above p. 63.

4 (1)   ZEUS AND OTHER ACTORS: MASKS, F, G, E, B, H.
                                                Red-figure oenochoe, 400/390.
Leningrad.   B.D., no. 97; B.H.T., fig. 121; P.C.F., fig. 80; Bethe, *Griechische Dichtung*,
pl. 8; Van Hoorn, *Choes*, no. 585; W.E.A.
See above pp. 61, 62, 63, 64, 66, 67, 115.

5 (399)   MAN ROWING FISH.   Polychrome oenochoe, 400/390.
British Museum 98.2–27.1.   Crosby, *Hesperia* 24 (1955), 82; W.W.S. III.
See above pp. 57, 102.

6 (402)   MEN CARRYING MEAT ON A SPIT.   Polychrome oenochoe, 400/390.
Athens, Agora Museum P 23907.   Crosby, *Hesperia*, 24 (1955), 80; W.W.S., III.
See above pp. 37, 102.

7 (403)   DIONYSOS AND PHOR (-TAX? MION?).   Polychrome oenochoe, 400/390.
Athens, Agora Museum, P 23985.   Crosby, *Hesperia*, 24 (1955), 81; W.W.S., III.
See above p. 61.

8 (99)   OLD MAN WITH STICK: MASK E.   Red-figure oenochoe, 400/390.
Athens, N.M. 17752.   Karouzou, *A.J.A.*, 50 (1946), 132 ff.; Van Hoorn, *Choes*, no. 117;
W.E.A.
See above p. 62.

9 (4)   MEMBERS OF FEMALE CHORUS: MASK T.
                                                Red-figure bell-krater, 390/370.
Heidelberg B 134.   Luschey, *Ganymed*, 74; W.L.G.C., pl. 2b; *Schweitzerfestschrift*, 261.
See above pp. 61, 65, 67; pl. 15a.

10 (24)   POET WITH MASKS A AND B.   Marble grave relief, 390/70.
Lyme Hall, Stockport.   P.C.F., fig. 89; Webster, *Studies presented to D. M. Robinson*,
I, 590; W.L.G.C., pl. 2.
See above pp. 56, 62, 64, 119; pl. 16.

11 (5–12)   (a) NURSE (U), (b) GIRL (V), (c) HERAKLES, (d) DISTRESSED MAN (L),
                   (e) MAN WITH BASKET (K), (f) MAN WITH WATERPOT (K),
                   (g) SEATED SLAVE (K).   Terra-cotta statuettes, 375/350.
New York 13.225.20 etc.   B.H.T., figs. 122–128; P.C.F., figs. 84–8, 112, 140, 141;
Webster, *Greek Terra-cottas*, pls. 27–33. Replicas or copies are known of (a) from Delphi, (b)
Olynthos, South Russia, Cyrenaica, (c) Paestum, (d) Olynthos (locally made, *Olynthos*, xiv,
378c, 380g), (f) Sicily, (g) Rhodes.
See above on (a) pp. 65, 70, 116, 144, (b) pp. 66, 70, 142, (c) pp. 56, 70, (d) pp. 63, 67, 70,
142; pl. 17a, (e) pp. 64, 70, (f) pp. 64, 67, 70, 71, (g) pp. 64, 70.

12 (13–18) (a) GIRL (V), (b) OLD WOMAN (R), (c) MAN WITH CLOAK OVER HEAD
            (D?), (d) PARASITE (Q), (e) SEATED MAN WITH PURSE (C), (f) MAN
            WITH SKIN CLOAK (L), (g) SEATED SLAVE (N).
                                        Terra-cotta statuettes, 375/350.
New York 13.225.28 etc.   B.H.T., figs. 129–135. Replicas or copies are known of (a) from
Olynthos, (b) from Paestum, (d) Olynthos, Egypt, (e) South Russia, perhaps Larisa, (f)
Olynthos, S. Russia, Paestum.
    See above on (a) pp. 73, 142, (b) pp. 56, 65, 73, (c) p. 73, (d) pp. 60, 64, 73, 82, 142,
(e) pp. 64, 73, 77, 158, (f) pp. 56, 67, 73, 142, (g) p. 71.

13 (20)   HERAKLES.   Terra-cotta statuette, 375/350.
British Museum 741 (Old C 80).   P.C.F., fig. 82. Found in Melos, replicas or copies
known from Athens (Pnyx), Larisa, Delphi, Thebes, Tarentum.
    See above pp. 61, 139, 144, 158; pl. 17c.

14 (21)   OLD MAN: MASK E.   Terra-cotta statuette, 375/50.
Oxford.
    See above pp. 62, 67; pl. 17b..

15 (256)   BEARDED MAN WITH HAND TO BROW: MASK L.
                                        Terra-cotta statuette, 375/50.
Athens, Agora Museum, T 1683.   D. B. Thompson, Hesperia, 21 (1952), 141, pl. 38,
no. 44; cf. British Museum Catalogue, no. 739.
    See above p. 63; pl. 18c.

16 (204)   BEARDED MAN WITH TORCH: MASK D.
                                        Terra-cotta statuette, 375/50.
Munich, inv. 6929.   B.D., no. 75; B.H.T., fig. 116.
    See above p. 63.

17 (232)   BEARDED MAN WITH BASKET: MASK P.
                                        Terra-cotta statuette, 375/50.
Boston 13.99.   B.H.T., fig. 93.
    See above p. 64.

18 (22)   PROCURESS AND BEARDED MAN: MASKS, U, H.
                                        Terra-cotta statuettes, 375/50.
Würzburg.   B.D., no. 92; B.H.T., fig. 103; P.C.F., fig. 108.
    See above p. 65.

19 (222)   OLD WOMAN: MASK Y.   Terra-cotta statuette, 375/50.
Berlin 7089.   B.D., no. 93; B.H.T., fig. 105.
    See above p. 65.

20 (272)   WOMAN WITH ELABORATE HAIRDRESSING: MASK X.
                                        Terra-cotta statuette, 375/50.
? Athens.   B.C.H., 11 (1887), 442, no. 8, pl. 3, 8; Winter, Typen, 462/9.
    See above p. 65.

21 (C 154) GIRL WITH LAMPADION HAIR.   Terra-cotta statuette, 375/50.
Berlin 6901.   B.D., no. 158; B.H.T., fig. 279; S.C.T., 120, n. 93 .
    See above pp. 65, 91.

22 (268)   GIRL WITH HAIR TIED OVER FOREHEAD: MASK W.
                                        Terra-cotta statuette, 375/50.
British Museum 745.   P.C.F., fig. 142.
    See above, pp. 66, 117.

23 (259)   MAN IN PILOS WITH BOX AND BASKET, BLANKETS ON HIS BACK;
           MASK L.   Terra-cotta statuette, 375/50.
Athens, Agora Museum, T 1685.   D. B. Thompson, Hesperia, 21 (1952), 141, pl. 38,
no. 43; cf. British Museum Catalogue ,no. 738=P.C.F., fig. 123; Olynthos 14, no. 381.
    See above p. 67, pl. 18a.

24 (212) WREATHED MAN CARRYING RAM; MASK K.

Terra-cotta statuette, 375/50.
Louvre CA 219. P.C.F., fig. 139.
See above p. 68.

25 (261) SHEPHERD BLOWING PIPE: MASK K. Terra-cotta statuette, 375/50.
Louvre CA 376. *Encyclopédie Photographique*, 207 G.
See above p. 68.

26 (205) TELEPHOS WITH BABY: MASK N. Terra-cotta statuette, 375/50.
Munich, inv. 5394. B.D., no. 76; B.H.T., fig. 118.
See above p. 71.

27 (254) MAN SITTING ON ALTAR WITH HAND TO EAR: MASK B.

Terra-cotta statuette, 375/50.
Athens, Agora Museum, T 1684. D. B. Thompson, *Hesperia*, 21 (1952), 141, pl. 38,
nos. 45–7; cf. *British Museum Catalogue*, no. 743=P.C.F., fig. 132; no. 1529, local variant from
Cyrenaica.
See above p. 71; pl. 18*b*.

28 (237) MAN WITH PITCHER: MASK N. Terra-cotta statuette, 375/50.
Louvre, from Cyprus. B.H.T., fig. 114; cf. Schefold, *Larisa am Hermos*, 108, pl. 9, 18;
British Museum Catalogue, no. 1532, local variant from Cyrenaica.
See above pp. 72, 145, 158.

29 (19) MAN WITH CLOAK OVER HIS HEAD: MASK A?

Terra-cotta statuette, 375/50.
British Museum 737 (old C 239). B.H.T., fig. 90; Webster, *Greek Terra-cottas*, pl. 26;
cf. adaptation on plaque in Sikyon, *Praktika*, 1941/4, 63, fig. 3.
See above pp. 72, 137.

30 (239) BEARDED MAN IN FEMALE CLOTHING: MASK D.

Terra-cotta statuette, 375/50.
Louvre 298. B.H.T., fig. 117; Rumpf in *Mimus u. Logos*, 170 n. 23.
See above pp. 72.

31 (25) FIVE MASKS: M, R, N, O, S. Marble relief, 340.
Athens, Acropolis Museum. P.C.F., fig. 18; W.L.G.C., pl. 3.
See above, pp. 56, 61, 62, 64, 65, 66, 73, 81, 117, 142; pl. 19.

31*a* (429) CHORUS OF SOLDIERS; MASKS A, M. Marble relief, 350/25?
Athens, Agora Museum, S 1025, 1586. W.W.S., III.
See above, pp. 56, 62, 67; pl. 18*d*.

II. SICILY AND ITALY

32 (27) CHEIRON GOES UPSTAIRS: MASKS P, G, E, R, T.

South Italian bell-krater, 400/375.
British Museum F 151. B.D., no. 109; B.H.T., fig. 362; Beare, *Roman Stage*, 15.
See above pp. 108, 109, 113; pl. 15*b*.

33 (28) BINDING A THIEF: MASKS, CLEAN-SHAVEN, E, U, AND (IN THE
BACKGROUND) B. South Italian kalyx-krater, 400/375.
New York 24.97.104. B.H.T., fig. 381; T.F.I., no. B 75, pl. 28*b*; Webster, *Schweitzer-
festschrift*, 260; Beazley, *A.J.A.*, 56 (1952), 193.
See above pp. 69, 98, 103, 108, 109, 113.

34 (109) HERAKLES WITH A SLAVE ON A DONKEY: MASKS, HERAKLES, B.

Apulian bell-krater, 400/375.
Berlin F 3046. B.D., no 106; B.H.T., fig. 356.
See above pp. 102, 108.

35 (186) SATYR FLUTING: MASK, TETTIX (26).   Apulian guttus, 375/50.
Ruvo, Jatta Coll. 1528.   Robert, *Masken der neueren Komödie*, fig. 108.
See above pp. 59, 85.

36 (108) PRIAM AND NEOPTOLEMOS: MASKS, L AND CLEAN-SHAVEN.
                                                Apulian bell-krater, 375/50.
Berlin F 3045.   B.D., no. 111; B.H.T., fig. 361; cf. with Priam, Attic terra-cotta,
British Museum Catalogue, no. 725.
See above pp. 62, 102.

37 (105) BIRTH OF HELEN: MASKS, T, E, B.   Apulian bell-krater, 375/50.
Bari 3899.   B.D., no. 110; B.H.T., fig. 365.
See above pp. 61, 65, 108, 109.

38 (185) THIASOS WITH ACTOR AND OLD WOMAN.   Apulian askos, 375/50.
Ruvo, Jatta Coll. 1402.   B.H.T., fig. 400.
See above pp. 99, 130.

39 (115) MEN CARRYING MEAT ON SPIT: MASKS, P, B.
                                                Apulian bell-krater, 375/50.
Leningrad, inv. 2074.   B.D., no. 123; B.H.T., fig. 378.
See above p. 102.

40 (192) MAN RIDING FISH: MASK B.   Apulian vase, 375/50.
Whereabouts unknown.   B.D., no. 114; B.H.T. fig. 372.
See above p. 102.

41 (158) MAN WITH WOMAN AT DOOR: MASK D. Apulian skyphos, 375/50.
British Museum F 124.   B.H.T., fig. 388.
See above p. 108.

42 (34) LONG-NOSED WOMAN PURSUING PARASITE.
                                                Apulian bell-krater, 350/325.
Berlin F 3047.   B.D., no. 122; B.H.T., fig. 375.
See above pp. 65, 82, 112.

43 (151) OLD MAN, YOUTH WITH BUNDLE, WOMAN.
                                                Apulian kalyx-krater, 350/325.
Naples 118333.   B.H.T., fig. 385.
See above pp. 108, 143.

44 (104) ZEUS AMMON.   Apulian bell-krater, 350/325.
Bari 2970.   B.H.T., fig. 369.
See above p. 109.

45 (146) GRAVE RELIEF OF YOUTH, WITH MASK A IN BACKGROUND.
                                                Apulian volute-krater, 350/325.
Lecce.   C.V., iv Dr, pls. 33-4; Messerschmidt, *R.M.*, 46 (1931), 72, fig. 32; cf. grave
relief of youth with 'Hermes' mask in background, Apulian amphora, Madrid, P.C.T.,
fig. 32.
See above p. 119.

46 (373) LAMPADION MASK (42).   Gnathia kotyle, 350/25.
Naples 1172.
See above p. 91.

47 (76) SNUB-NOSE MASK WITH WIMPLE (44).   Gnathia kantharos, 350/25.
Naples 80895.   Picard, *B.C.H.*, 1911, 226, no. 50; W.G.M., no. 28.
See above p. 92.

48 (50) MAN WITH CAKE: MASK P.   Gnathia kalyx-krater, 350/25.
British Museum F 543.   C.V., iv Dc, pl. 2/2; W.G.M., no. 38.
See above p. 117.

49 (88)   ZEUS (?) WITH TORCH: MASK D.   Gnathia oenochoe, 350/25.
Taranto 8953.   B.H.T., fig. 395; W.G.M., no. 41
See above p. 117.

50 (86)   REVELLER WITH TORCH: MASK H?   Gnathia kalyx-krater, 350/25·
New York 51.11.2.   C.V., Vienna University, pl. 18; W.G.M., no. 39.
See above p. 117.

51 (48)   MASK OF WOMAN WITH HAIR TIED OVER FOREHEAD: W.
                                                     Gnathia bowl, 350/325.
British Museum F 586.   C.V., IV Dc, pl. 2/4; W.G.M., no. 11, pl. 45 f.
See above p. 117; pl. 11d.

52 (63)   MASK OF YOUTH WITH FAIR, WAVY HAIR: O.
                                                 Gnathia bell-krater, 350/325.
Haileybury College.   W.G.M., no. 9a, fig. 5.
See above pp. 117, 143; pl. 11e.

53 (52)   MASK OF YOUNG PAN (THREE-QUARTER).
                                               Gnathia fragment, 350/325.
Oxford, Sir John Beazley.   W.G.M., no. 1, pl. 45a.
See above p. 117.

54 (95)   MASK OF YOUNG PAN (FRONTAL).   Gnathia bell-krater, 350/325·
Lecce 1034.   W.G.M., no. 1a.
See above p. 117.

55 (53)   MASK OF HERMES (?).   Gnathia bell-krater, 350/325.
Milan, Ambrosiana.   W.G.M., no. 9; cf. P.C.T., fig. 32.
See above p. 117.

56 (374)   MASK OF HERMES (?).   Gnathia bowl, 350/325.
Naples 112813.
See above p. 117.

57 (49)   MASK OF WEDGE-BEARDED OLD MAN: A   Gnathia bowl, 350/325.
Leiden, G.N.V. 111.   W.G.M., no. 6, pl. 45d.
See above p. 119; pl. 11c.

58 (385)   PARASITE.   Paestan terra-cotta statuette, 4th cent.
Paestum, MN, Case 49.
See above pp. 82, 112.

59 (390)   WOMAN WITH LONG HAIR.   Paestan terra-cotta statuette, 4th cent.
Paestum, MN, Case 44.   Cf. 84 below (Cyrenaica) and Athens, N.M. 16268 (Attic).
See above pp. 65, 89, 112.

60 (32)   ZEUS, HERMES, AND ALKMENE: MASKS G, RUSTIC, X.
                                               Paestan bell-krater, 360/340.
Rome, Vatican U 19.   B.D., no. 101; B.H.T., fig. 368; T.P.P., pl. 9, 10; T.P.P.S.,
no. 59; Beare, Roman Stage, p. 46.
See above pp. 80, 108, 114 f.; pl. 20.

61 (149)   TWO MEN ROBBING A MISER: MASKS L, 17, 16, B, AND 41 IN THE
                BACKGROUND.   Paestan kalyx-krater, 360/340.
Berlin F 3044.   B.D., no. 116; B.H.T., fig. 373; T.P.P., pl. 5; T.P.P.S., no. 37
See above pp. 82, 108, 109, 114 f., 118.

62 (31)   HERAKLES AND APOLLO: MASKS, HERAKLES, 16, B.
                                               Paestan bell-krater, 360/340.
Leningrad 1777.   B.D., no. 105; B.H.T., fig. 355; T.P.P., fig. 16; T.P.P.S., no. 45
See above pp. 107, 108, 114.

63 (30)   RAPE OF AJAX: MASKS, D, V.   Paestan fragments, 360/340.
Villa Giulia.   B.H.T., figs. 366–7; T.P.P., pl. 6; T.P.P.S., no. 38.
See above pp. 112, 114.

64 (145) SYMPOSION WITH MASKS IN THE BACKGROUND: B, S, A.
Paestan bell-krater, 350/25.
Vatican, Old no. 120.   B.H.T., fig. 401; T.P.P., pl. 18; T.P.P.S., no. 148.
See above pp. 118, 152.

65 (122) PHLYAX BETWEEN DIONYSOS AND MAENAD.
Paestan bell-krater, 320/300.
Naples 1778.   T.P.P., fig. 57; T.P.P.S., no. 408.
See above p. 99.

66 (43) OLD MAN, SLAVE, AND PEACE: MASKS, L, B.
Campanian kalyx-krater, 370/30.
Glasgow 03.70 f.   Pace, *Arte e Civiltá*, 2, 469, figs. 338–40; T.P.P.S., 29.
See above p. 63.

67 (29) HERAKLES AND AUGE: MASKS, HERAKLES, V, Y, N.
Campanian kalyx-krater, 350/25.
Lentini.   B.D., no. 108; B.H.T., fig. 358; Beazley, *J.H.S.*, 43 (1943), 107; T.P.P.S., 29.
See above pp. 107, 109, 116.

68 (172) THREE ACTORS APPROACHING A HOUSE.
Campanian oenochoe, 350/25.
Rome, Vatican U 49.   Wieseler, *Annali*, 1853, pl. AB, 8.
See above p. 108.

69 (39) SYMPOSION WITH MASK E IN THE BACKGROUND.
Campanian bell-krater, 350/325.
Cambridge AE/26.   P.C.F., fig. 91a.
See above p. 118.

70 (269) SEATED MAN.   Tarentine terra-cotta statuette, 370/330.
British Museum 1359 (old D 323).
See above p. 112.

III. MAINLAND GREECE

71   (a) ODYSSEUS AND KIRKE. (b) ODYSSEUS BLOWN OVER THE
WAVES.   Boeotian skyphos, 450/25.
Oxford 262.   B.D., no. 128; B.H.T., fig. 137.
See above p. 139.

72 (103) BEARDED MAN; MASK B?   Corinthian fragment, 375/350.
Corinth.   Luce, *A.J.A.*, 34 (1930), 342, fig. 6.
See above pp. 132, 135.

73 (102) MEN AT A MIXING BOWL ASSAILED BY GEESE.
Corinthian bell-krater, 375/350.
Athens, N.M. 1391.   B.D., no. 126; B.H.T., fig. 136.
See above pp. 132, 135.

74 (369) BEARDED MAN WITH BASKET ON HEAD.
Corinthian terra-cotta statuette, 375/50.
Corinth.   Morgan, *Hesperia*, 22 (1953), 131, pl. 46c.
See above p. 136.

75 (346) ACTOR IN FLARED CHITON.   Corinthian terra-cotta statuette, 375/350.
Corinth.   *Corinth*, XV, ii, Group xix, 18. Cf. *British Museum Catalogue*, 263 (=old C 9).
See above p. 136.

76 (244) MAN CARRYING WATERPOT.   Boeotian terra-cotta statuette, 375/350.
Munich SL 203.   *Sammlung Loeb*, II, 18, pl. 82/1. Cf. *Olynthos*, xiv, no. 380 A–C.
See above pp. 139, 142.

77 (274) OLD MAN WITH POINTED SHOES.
Boeotian terra-cotta statuette, 375/350.
Thebes, from Halai, V.1.2.   Goldman, *Hesperia*, 11 (1942), pl. 33/2; P.C.F., fig. 90.
See above p. 139.

78 (327) MAN WITH PILOS RIDING A MULE: MASK K.
Boeotian terra-cotta statuette, 375/350.
Copenhagen, N.M., inv. 759.   Breitenstein, *Catalogue*, no. 325; *Acta Archaeologica*, 9 (1938), 127 ff.   Cf. *Olynthos*, VII, nos. 330–2; XIV, nos. 376–7.
See above pp. 61, 142.

79 (352) MAN CARRYING BASKET ON HIS HEAD: MASK B.
Olynthian terra-cotta statuette, 375/350.
Olynthos, inv. 34.138.   *Olynthus*, XIV, no. 364 (*b*) and (*c*).
See above p. 142.

80 (26) MASK OF YOUTH, O.   Olynthian terra-cotta mould, 375/350
Olynthos, inv. 494, 497.   *Olynthus*, IV, no. 421.
See above pp. 61, 117, 180.

81 (364) YOUTH IN LONG CLOAK: MASK Z.
Olynthian terra-cotta statuette, 375/350.
Olynthos, inv. 38.148.   *Olynthus*, XIV, no. 388.
See above pp. 64, 81, 143.

IV. THE ISLANDS

82 (340) MAN WITH HIMATION OVER LEFT SHOULDER.
Cyprian terra-cotta statuette, 4th cent.
Nicosia D 113.
See above p. 145.

83 (341) MAN WITH SPEAR AND PHIALE: MASK M.
Cyprian bronze statuette, 4th cent.
Nicosia D 266.
See above p. 145.

V. ASIA AND AFRICA

84 (270) WOMAN WITH LONG HAIR.   Cyrenaic terra-cotta statuette, 250/330.
British Museum 1531 (Old C 825).   Cf. no. 59 above (Paestum) and Athens, N.M. 16268 (Attic).
See above pp. 65, 89, 112.

C. NEW COMEDY

I. ATHENS

1 (186) MASK OF WREATHED YOUTH WITH RAISED BROWS AND WAVY
HAIR (15).   Attic terra-cotta mask, 3rd cent.
Heidelberg TK 98.   Luschey, *Ganymed*, 76, figs. 5–7.
See above p. 81.

2 (151) MASK OF OLD WOMAN (28).   Attic terra-cotta mask, 3rd cent.
Bonn.   B.H.T., fig. 276; Luschey, *Ganymed*, 77.
See above p. 85.

3 (187)   MASK OF OLD WOMAN (36 OR 37).   Attic terra-cotta mask, 3rd cent.
Copenhagen, N.M., Inv. Chr. viii, 922.   Breitenstein, *Catalogue*, no. 599; Luschey,
Ganymed, 77, fig. 8.
See above p. 89.

4 (210)   MASKS: 7, 10 3, 4, 16, 25, 33 (TWICE), 41 (TWICE).
Attic gold necklace, 3rd/2nd cent.
Hamburg 1917, 195, from Thessaly.   *A.M.*, 1925, 174, pl. 8/9; S.C.T., 188 n. 8.
See above p. 87.

5 (439)   MASKS OF RUSTIC (14), LITTLE HETAIRA (39), HOUSEKEEPER (30).
Attic terra-cotta brazier, 2nd cent.
Mykonos, from Delos.   Marcadé, *B.C.H.*, 76 (1952), 623, fig. 25; Rumpf, *A.E.*, 1954.
See above p. 80.

II. SICILY AND ITALY

6 (28)   MASK OF WOMAN WITH MELON HAIR (39).
Gnathia oenochoe, 300/275.
Manchester, MWI 6949.   Webster, *Greek Interpretations*, pl. 8; W.G.M., no. 35.
See above p. 120.

7 (29)   MASK OF WOMAN WITH WREATH OF HAIR (37).
Gnathia oenochoe, 300/275.
Ann Arbor, University of Michigan.   *C.V.*, pl. 29 7; W.G.M., no. 8.
See above pp. 89, 120.

8 (301)   MASKS 3, 9, 11, 22, 25, 33.   Tarentine silver cup, 300/275.
Lost.   Nachod, *R.M.*, 1918, 115, pls. 7–8; Willeumier, *Tarente*, 338 f.
See above pp. 75, 121.

9 (96)   COOK: MASK 25.   Tarentine terra-cotta statuette, 3rd/2nd cent.
Taranto.   B.D., no. 87; B.H.T., fig. 97.
See above p. 121.

10 (99)   SLAVE WITH CHILD: MASK 22.
Tarentine terra-cotta statuette, 3rd/2nd cent.
Taranto, from same grave as no. 9.   B.D., no. 89c; *N.Sc.*, 1897, 216.
See above p. 121.

11 (17)   GARRULOUS WIFE: MASK 31.
Terra-cotta statuette from Capua, 3rd/2nd cent.
Berlin 7041.   B.D., no. 156; B.H.T., fig. 244.
See above pp. 89, 122.

12 (132)   SICILIAN PARASITE: MASK 20.
Terra-cotta statuette from Capua, 3rd/2nd cent.
Berlin 7395.   B.D., no. 145; B.H.T., fig. 250; S.C.T., 183 n. 49; P.C.F., fig. 119.
See above pp. 82, 122.

13 (19)   MASK OF GREYING GARRULOUS WOMAN: 36.
Terra-cotta mask from Tarquinia, 3rd/2nd cent.
Berlin 7138.   B.D., no. 173; B.H.T., fig. 282; S.C.T., 197 n. 51; P.C.F., fig. 148.
See above pp. 89, 122.

14 (474)   MASK OF ADMIRABLE YOUTH: 10.
Paestan terra-cotta mask, 3rd/2nd cent.
Paestum, MN, Case 38.
See above p. 122.

15 (475)   MASK OF WOMAN WITH MELON HAIR: 39.
Paestan terra-cotta mask, 3rd/2nd cent.
Paestum, MN, Case 38.
See above p. 122.

16 (476)   MASK OF SLAVE: 22.   Paestan terra-cotta mask, 3rd/2nd cent.
Paestum, MN, Case 38.
See above p. 122.

17 (477)   MASK OF DELICATE YOUTH: 13.
                                                Paestan terra-cotta mask 3rd/2nd cent.
Paestum, MN, Case 45.
See above p. 122.

18 (21)   MASK OF MEDDLESOME OLD MAN: 7.
                                Terra-cotta mask from Pompeii, 3rd/2nd cent.
Pompeii.   Rohden, *Terrakotten von Pompeii*, pl. 15, 2; S.C.T., 194, n. 66; cf., *ibid.*,
pl. 10, 1; Robert, *Masken*, fig. 101.
See above pp. 77, 122.

19 (4)   MENANDER, *WOMEN AT BREAKFAST*: MASKS 39, 35, 29.
                        Mosaic by Dioskourides, 2nd cent. (from original, 300/275).
Naples 9987.   B.D., no. 136; B.H.T., fig. 242; P.C.T., fig. 86; P.C.F., fig. 95; S.C.T.,
no. 10; Beazley, *Etruscan Vase-painting*, 235; Rumpf, *J.H.S.*, 67 (1947), 16; Webster, *Studies
in Menander*, 91.
See above pp. 23, 45, 74, 85, 87, 90, 104, 122, 153, 162; pl. 21.

20 (5)   KOMASTS: MASKS 39, 10, 13.
                        Mosaic by Dioskourides, 2nd cent. (from original, 300/275).
Naples 9985.   B.D., no. 135; B.H.T., fig. 239; S.C.T., no. 8; P.C.T., fig. 85; W.L.G.C.,
120; Beare, *Roman Stage*, 220.
See above pp. 23, 45, 74, 79, 90, 122, 154; pl. 22.

21 (226)   MASKS: 4, 10, 11, 21, 22, 33, 39.   Border of Dove mosaic, 2nd cent.
Naples 114281.   S.C.T., 183 n. 61, 184 n. 82b, 190 n. 43c, 190 n. 45, 194 n. 60; Rumpf,
M.U.Z., 166, pl. 56/1.   Cf. borders of the mosaic of the 'seven sages' (Schefold, *Bildnisse*,
154/1), of the tiger rider (*Antike*, 1937, 57, fig. 14), of the lion-hunt (S.C.T., pl. 11).
See above pp. 87, 119, 152.

22 (172)   ACTORS IN SCENERY: MASKS 27, 3, 4.   Terra-cotta relief, 1st cent.
Rome.   B.H.T., figs. 425; P.C.T., figs. 78–9; S.C.T., 173.
See above pp. 28, 76.

23 (30)   SCENE FOR COMEDY. Paintings from cubiculum, Boscoreale, 1st cent. B.C.
New York.   B.H.T., figs. 345–6; P.C.T., fig. 90; Rumpf, *J.H.S.*, 67 (1947), 18; *M.U.Z.*,
pl. 54/4.
See above pp. 26, 140, 162; pl. 23.

24 (42)   MASK OF RUSTIC: 14.   Silver cup from Boscoreale, 1st cent. B.C.
Louvre.   Héron de Villefosse, *Mon. Piot*, 5 (1899), 58; Schefold, *Bildnisse*, 167, fig. 2;
Webster, *Schweitzerfestschrift*, pl. 57.
See above p. 80.

25 (26)   SOLDIER SLAVE (27) AND LEADING SLAVE (22).
                                                Painting, 1st cent. A.D.
Pompeii, House of the Great Fountain.   B.D., no. 134; B.H.T., fig. 237; S.C.T.,
no. 14; P.C.F., fig. 98; Rumpf in *Mimus und Logos*, 164.
See above pp. 56, 80.

26 (31)   OLD SLAVE (21), YOUNG SLAVE (22), AND FLUTE-PLAYER (39).
                                                Painting, 1st cent. A.D.
Naples 9035.   B.D., no 133; B.H.T., fig. 228; S.C.T., no. 5.
See above p. 83.

27 (41, 285) YOUTH AND GIRL MASKS 10, 33.   Terra-cotta statues, 1st cent. A.D.
Naples 22248–9.   B.H.T., fig. 409; S.C.T., 183 n. 66, 197 n. 56, pl. 7.
See above pp. 87, 122.

28 (32) SLAVE (27) WATCHES OLD MAN (3) LEAVING WOMAN (31).

Painting, 1st cent. A.D.

Bonn E 168. B.H.T., fig. 229; P.C.F., fig. 101; S.C.T., no. 7.
See above pp. 79, 89.

29 (34) HETAIRA (38) AND COOK (25). Painting, 1st cent. A.D.

Palermo. B.D., no. 131; B.H.T., fig. 243; P.C.F., fig. 96; S.C.T., no. 6.
See above p. 90.

30 (33) OLD SLAVE (21) WATCHED BY WOMAN (42) AND YOUTH (10).

Painting, 1st cent. A.D.

Naples 9037. B.D., no. 132; B.H.T., fig. 238; P.C.F., fig. 97; S.C.T., no. 1.
See above pp. 90, 123.

31 (156) MASK OF SNUB-NOSED GIRL (43). Marble mask, 1st cent. A.D.

Naples 6612. B.D., no. 175; B.H.T., fig. 281; P.C.F., fig. 152; S.C.T., 197 n. 41.
See above p. 92.

32 (458) MASKS OF TWO OLD MEN (3) FLANKING MASK OF DIONYSOS.

Marble masks, 1st cent. A.D.

Herculaneum, Insula vi, 11. Maiuri, Herculaneum, 44, pl. 20.
See above p. 125.

33 (37) OLD SLAVE (21) AND BOY (13). Painting, 1st cent. A.D.

Pompeii, House of the Centenary, atrium. P.C.F., fig. 100; S.C.T., no. 16.
See above p. 122.

34 (183) WOMAN (33), SLAVE BY ALTAR WITH BIRD (21), SLAVE IN HAT (21).

Painting, 1st cent. A.D.

Pompeii, House of the Centenary, atrium. Dieterich, Pulcinella, pl. 3; S.C.T., no. 15.
See above pp. 83, 122.

35 (184) YOUNG MAN (12) AND OLD SLAVE (21). Painting, 1st cent. A.D.

Pompeii, House of the Centenary, triclinium. B.H.T., fig. 519; S.C.T., no. 17.
See above p. 123.

36 (38) OLD MAN (4) INTERROGATING SLAVE (27).

Painting, 1st cent. A.D.

Pompeii, House of the Centenary, triclinium. Robert, Masken, fig. 86; S.C.T., no. 18.
See above pp. 83, 123.

37 (7) SLAVE (27) WATCHES FAT OLD WOMAN (29) AND GIRL (39).

Painting, 1st cent. A.D.

Pompeii, House of the Centenary, triclinium. Robert, Masken, fig. 88; S.C.T., no. 19.
See above pp. 86, 123.

38 (185) OLD WOMAN (29) SOLILOQUISING. Painting, 1st cent. A.D.

Pompeii, House of the Centenary, triclinium. S.C.T., no. 20.
See above p. 123.

39 (6) OLD MAN (3) AND SLAVE (21). Painting, 1st cent. A.D.

Pompeii, House of the Centenary, triclinium. P.C.F., fig. 99; S.C.T., no. 21.
See above p. 123.

40 (482) MASKS (13, 10, 33) GROUPED ROUND A COLUMN.

Painting, 1st cent. A.D.

Pompeii, I, vi, 11. N.Sc. 1929, 404 f.
See above p. 123.

41 (33a) OLD SLAVE (21), WOMAN (42), YOUTH (10).

Painting, 1st cent. A.D.

Pompeii, I, vi, 11. B.H.T., fig. 524; Maiuri, Pompeii, fig. 68; S.C.T., no. 2.
See above p. 123.

42 (180) OLD MAN (7). Painting, 1st cent. A.D.

Pompeii, I, vi, 11. N.Sc., 1929, 407; S.C.T., no. 4.
See above pp. 77, 124.

43 (179)   PARASITE (18) VISITS COOK (25).   Painting, 1st cent. A.D.
Pompeii, I, vi, 11.   *N.Sc.*, 1929, pl. 22; S.C.T., no. 3.
See above p. 124.

44 (192, 381) GROUPS OF COMIC MASKS.   Painting, 1st cent. A.D.
Pompeii, I, ii, 6.   Robert, *A.Z.*, 1878, 13 f. (*a*) Robert, pl. 4/1; P.C.F., fig. 151; S.C.T.
197 n. 57. (*b*) Robert, pl. 5/2; S.C.T., 193 n. 44; 194 n. 73; 197 n. 63.
See above p. 125.

45 (238, 339) (*a*) MASK 27, (*b*) MASKS 22, 3, 10.   Marble reliefs, 1st cent. A.D.
Pompeii, House of the Golden Cupids.   *N.Sc.*, 1907, (*a*) 558, fig. 8, (*b*) 560, fig. 10.
See above p. 126.

46 (338, 291, 336) (*a*) MASK 16, (*b*) MASK 13, (*c*) MASK 33.
                                                  Marble masks, 1st cent. A.D.
Pompeii, House of the Golden Cupids.   *N.Sc.*, 1907, (*a*) 583, fig. 32, (*b*) 588, fig. 37; S.C.T.
184 n. 72, (*c*) 589, fig. 38; S.C.T., 197 n. 62.
See above p. 127.

47 (292, 337) (*a*) MASKS 4, 13, 27, (*b*) MASKS 22, 41, 3.
                                                  Marble reliefs, 1st cent. A.D.
Pompeii, House of the Golden Cupids.   *N.Sc.*, 1907 (*a*) 580, fig. 22; S.C.T., 184 n. 73,
197 n. 55, (*b*) 583, fig. 26; S.C.T., 198 n. 73.
See above p. 127.

48 (1)   OLD MAN (3) RESTRAINS FATHER (4) FROM ATTACKING SON (16),
            WHO IS SUPPORTED BY SLAVE (27).
                                                  Marble relief, 1st/2nd cent. A.D.
Naples 6687.   B.D., no. 130; B.H.T., fig. 225; P.C.T., fig. 77; P.C.F., fig. 94; S.C.T.,
66, 80, 88; Beare, *Roman Stage*, 38.
See above pp. 20, 75, 81, 83; pl. 24*a*.

49 (3)   MENANDER WITH MASKS OF YOUTH (11), WOMAN (34), OLD MAN (4).
                                      Marble relief (original 300/275), 1st to 2nd cent.
Rome, Lateran 487.   B.D., no. 129; B.H.T., fig. 223; P.C.F., fig. 93; S.C.T., 59, 92,
119; Beare, *Roman Stage*, 176; Bieber, *Festschrift Andreas Rumpf*, 14 f.
See above pp. 74, 75, 78, 79, 87; pl. 24*b*.

50 (402)   MASK OF CURLY-HAIRED WIFE (32).   Marble mask. 2nd cent. A.D.
Rome, Terme 202.   S.C.T., 107, 196 n. 28, pl. 12.
See above p. 89.

51 (39)   MASK OF GOLDEN HETAIRA (40).   Marble mask, 2nd cent. A.D.
Rome, Vatican, Gall. dei Busti 313.   B.D., no. 177; B.H.T., fig. 284; P.C.F., fig. 156.
See above p. 90.

III. MAINLAND GREECE

52 (100)   MASK OF BALD SLAVE WITH WREATH (25).
                                          Boeotian Terra-cotta, 325/275.
Thebes, from Halai.   Goldman, *Hesperia* 11 (1942), pl. 20; P.C.F., fig. 91.
See above p. 140.

53 (46)   MUSE WITH SLAVE MASK (22).   Corinthian bronze mirror, 300/275.
British Museum 295.   Züchner, *Klappspiegel*, no. 144, fig. 48.
See above p. 136.

54 (9)   MASK OF FLATTERER (17).   ? Boeotian terra-cotta mask, 3rd/2nd cent.
University College, London.   W.L.G.C., pl. 4*b*.
See above p. 82.

55 (95)   MASK OF FLATTERER (17).   Boeotian terra-cotta mask, 3rd/2nd. cent.
Athens, from Elateia.   B.C.H., 11, pl. 3, fig. 10.
See above p. 140.

56 (15)   COOK (25) WITH BASKET.
                                    ? Megarian terra-cotta statuette, 3rd/2nd cent.
Berlin 7042.   B.D., no. 86; B.H.T., fig. 98; P.C.F., fig. 81.
See above p. 85.

57 (58)   SOLDIER (15), GIRL (33), AND YOUTH (? 13) IN MENANDER'S
             ACHAIOI.   Mosaic from Oescus, 2nd/3rd cent. A.D.
Ivanov, *Monuments de l'Art en Bulgarie*, ii (1954) Toynbee, *J.R.S.*, 45 (1955), 204.
See above p. 80.

IV. THE ISLANDS

58 (430)   PROCURER (8).   Cyprian terra-cotta statuette, 3rd cent.
Nicosia 1934–vii–12–3.
See above p. 145.

59 (434)   MASK OF YOUTH WITH SMOOTH BROWS AND WAVY HAIR (16).
                                    Cyprian terra-cotta mask, ? 3rd cent.
Nicosia D 216.
See above p. 145.

60 (435)   MASK OF SLAVE (22).   Cyprian terra-cotta mask, ? 3rd cent.
Nicosia D 217.   Perhaps the mould for an actor's mask (W.W.S., II).
See above p. 145.

61 (225)   (*a*) MASKS 27, 29, PAN, 16, 3; SATYR, 11, 4, 8, 22, (*b*) SLAVE DANCING.
                                    Mosaic, 200/150 B.C.
Delos, House of the Masks.   Chamonard, *Délos XIV*, pls. 4–7; S.C.T., 93; 184 n. 82,
190 n. 43, 191 n. 64, 192 n. 9, 193 n. 47, 194 n. 61, 199 n. 11.
See above pp. 152ff., 161.

62 (66)   SOLDIER (15).   Terra-cotta statuette from Delos, 2nd cent.
Mykonos.   B.D., no. 57; B.H.T., fig. 207; P.C.F., fig. 50; Rumpf in *Mimus und Logos*,
164.
See above pp. 80, 146.

V. ASIA MINOR AND AFRICA

63 (107)   MASK OF SLAVE (22).   Terra-cotta mask from Larisa, late 4th cent.
Larisa.   *Larisa am Hermos*, 3, 115, pl. 9, 21.
See above p. 159.

64 (383)   MASK OF OLD MAN (3).
             Terra-cotta mask from Chatby Cemetery, Alexandria, late 4th cent.
Alexandria 15915.   Breccia, *Terrecotte*, no. 363, pl. 46; S.C.T., 193 n. 48.
See above p. 159.

65 (22)   PROCURER (8).   Terra-cotta statuette from Myrina, 2nd cent.
Louvre 199.   B.D., no. 146 P.C.F., fig. 106; S.C.T., 192 n. 4.
See above pp. 77, 160.

66 (23)   EIKONIKOS (19).   Terra-cotta statuette from Myrina, 2nd cent.
Athens, N.M. 5045.   B.D., no. 141; B.H.T., fig. 230; P.C.F., fig. 113; S.C.T., 184 n. 92.
See above pp. 78, 160.

67 (254, 389) (*a*) CURLY-HAIRED YOUTH (12), (*b*) WIMPLED HETAIRA (41).
             Terra-cotta masks on disks from Selymbria, 2nd cent.
Berlin 6623, 6622.   B.D., no. 67; P.C.F., fig. 55; S.C.T., 182 n. 24, 197 n. 66, pl. 6/2.
See above pp. 79, 90, 160.

68 (25)   SOLDIER (15).   Terra-cotta statuette from Myrina, 2nd cent.
Athens, N.M. 5025.   B.D., no. 56; B.H.T., fig. 205; P.C.F., fig. 49; S.C.T., 182 n. 26.
See above pp. 80, 161.

69 (24)   PARASITE (18).   Terra-cotta statuette from Myrina, 2nd cent.
Athens, N.M. 5027.   B.D., no. 144; B.H.T., fig. 249; P.C.F., fig. 120; S.C.T., 181 n. 1.
See above p. 82, 161.

70 (216)   STRAIGHT-HAIRED SLAVE (23).
Terra-cotta statuette from Myrina, 2nd cent.
Louvre 214.   Robert, *Masken*, fig. 34; S.C.T., 189 n. 29.
See above pp. 84, 161.

71 (27)   CURLY-HAIRED SLAVE (24).
Terra-cotta statuette from Myrina, 2nd cent.
Athens, N.M. 5048.   B.D., no. 150; B.H.T., fig. 236; S.C.T., 189, n. 32.
See above p. 84.

72 (40)   MASK OF TETTIX (26).   Marble frieze from Pergamon, 2nd cent.
Berlin.   B.D., no. 166; B.H.T., fig. 273; P.C.F., fig. 53c; S.C.T., 188 n. 9; Rumpf,
Symbola Coloniensia, 98.
See above pp. 85, 161.

73 (12)   MASK OF HOUSEKEEPER (30).
Terra-cotta mask from Cyrenaica, 2nd cent.
British Museum C 749.   S.C.T., 199 n. 1; W.L.G.C., pl. 4c.
See above p. 85.

74 (196)   MASK OF WOMAN WITH MELON HAIR (39).
Terra-cotta mask from Smyrna, 2nd cent.
Oxford.   P.C.F., fig. 157.
See above p. 91.

75 (128)   HETAIRA'S MAID (44)   Terra-cotta statuette from Myrina, 2nd cent.
Athens, N.M. 5032.   B.D., no. 157; B.H.T., fig. 246; P.C.F., fig. 149; S.C.T., 195 n. 1.
See above pp. 92, 161.

76 (72)   OLD MAN (4) DRESSED AS EUNUCH
Bronze statuette from Egypt, ? 1st cent. A.D.
Berlin 71 (N).   Robert, *Masken*, fig. 103; Rumpf in *Mimus und Logos*, 168, pl. 7a.
See above p. 77.

77 (71)   MASK OF *EIKONIKOS* (19).   Marble mask from Carthage, ? 2nd cent. A.D.
Louvre, Salle d'Afrique, 1836.   B.H.T., fig. 537; Rumpf in *Mimus und Logos*, 166.
See above p. 78.

78 (70)   MASK OF CURLY YOUTH (12).
Marble mask from Ephesos, ? 2nd cent. A.D.
Vienna.   Rumpf in *Mimus und Logos*, 166, pl. 7b.
See above p. 79.

F. ORIGINS

I. ATHENS

1 (9)   PROTO-SATYRS.   Proto-Attic vase, ca. 650.
Berlin A 32.   *C.V.*, pls. 20–21; Beazley, *Development of Black-figure*, 9, pl. 3; Buschor,
B.S.A., 46 (1951), 36; W.G.C.C., 584.
See above pp. 133, 157.

2 (33)   CARNIVAL GIANTS: SATYR AND FAT-MAN.
Black-figure kylix, 560/40.
Florence 3897.   Nilsson, *Gesch. d. gr. Religion*, 1, 558; W.G.C.C., 584, fig. 2; Vallois,
B.C.H., 46 (1922), 96.
See above pp. 17, 19, 29f.; pl. 2.

3 (32)   CHORUSES OF MEN DRESSED AS WOMEN.
Black-figure kylix, 560/40.
Amsterdam 3356.   *C.V.*, Scheurleer, III, He, pl. 2, 4; W.G.C.C., 574, 585.
See above pp. 34, 36; pl. 3.

4 (30)   YOUTHS DRESSED AS MAENADS.   Black-figure pyxis, 560/40.
Eleusis 1212.   *Hesperia*, 7 (1938), 409; W.G.C.C., 585, fig. 4.
See above p. 33; pl. 4b.

5 (38)   KNIGHTS.   Black-figure amphora, 560/40.
Berlin 1697.   B.D., no. 71a; B.H.T., fig. 79; P.C.D., fig. 18; Beazley, *Development of Black-figure*, 74.
See above pp. 34, 57.

6 (10)   KOMASTS AND NYMPHS.   Black-figure mastos cup, 530/10.
Rome, Mus. Artistico-Industriale.   Von Mercklin, *R.M.*, 38 (1923), 82; W.G.C.C., 585, fig. 3; Beazley, *Attic Vase Paintings in Boston*, II, 84, 102; Brommer, *Antike und Abendland*, 4 (1954), 42 f.; W.W.S., IV.
See above p. 33; pl. 4a.

7 (36)   FEATHERED MEN.   Black-figure oenochoe, 500/480.
London B 509.   B.D., no. 71b; B.H.T., fig. 76; P.C.D., fig. 16; Haspels, *Attic black-figured Lekythoi*, 214, no. 187.
See above pp. 35, 57.

8 (37)   COCKS.   Black-figure amphora, 500/480.
Berlin 1830.   B.D., no. 71c; B.H.T., fig. 77; P.C.D., fig. 17.
See above pp. 35, 57.

9 (40)   MAN WEARING PHALLOI.   Red-figure fragment, 490/470.
Athens, Akropolis Mus., 702.   *A.R.V.*, 143, no. 95.
See above p. 36f.

II. SICILY AND ITALY

III. MAINLAND GREECE

10 (48)   PADDED DANCERS.   Corinthian aryballos, 625/600.
British Museum A 1437.   P.C.D., figs. 37–9; Payne, *Necrocorinthia*, no. 515.
See above pp. 37, 134.

11 (46)   PADDED DANCERS AND FRUITSTEALERS.
Corinthian krater, 600/575.
Louvre E 632.   B.D., no. 72b; B.H.T., figs. 84–5; Payne, *Necrocorinthia*, no. 1178.
See above pp. 129, 132.

12 (2)   PADDED DANCERS.   Corinthian skyphos, 600/575.
Louvre CA 3004.   Amandry, *Mon. Piot*, 41 (1944), 23 ff.; W.G.C.C., 580 fig. 1.
See above pp. 100, 133; pl. 5a.

13 (17)   RETURN OF HEPHAISTOS.   Corinthian krater, 600/575.
British Museum B 42.   Payne, *Necrocorinthia*, no. 1176.
See above p. 133.

14 (4)   RETURN OF HEPHAISTOS.   Corinthian amphoriskos, 600/575.
Athens, N.M. 664.   B.D., no. 72a; B.H.T., fig. 83; Payne, *Necrocorinthia*, no. 1073.
See above p. 133.

15 (41)   KOMAST WEARING PANTHER SKIN.
Corinthian moulded vase, 600/575.
Louvre.   Pottier, *B.C.H.*, 1895, 225, fig. 3; Payne, *Necrocorinthia*, 180, pl. 44, 48.
See above pp. 37, 135, 157.

GTP—N

16 (47)   RETURN OF HEPHAISTOS.   Corinthian mastos, 575/50.
Paris, Musée Rodin 503.   *C.V.*, pl. 7.
See above p. 133.

17 (5)   PADDED DANCERS AND WOMEN.   Corinthian krater, 575/50.
Dresden.   Payne *Necrocorinthia*, no. 1477; Buschor, *Griechische Vasen*, fig. 80.
See above p. 134.

18 (D 16)   SATYRS AND MAENADS.   Chalkidian krater, 560/40.
Brussels A 135.   Rumpf, *Chalkidische Vasen*, no. 13, pls. 27-30.
See above p. 134.

19 (44)   DANCERS AND SATYRS.   Boeotian puzzle cup, 575/50.
Berlin, inv. 3366.   Bielefeld, *Festschrift Zucker*, 27 f.
See above p. 138.

20 (42)   DANCERS AND SATYRS.   Boeotian aryballos, 575/50.
Göttingen University 533*g*.
See above p. 138; pl. 5*b*.

21 (12)   FEMALE MASK.   Laconian terra-cotta mask, 560/40.
British Museum 1038.   Cf. P.C.D., figs. 19-25; Barnett, *J.H.S.*, 68 (1948), 6, n. 35;
W.G.C.C., 577; W.W.S., II.
See above p. 130; pl. 6*a*.

22 (3)   SATYRS ATTACKING WOMEN..   Laconian cup, 560/40·
Sparta.   Lane, *B.S.A.*, 34 (1933), pl. 39*a* and 40; W.G.C.C., 576.
See above pp. 129, 133, 156.

IV. THE ISLANDS

V. ASIA MINOR AND AFRICA

23 (51)   PHALLIC DAIMON.   Samian plastic vase, 700/675.
Samos.   Buschor, *B.S.A.*, 46 (1951), 32 f.
See above pp. 131, 157.

24 (15)   GORGON-HEADED QUEEN OF BEASTS.   Rhodian plate, 600/575.
British Museum A 748.   Rumpf, *J.D.A.I.*, 48 (1933), 76, no. 18; Nilsson, *Geschichte d.
gr. Religion*, 1, 211, 286, pl. 30/2.
See above pp. 131, 156.

25 (49)   FEMALE MASK.   Samian terra-cotta mask, 560/40.
Kassel.   Boehlau, *Nekropolen*, 47, 157; pl. 13/1.
See above pp. 130, 156.

26 (50)   SATYR MASK.   Samian terra-cotta mask, 525/500.
British Museum 523.   W.W.S., II.   Cf. Buschor, *Altsamische Standbilder*, fig. 201.
See above p. 157; pl. 6*b*.

INDEX

[PLATE I

PLATE 2]

(*a*) SATYR RIDING PHALLOS POLE

(*b*) KOMAST RIDING PHALLOS POLE

(F 2)

[PLATE 3

MEN   DRESSED   AS   WOMEN   DANCING

(F 3)

PLATE 4]

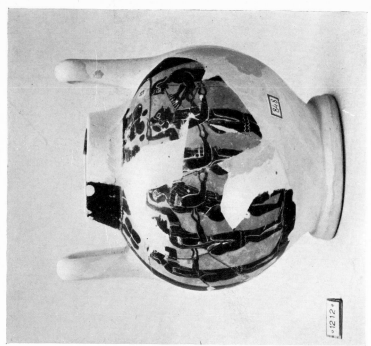

(b) MEN DRESSED AS MAENADS
(F 4)

(a) KOMASTS AND NYMPHS
(F 6)

[PLATE 5

(*a*) CORINTHIAN PADDED DANCERS (F 12)

(*b*) BOEOTIAN PADDED DANCERS (F 20)

PLATE 6]

(*a*) FEMALE MASK FROM SPARTA

(F 21)

(*b*) SATYR MASK FROM SAMOS

(F 26)

[PLATE 7

IPHIGENEIA IN TAURIS

(A 8)

PLATE 8]

ACTORS AND CHORUS OF SATYR PLAY

(A 9)

[PLATE 9

ACTOR DRESSED FOR FEMALE PART IN TRAGEDY

(A 20)

PLATE 10]

MEN AND WOMEN IN PALACE SETTING

(A 35)

[PLATE II

(a) MASK OF FIRST SHORN
MAIDEN (A 45)

(b) MASK OF SECOND SHORN
MAIDEN (A 48)

(c) MASK OF WEDGE BEARDED
OLD MAN (B 57)

(d) MASK OF FIRST FALSE-MAIDEN (B 51)

(e) MASK OF FAIR, WAVY-HAIRED YOUTH (B 52)

Plate 12]

PERSONIFICATION OF TRAGEDY

(A 78)

[PLATE 13

ACTOR DRESSED TO PLAY YOUNG KING IN TRAGEDY

(A 57)

PLATE 14]

[PLATE 15

(*a*) FEMALE CHORUSMEN OF COMEDY

(B 9)

(*b*) CHEIRON GOES UPSTAIRS

(B 32)

PLATE 16]

COMIC POET WITH MASKS

(B 10)

[PLATE 17

(*a*) OLD COUNTRYMAN
DISTRESSED (B 11*d*)

(*b*) OLD MAN
(B 14)

(*c*) HERAKLES

(B 13)

PLATE 18]

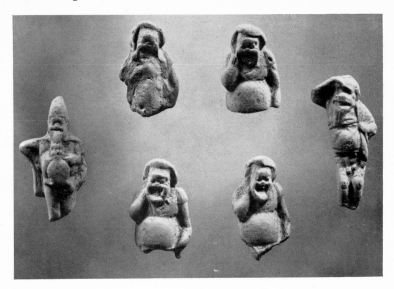

(*a*) TRAVELLER
(OR SOLDIER)

(B 23)

(*b*) MAN SEATED
ON ALTAR

(B 27)

(*c*) MAN
ESPYING GIRL

(B 15)

(*d*) CHORUS OF SOLDIERS

(B 31*a*)

[PLATE 19

FIVE COMIC MASKS

(B 31)

PLATE 20]

ZEUS, HERMES, AND ALKMENE

(B 60)

[PLATE 21

WOMEN AT BREAKFAST

(C 19)

PLATE 22]

REVELLERS

(C 20)

[PLATE 23

COMEDY SCENERY, BOSCOREALE

(C 23)

PLATE 24]

(a) ACTORS IN COMEDY (C 48)

(b) MENANDER WITH MASKS AND PERSONIFICATION OF
COMEDY (C 49)